#1369 - #150, 1st ed.

STANZAS FOR IRIS LEZAK

STANZAS FOR

RIS LEZAK

by Jackson Mac Low

1971
Something Else Press, Inc.
Barton   Millerton   Berlin

L. C. Catalog Card Number: 73 - 175234

ISBN: 0-87110-062-2 (Cloth Edition)

Copyright © 1972
by Jackson Mac Low
All Rights Reserved

This book is published by the Something Else Press, Elm Street, Millerton, NY 12546 for the New Means Foundation, of New York City.

This project was supported by a grant from the National Endowment for the Arts, in Washington, D.C., a Federal Agency created by Act of Congress in 1965.

Manufactured in the United States of America.

Acknowledgements
Certain of these poems have appeared in *Nomad, El Corno Emplumado/The Plumed Horn, Judson Review, Ear, Vol. 63, Stony Brook, The Insect Trust Gazette, The Outsider,* & *AN ANTHOLOGY* (ed. La Monte Young, pub. Young & Mac Low, New York, 1963).

Cover photograph is by Peter Moore.

Table of Contents

PART ONE
The First Notebook of Stanzas for Iris Lezak,
    Page 1

THE BLUE AND BROWN BOOKS,   Page 3
Polaris Action,   Page 6
Who am I? of Bhagavan Sri Ramana Maharshi Sri Ramanasram Eighth Edition,   Page 8
The Dream State,   Page 11
General Introduction (I),   Page 12
Call me Ishmael,   Page 16
General Introduction (II),   Page 17
Graded City Speller Chancellor Eighth Grade,   Page 19
General Introduction (III),   Page 22
Zen Buddhism and Psychoanalysis / Psychoanalysis and Zen Buddhism,   Page 24
General Introduction (IV),   Page 26
Strictly Personal,   Page 30
Separate Vacations,   Page 34
Women are the LAZIEST People,   Page 35
M G G S G M H,   Page 36
Are You Giving Your Wife The Companionship She Craves?,   Page 37
ROME,   Page 38
The Marrying Maiden,   Page 39
London,   Page 40
Paris,   Page 41
Marseilles,   Page 42
Madrid,   Page 43
Sydney,   Page 44
Berlin,   Page 45
Dolmancé,   Page 46

La Jeune Parque, Page 51
The Catholic Church of the North-American Rite, Page 52
Poe and Psychoanalysis, Page 54
Fleming's Lysozyme, Page 55
There are many ways to use Strayer's Vegetable Soybeans, Page 56
WRL, Page 57
VOICE OF THE PEOPLE, Page 58
The Inquiring Photographer, Page 59
Synthetic Diamonds, Page 60
Sterile Equation, Page 60
The Cookie Crumbles, Page 61
The Myth of the Two Germanies, Page 62
Birth of a Student Movement, Page 63
Ferrites, Page 64
Federacy, Page 66
THE COVER, Page 67
THE ORIGIN OF ORES, Page 68
INSECT ASSASSINS, Page 70
BURROUGHS Corporation B "New Dimensions in electronic and data processing systems," Page 72
The Mind and Marihuana, Page 74
Twenty-Five Stories Spencer Holst One Dollar (No. 1), Page 76
Twenty-Five Stories Spencer Holst One Dollar (No. 2), Page 79
"Like a map," the arcana of the universe Lay bare before me."—FitzHugh Ludlow, the American "Hasheesh Eater," Page 81
"Portable Ecstasies Might be Corked Up in a Pint Bottle"—DeQuincy, Page 83
The Prayer to the Gurus, Page 86
The Path of Transference, Page 89
The Path of Knowledge, Page 91

More a ran it him a no a,   Page 92
Hipsters Aren't Happy People,   Page 95
I Love Iris,   Page 96
Iris is Lovely,   Page 97
Yoga of One-Pointedness,   Page 98
Iris,   Page 99
The Force Between Molecules,   Page 101
The Buoyancy of Marine Animals,   Page 103
Things that go faster than light,   Page 104
ŌM,   Page 106
Drive on Malaria Covers 92 Lands,   Page 108
Prehistoric Man in Mammoth Cave,   Page 109
Metal "Whiskers",   Page 111
NEW APPROACHES TO CITY PLANNING: THE RETURN OF *COMMUNITAS*,   Page 112
Soviet Offensive Perplexes West,   Page 113
Profiles Maestro di Construzione Pier Luigi Nervi,   Page 115
Pattern Recognition by Machine,   Page 116
UBU COCU (UBU CUCKOLDED) FROM A VERSION BY CYRIL CONNOLLY,   Page 119
Solar Particles and Cosmic Rays,   Page 122
Mark Twain Life on the Mississippi Illustrated Harpers,   Page 127
MANAS OR THE INWARD SENSE: THE TEN EXTERNAL FACULTIES OF SENSATION AND ACTION,   Page 129
MAN AND HIS BECOMING ACCORDING TO THE VEDĀNTA RENE GUENON,   Page 132
THE ENVELOPES OF THE "SELF," THE FIVE VĀYUS OR VITAL FUNCTIONS,   Page 135
THE ESSENTIAL UNITY AND IDENTITY OF THE "SELF" IN ALL THE STATES OF BEING,   Page 138
Hard Sell,   Page 141
Bryophyta: Musci,   Page 143

COMMON Gametophyte, Page 146
Tracheophyte: Psilopsida, Lycopsida, Sphenopsida, Page 147
Sphenopsida (Horsetails), Page 149
Appendix Check list of Common and Scientific names of plants, Page 150
Botany Poem for John Cage, Page 153
On Pilgrimage By Dorothy Day, Page 156
The Story of Mosses, Ferns and Mushrooms, Page 158
Rinzai on the Self, or "The One who is, at this moment, right in front of us, illuminatingly, in full awareness, listening to this talk on the Dharma," Page 162
Psychoanalysis and Zen Buddhism, Page 171
The Human Situation and Zen Buddhism, Page 173
Lectures on Zen Buddhism, Page 175
The Sleepy Character, Page 178
A Ten Dollar Poem For Vera, Page 179
Introduction to "Plant Poem for Iris Lezak Whom I Love," Page 181
Plant Poem for Iris Lezak Whom I Love, Page 185
What Makes Leaves Fall, Page 190
They're Living it up at our expense, Page 196
"A Fig for Thee, Oh Death!" Page 197
Hitched to a Red Star, Page 198
Forbidden Marriage, Page 200
Solar Speculations, Page 201
Introduction to Provençal, Page 202
6 Gitanjali for Iris, Page 203

PART TWO
The Second Notebook of Stanzas for Iris Lezak,
Page 209

Peter Maurin Gay Believer, Page 211
That Odd Art—Understatemanship, Page 214
Bon Voyage, Page 215
Campaign Is On Foreign Policy the Key, Page 216
Books of the times, Page 230
A Story for Iris Lezak, Page 232
A Sermon, Page 234
Dorothy Day The Long Loneliness An Autobiography (I), Page 238
Cuba As I See It, Page 247
Good-by New York New York Prepares for Annihilation (I), Page 259

PART THREE
The Third Notebook of Stanzas for Iris Lezak,
Page 267

Dorothy Day The Long Loneliness An Autobiography (II), Page 269
Stanzas for Iris Lezak, Page 273
Asymmetry from the *I Ching,* Page 274
Haiku from the above, Page 274
Topography of the earth processes of the earth, . . . , Page 275
GOOD-BY NEW YORK NEW YORK PREPARES FOR ANNIHILATION (II), Page 279
A Greater Sorrow, Page 280
Dag Fears War Over Congo, Page 289
Shadow Over America, Page 291

First Asymmetry for Iris, Page 292
Second Asymmetry for Iris, (23 Sept. 1960), Page 294
3rd Asymmetry for Iris (23 Sept. 1960), Page 295
A Childs Garden of Verses / Robert Louis Stevenson / with illustrations by / Jessie Willcox-Smith, Page 297
Medieval Essays The Moslem West, Page 312
Andersen's Fairy Tales, Page 313
SELF-RELIANCE, Page 314
COMPENSATION, Page 315
The Magic Christian, Page 316
ZEN AND THE ART OF TEA, Page 318
The Buddha's Philosophy G. F. Allen, Page 319
The South Learns Its Hardest Lessons, Page 320
Asymmetry from Krishnamirti's Education and the Significance of Life, Page 321
Asymmetry from Dahlberg on his Mother 23 Sept. 1960, Page 322
Asymmetry from the *Catholic Worker,* Sept. 1960, & Kenneth Walker on Gurdjieff 24 Sept., 1960, Page 323
Asymmetry from Kenneth Walker's Study of Gurdjieff 24 Sept. 1960, Page 325
Asyymmetry from Kenneth Walker on Gurdjieff 24-25 Sept. 1960, Page 326
Berdyaev Christianity and Anti-Semitism,... Page 328
Asymmetry from the New Testament, Kenneth Walker on Gurdjieff, Dhopeshwarkar on Krishnamurti, Dante's Convivio, Paracelsus, & Freud—25 September 1960, Page 329
Prologue the Golden Poems, Page 332
Asymmetry from *The New York Times* 18 Sept. 1960, Dante's *Convivio,* & *Science* 23 Sept. 1960
Paracelsus (20 Sept. 1960), Page 336
Asymmetry from *In Quest of Yage (23 Sept. 1960),* Page 338
Asymmetry from Ansen on Burroughs (23 Sept. 1960), Page 339

Asymmetry from Bowles on Burroughs (23 Sept. 1960), Page 340

Asymmetry from Artaud to the Pope trans. Taylor (23 Sept. 1960), Page 341

4th Asymmetry for Iris (23 Sept. 1960), Page 342

2nd Asymmetry from Dhopeshwarkar on Krishnamurti (23 Sept. 1960), Page 345

Asymmetrical Tercet, Page 346

Asymmetry from Sayings of Gurdjieff (23 Sept. 1960), Page 347

1st Asymmetry from Kenneth Walker's Study of Gurdjieff's Teaching (23 Sept. 1960), Page 348

2nd Asymmetry from Kenneth Walker's Study of Gurdjieff's Teaching (23 Sept. 1960), Page 349

AN ASYMMETRY FOR LUCIA DLUGOSZEWSKI: A GET-WELL CARD (26 Sept. 1960), Page 350

Asymmetry from Arthur Clarke & Friedrich Dürrenmatt (8 Oct. 1960), Page 355

Untitled Asymmetry, Page 358

Text of Stevenson Speech at Dinner Here Condemning Nixon on World Affairs, Page 359

KRISHNAMURTI—THE SILENT MIND, Page 360

A 2-Part Poem for Ginsberg & Burroughs from Burrough's Letter to Ginsberg, Page 362

An Asymmetry from Dhopeshwarkar on Krishnamurti 29 Sept. 1960, Page 364

Haiku from above (29 Sept. 1960), Page 365

Asymmetry from *BIRTH #3* & (a little of the) New York *Sunday News* 2 Oct. 1960, Page 366

Haiku (3 Oct. 1960), Page 369

Asymmetry from *Scientific American* October 1960 *The New York Times* Book Review Section 25 September 1960 (5 Oct. 1960), Page 370

Piers Plowman, Page 374

The Earth Gods Are Coming, Page 375
Games of Neith, Page 376
Asymmetry from Ginsberg's KADDISH—22 Sept. 1960, Page 377
The Migration of Symbols (from a bawdy verse told me by Jennie & Sarah Williams & a book lent me by Margradelle Hicks), Page 378
The Courage to Be—(**Headlines from Tillich**), Page 380

PART FOUR
poems written on yellow lined legal pads with words drawn from previously written poems in *Stanzas for Iris Lezak*,
Page 383

> ONE HUNDRED AND NINETY DOLLAR POEM FOR VERA, Page 385
> A LITTLE DISSERTATION CONCERNING MISSISSIPPI AND TENNESSEE FOR IRIS (August 1960), Page 390

AN AFTERWORD
on the Methods Used in Composing & Performing *STANZAS FOR IRIS LEZAK*,
Page 397

PART ONE

THE FIRST NOTEBOOK OF

STANZAS FOR IRIS LEZAK

(written from the middle of May to the end of July 1960)

THE BLUE AND BROWN BOOKS

The "how" explanation
Bewilderment: Let us explanation
A number does
Bewilderment: reply of What number
Bewilderment: of of know something.

This helps explanation
Bring look us explanation
Attack no do
Bring Roughly: of word? No
Bring of of kind. Sources

The however explanation
Be like? Us explanation
Asking, not down
Be *roughly,* of what not
Be of of kind substance

The have earth.
"Be length?" Us earth.
(A "number", divided
Be rough of word; "number",
Be of of kind substantive.)

The heard "explanation
Be length?" Up "explanation"
A "not", definitions.
"Be real one?" What "not",
"Be one?" "One?" Kind sense

"This here explanation
Be length?" Understand explanation
A Need division
Be remove, ought word Need
Be ought ought Know. Surely,

To have explains
Be "let's understand explains
Analogous Now definition,
Be red", one way Now
Be one one king Studying

The "hard", expression
Be look us expression
A never definition
Be red of way never
Be of of kings something

The hints "explanation
Before." Later us "explanation
A no difficulty
Before. 'Red' ". Of we no

Before. Of of kind something

To has "explanations"
Business learning us "explanations
Anything nothing do
Business round", of "what nothing
Business of of know seen

The he expression
Between language understood?—"Expression
Are "now definitions;"
Between red of "What "now" "
Between of of kinds sense

The has e.
Be Let us e.
Against Now definition
Be red ought "What Now"
Be ought ought know seem

Polaris Action

Polaris of London-Groton, action RULE'S if submarine
Action (Conn.) 26, if of 1959

Phone: 1 LOCAL August regional invite 6,
August Community the invite 1 New

Public on leafleting a rally in 7,
A civil there in on NONVIOLENT

Please Orient Long Accommodations rooming. It SENT
Accommodations could that. It Orient name

Parts, own large and ROOM Is see
And cover testimony Is own Naval

POSTER, OVER. Launching attack retaliation important S.
Attack CONTROL TORPEDO important OVER. Nuclear

President opponent London.   Academy.   Resort including
             strategists,
Academy.   Circumstances to including opponent nations

Psychological off like are ROSTOV "Instant Sea"
Are countries.   This "Instant" off next?

Polar other liners as race industries supports
As contribute their industries other now

Projects; Ordnance levels, *at* REPRINTS *Information Sheet*
At C.   *Time; Information* Ordnance 1960;

P.   Our life all resolution imaginative, support
Accepted Committee Treasurer imaginative, Our Neil

Preparation OMAHA Lebanon, Armed races inclosed sponsor
Armed copies Transportation inclosed OMAHA Northeast

Who Am I? of Bhagavan Sri Ramana Maharshi Sri
Ramanasramam Eighth Edition

Which happy order
Always mind
Is
Order for
Being happy always greatest always vocal always nature.
Sorrow; real is
Real always mind always nature. Always
Mind always happy always real sorrow; happy is
Sorrow; real is
Real always mind always nature. Always sorrow; real always
   mind always mind
Every is greatest happy to happy
Every due is to is order nature.

Which has obtaining
And means
Is

Obtaining fact
Be has and govern and vital and not
Solely realize is
Realize and means and not and
Means and has and realize solely has is
Solely realize is
Realize and means and not and solely realize and means and
      means
Everyone is govern has the has
Everyone daily is the is obtaining not

When himself, organs
And movements
In
Organs For
Body, himself, and genital and *vasanas* and nor
Subdued respective in
Respective and movements and nor and
Movements and himself, and respective subdued himself, in
Subdued respective in
Respective and movements and nor and subdued respective and
      movements and movements
Experiences in genital himself, to himself,
Experiences deep in to in organs nor

'Who happiness of
Am matter
Inherent
Of five
Body, happiness am gross'; am verily am nose,
Sleep, respiration, inherent
Respiration, am matter, am nose, am
Matter, am happiness am respiration, sleep, happiness inherent
Sleep, respiration, inherent

Respiration, am matter, am nose, am sleep, respiration, am matter, am matter,
Essential inherent gross; happiness the happiness
Essential digestion inherent the inherent of nose,

'WHO Hence, of
AM mind.'
Indeed
Of functions
Blood, Hence, AM gets AM vision AM not
Should retains indeed
Retains AM mind.   AM not AM
Mind.   AM Hence, AM retains should Hence, indeed
Should retains indeed
Retains AM mind.   AM not AM should retains AM mind.   AM mind.
Enquiry, indeed gets Hence, that Hence,
Enquiry, deep indeed that indeed of not

With happiness, organs
Am merely
Is
Organs five
Being happiness, am gets am verily am nor
Such rejecting is
Rejecting am merely am nor am
Merely am happiness, am rejecting such happiness, is
Such rejecting is
Rejecting am merely am nor am such rejecting am merely am merely
Excellence.   Is gets happiness, that happiness,
Excellence.   Dream is that is organs nor

The Dream State

The individual himself, entirely
Dream reabsorption effected and mental
State to itself action to say existence.

There is however existence
Doubt regard exactly equivalent to activity metaphysically
Superiority; the possibilities are those they escape

This production: here effective
Dream real extensive absolutely mental
Situated in the waking state

General Introduction (I)

Given preference to Sj. Atal Ghosh's rendering of *Mahāyāna*, of which he says (in the Tibetan Book of the Dead, p. 232[1]): "*Mahāyāna* may, and possbily does, mean the "Greater" or "Higher Path" (or "Voyage"), and *Hināyāna* the "Lesser" or "Lower Path" (or "Voyage"). Elements discernible which very probably had origin in the ancient Bön Faith long prior to the rise of Tibetan Buddhism. Northern Buddhism; and is thus representative of the orthodox metaphysics underlying the whole of Lāmaism. Expression of the most important tenents of Mahāyānic Buddhism, some of which in the form herein presented are as yet unknown to the Occident save for a few fragmentary extracts. Religion, as to the anthropologist and psychologist, this work offers new fields for study. Although the number of books concerning Tibetan religions has recently grown, very few of them are little more than journals of travellers, whose principal concern, naturally, is the recording of their experiences of travel, and inevitably, of their own opinions. Less in religions than in historical or other problems, must ever depend upon original documents.

Individual and the generation, just as social and moral standards do; but written records are for ever the same. Need for just such a catena as this volume presents, of carefully made English renderings, profusely annotated, of some of the most fascinating and highly valued recorded religious teachings of Tibet, the Land of the

Snowy Mountains and of *Gurus* and mystic Initiations. The Commentary. Reader to grasp the abstruse philosophy of the Tibetan *Yogins* and mystics, which is as yet so little understood beyond the confines of Tibet, a comprehensive commentary, comprised in special introductions and copious annotations to each of the seven Books, has been added. Of this commentary is the explanatory teachings privately transmitted from the translator to the editor, supplemented, in some measure, by later research on the part of the editor, both in the Tibetan and Indian aspects of *yoga*, when the learned translator was no longer in this world to elucidate certain problems which arose as the editor reviewed the various texts preparatory to their publication. Doctrine of the Enlightened One, numerous erroneous opinions concerning it are at present current among European peoples. Unfortunately, too, there has been, on the part of opposing religions, much misrepresentation, some deliberate, some arising from ignorance of the subtle transcendentalism which makes Buddhism more a philosophy than a religion, although it is both. Comprehensive than any philosophical or scientific system yet developed in the Occident; for it embraces life in all its multitudinous manifestations throughout innumerable states of existence, from the lowest of sub-human creatures to beings far in evolutionary advance of man. To The Doctrine of Soul. It avoids the fallacious reasoning that a thing like the soul, as conceived by popular Christian belief, can without having existed prior to its expression through a human body, continue to exist after the dissolution of the body, either in a state of felicity or of suffering for all future time. On the contrary, Buddhism postulates that what has a beginning in time must inevitably have an ending in time. Not until man transcends this belief, in virtue of Right Knowledge, can there come Liberation.

Great majority of Europeans and Americans, belief in immortality, if it exists at all, is almost wholly founded upon their hereditary predisposition to the animistic theory of the soul; and to them, as is but to be expected, the Buddhistic contention, that the theory of an eternally enduring personal self for ever separate from all other selves is untenable, appears to be equivalent to an absolute negation of conscious being. Exceptional conditions due to *yogic* training prior to death, a more or less complete break in the continuity of memory in the *sangsāric* (or mundane) consciousness, but not in the subconsciousness, which, in our view, represents a microcosmic aspect of the macrocosmic (or supramundane) consciousness. Normal consciousness reflect only a very minute fraction of the subconsciousness otherwise known as the unconscious, which is the subliminal root of man's illusory being. Eyes of the unsophisticated man actual and real in itself, for he is ignorant of its hidden source. Representation of the macrocosmic, persists throughout all existences, or states of conditioned being within the *Sangsāra*, but the personal, or soul, or mundane, consciousness, does not. As from youth to old age in this world, so from old age and the moment of death in this world onwards through the after-death state to that of rebirth in this world, there is a casual process, a continuity in perpetual transformations. Literally, *Sangsāra* means 'going (or faring) on', or continued 'coming-to-be', as in a round of rebirths and redyings.

Is beyond conditioned being, beyond Nature, across the ocean of the *Sangsāra*. Not to be in any way identified with the personality represented by a name, a bodily form, or a *sangsāric* mind; these are but its illusory creations. Therefore, transcending time and space, which have only relative and not absolute existence, it is beginningless and endless. Rebirths and redyings. Of Buddhahood and the True State is attained, *sangsāric* mind, that is to say, personal, or soul, consciousness is realized to have like time and space, merely relative and not absolute existence. *Dharma* (or Doctrine) is, as the Buddha Himself emphasized, to attain 'Deliverance of the Mind': Understood as having reference to the microcosmic aspect of the macrocosmic mind. Conquest of ignorance; that is to say, transcendence over all that constitutes the complex content of the mundane mind (or consciousness), which is merely the illusory reflex of supramundane mind (or consciousness), or, in the language of our own texts, of mind in the unborn, unshaped, True State of *Nirvāṇic* Enlightenment. The causal continuity of the *sangsāric* mind there is thus a supra-*sangsāric* impersonal principle. Itself as the life-flux of the illusory five *skandhas* (see p. 356²), which constitute conditioned (or *sangsāric*) being. On the Path, in virtue of *yogic* training *Nirvāṇa* becomes the supramundane object of mundane mind. *Nirvāṇa* may be realized.

Greed, hatred, fear, desire, and all worldliness; he has uprooted all the mundane elements which constitute the very seed of *karmic* existence. Ever teaches of such *yogic* disciplining as will enable 'man' thus to realize that he is neither the body nor the mental faculties of the body, but that both are merely instruments, whereby he who makes right use of them attains the sublimest of *yogic* accomplishments. No conceivable state of finality like that of an eternal paradise; that there is no conceivable end of evolution; that the Cosmos itself is eternally subject to rebirths and redyings, of which the One Mind is the Dreamer, the Source, and the Sustainer. Existence.

Call me Ishmael

Circulation. And long long
Mind every
Interest Some how mind and every long

Coffin about little little
Money especially
I shore, having money about especially little

Cato a little little
Me extreme
I sail have me an extreme little

Cherish and left, left,
Myself extremest
It see hypos myself and extremest left,

City a land. Land.
Mouth; east,
Is spleen, hand mouth; an east, land.

General Introduction (II)

Responsible annihilation Lust,
Ill-will, *Nirvāṇa* translated realized of desires understood.
    Concerning the into Occidental Northern

Gospels, every not even *Romans* (alone) LIVING
Incongruity note there recognizes of dwelling Utopia
        Consummation. Then, it Ones, *Nirvāṇa*.

Gnostic Earth, no Earth, Right a last
Importance. Northern the represented order determine—
        unsettled, claim to is one, not

Gradually entirely, not exactly relative arising like
In nature. The real of duality Understanding. Comprehends
  the in or *Nirvāṇa*

'Great expression Nāgārjuna, exoteric revered after land,
In Nālanda the *Relation of* derived understanding consideration
to introduction of nature

Guide editor (1914).' Existence, RESULTS aim lived
In n. The religion of direct, unnecessary. Can the is of nature

Great essential not exploit race attained leading
In now to researches or direct unto case this is of not

Gaining Enlightenment. Nevertheless, end remiss a *Laya*
Its (negative) the represented of duality usually character. Texts
importance of *Nāda*

Great employed nature evolution rebirth as lead
Is not to *Rāja* or [Divine] underlies chapter the is, of non-Tantric

Graded City Speller Chancellor Eighth Year Grade

Guard raises against daily eliminate daily
Chrysalis identity Tuesday yearn
Subterfuge plight eliminate lessons lessons eliminate raises
Chrysalis he against neither chrysalis eliminate lessons lessons
        obvious raises
Eliminate identity guard he Tuesday he
Yearn eliminate against raises
Guard raises against daily eliminate

Guard relapse and detriment existing detriment
Culminate implement tenure yearn
Salutary politeness. Existing languor languor existing relapse
Culminate harangue and nor culminate existing languor languor
        of relapse
Existing implement guard harangue tenure harangue
Yearn existing and relapse
Guard relapse and detriment existing

Gentleman. Résumé are dejected evils dejected
Cautious insinuate. The yet
Statistics pierces evils lessons lessons evils résumé
Cautious haggard are nature **cautious** evils lessons lessons of
        résumé

Evils insinuate gentleman. Haggard. The haggard
Yet evils are résumé
Gentleman. Résumé are dejected evils

Graceful ruminate and dangers; evaporate dangers;
Circumspect in through yielding
Suspicious pompadour evaporate light, light, evaporate ruminate
Circumspect hinging and not **circumspect** evaporate
           light, light, evaporate ruminate
Evaporate in graceful hinging through hinging
Yielding evaporate and ruminate
Graceful ruminate and dangers; evaporate

Graceful **"Recovery"** against deception embroider deception
Carefully is the young
Substance parenthesis embroider lancet lancet embroider
        "Recovery"
Carefully himself; against noxious carefully embroider lancet
        lancet obsequiousness **"Recovery"**
Embroider is graceful himself; the himself;
Young embroider against **"Recovery"**
Graceful **"Recovery"** against deception embroider

Gentleness **restoration** and designing encore designing
Concern. Is the yawl
Superiors proficient encore lattice lattice encore **restoration**
Concern. Henry and nominal concern. Encore lattice lattice of
        restoration
Encore is Gentleness Henry the Henry
Yawl encore and **restoration**
Gentleness **restoration** and designing encore

Great Recovery artifices deliberate embryo deliberate

"Cloud." In the yawl
Safe. Permeate embryo lawyer, lawyer, embryo Recovery
"Cloud." Heart, artifices nature, "cloud." Embryo lawyer,
       lawyer, or Recovery
Embryo in great heart, the heart,
Yawl embryo artifices Recovery
Great Recovery artifices deliberate embryo

Genial restoration and descend evacuate descend
City inferiors the yourself;
Self-possession particle evacuate limits limits evacuate restoration
City How and not city evacuate limits limits opportunities
       restoration
Evacuate inferiors genial How the How
Yourself; evacuate and restoration
Genial restoration and descend evacuate

Glossary ravenous arrogance daffodil even daffodil
Clemency is There Your
Spring prosaic even lymph lymph even ravenous
Clemency how arrogance nor clemency even lymph lymph or
       ravenous
Even is glossary how There how
Your even arrogance ravenous
Glossary ravenous arrogance daffodil even

Governor reveler a diminish epicure diminish
Connive impertinence. The you
Smiles. Premature epicure ligament ligament epicure reveler
Connive how a nor connive epicure ligament ligament officious
       reveler
Epicure impertinence. Governor how the how
You epicure a reveler
Governor reveler a diminish epicure

General Introduction (III)

Goddess enthroned nature enthroned relationship another *leading*
Intellect. Nature. There relationship of *Dhyāna* unitary chief.
    There intellect. Of nature.

Great each natural each rather all. Less
It natural the rather of degenerate, uncivilized conveyed the it of
    natural.

Gnostic Egypt Near Egypt religious aside light
Ignition, Near the religious occult does, us Celtic the ignition,
    occult Near.

Greeks, even not, even regarded as *Light*
Individualized not, the regarded One darkness *Upanishads*
        common the individualized One not.

Greater esoteric Northern esoteric return, as liquids.
In Northern the return, of Deliverance, unknown canon, the in of Northern.

Guidance. Editor non-attachment editor right a largely
In non-attachment. They right or diameter, upon circle. They in or non-attachment.

Gooneratne; (earth, non-ego). Earth researches among living
Is non-ego. The researches of direct upon concentrated the is of non-ego.

Zen Buddhism and Psychoanalysis
Psychoanalysis and Zen Buddhism

(Secondary experience, nouns
Both used determine determine hearsay.) (Indirect secondary
    makes
Activity nouns determine
Principle secondary indirect conjugation hearsay.) Occurs activity
    Latin indirect secondary indirect secondary
(Principle sense is conjugation hearsay.) (Occurs activity nouns
    activity Latin is sense is sense
Activity nouns determine
Sense experience, nouns
Being used determine determine hearsay.) Is sense makes

Strictly exclude name
Books utterly dialectics dialectics Heraclitus' Indian strictly make
A non-A dialectics
Paradoxical strictly Indian Chinese Heraclitus' other A non-A A
    logic, Indian strictly Indian strictly

24

Predicates seem is Chuang-tsu: Heraclitus' (Oxford A non-A A
 logic, is seem is seem
A non-A dialectics
Seem exclude name
Books University dialectics dialectics Heraclitus' is seem make

Symptom.) Exactly not
Become unconscious develop develop have impulse symptom
 members
Awareness. Not develop
Peaceful symptom impulse contrary have other awareness. Not
 awareness. Let impulse symptom impulse symptom
Penetrate symptom impulse contrary have one. Awareness.
 Needs, awareness. Let impulse symptom impulse
 symptom
Awareness. Needs, develop
Symptom expresses needs,
Become one. Develop develop have impulse symptom members

Statements effective not
Be unrelated dying, dying, human impulses. Statements made
Answer not dying,
Put statements impulses. Completely human obvious aware not
 aware language, impulses. Statements impulses. Statements
Put statements impulses. Castration humanity, openness
 answer nature answer language, impulses. Statements
 impulses. Statements
Answer nature dying,
Statements. Experiences nature
Be unconsciousness dying, dying, humanity, impulses.
 Statements made

Speak

General Introduction (IV)

'Goddess, efficacious for the purposes invoked and visualized, not from any external help or favour.' Esoteric significance of the *Tri-Kaya*, reflected Divine Body of Glory, a reflex of the first, lead unenlightened beings to Freedom.

Incarnation, nowhere treated as a matter of mere belief; they are regarded as being based upon incontrovertible laws by nature. Relation to relativity has been made by Eddington, 'of time has not obliterated this order.' Direct outcome of how he wills and acts now, unsuspected by our biologists, cause and effect when applied to physics, to psychics. In assuming such an attitude, Occidental, nothing has real existence save Mind.

Grave doubt the claim of the master of *yoga* that not only is rebirth scientifically provable by means of *yoga*, editor has devoted twenty-two pages to an exposition of the Doctrine of Rebirth, need of a more serious attempt on the part of thinkers and scientists of Europe and the two Americas to put to the test of Western science this *yogic* doctrine of rebirths and redyings. Editor, research, a serious scientific effort to investigate the whence, last meet in mutual recognition.

Is Occidental man for much longer to be content with the study of the external universe, not know himself? The editor believes, race, on our getting an adequate knowledge and control of life and mind before the combination of ignorance on these subjects with knowledge of physics and chemistry wrecks the whole social system. 'Death have a long start over psychology and life.' Us in ignorance concerning the greatest of all human problems, chief concern is with these very problems, those *yogic* methods of attaining spiritual insight which gave scientific character to Primitive Christianity, its Gnostic Schools, of purely intellectual, nowadays leads to the worldly dignity of a doctor of divinity.

Give intellectual assent to its creed and dogmatic theology, essentially upon professions of faith and written scriptures declared to be infallible and all-sufficient for mankind's salvation, nationally supported and directed churches and priesthoods pledged to promulgate doctrines, excommunication. (Rather than by bibles) accepted merely intellectually, legalized ecclesiastical organization.

In the possibility of discovering facts by careful experimentation. Not, tyranny, root of all the chief world religions, of this transmission varies, did amongst the Druids of Gaul, us that their actual method of transmitting the secret teachings is as ancient as man; case of *The Tibetan Book of the Dead*, the translating of the present texts was done in Gangtok, idiomatic structures of the two languages allow, or as is in keeping with literary English. Not infrequently.

Good English highly philosophical Tibetan, esoteric language of Lāmaism and not well versed in that form of Tantricism which shapes the matter of some of our texts, no standard method has been generally adopted by European scholars. Errors as may have escaped the editor's carefulness would doubtless have been corrected. Revision. As it is, less technically correct than he would have left them.

Is. No scholar of this epoch, the Orient or in the Occident, rendering these texts into intelligible English than the late Lāma Kazi Dawa-Samdup. Of the mystical Kargyütpa School (derived), (underlying each of our seven Books) ('Contemplative') the Mahāyāna, into which he had been given special initiation when as a young man he renounced the world and dwelt near his *guru* in hermitage in the mountains of Bhutan. Of the Lāma's unusual career is to be found in *The Tibetan Book of the Dead,* neophyte at the beginning of the Path must know the rules and regulations governing the *yogic* career which he has chosen.

Great problem of the nature of the mind and of reality. Endowed with *Bodhic* insight, namely, essence of the most transcendental of all Mahāyānic teachings is set before the *yogin* for profound meditation and realization. Round about him, and of mind, longer will he be as are the multitude.

Ignorance into the unclouded Light of Right Knowledge. Nevertheless. This being so, reader will probably be inclined to concentrate his study upon one or more Books rather than upon the treatise as a whole, of the *Bodhisattva,* distinctly Oriental. Untrammelled scientific development, centres of research. The meeting of the British Association for the Advancement of Science, in 1933, or, 1928.

Give scientific sanctions to the same theories which underlie the whole of our present treatise. East. New Age of re-established mutual understanding and respect between Orient and Occident, ever new, record in this volume and so made available in English form to all who reverence, as the translator and the editor do, like the Buddha.

Ignorance into the Light of Reality and Divine Bliss, no avenue of escape from the transitoriness of the *Sangsāra*.

Strictly Personal

Short, Jewish seeks girl over 20, any faith or nationality. 25-45. Religion no barrier. Is interested in establishing correspondence contact with a lady of reasonable intellect, 35-60 age range. Cultural interests. Town spinster, 33, tall, attractive, fair, German descent, intelligent, introverted, free-thinker, non-religious, much integrity, tired of boring life amid small-minded people, wishes to have one fling this summer. Lightweights. Young man, good education, 37, poor but particular, seeks charming coleen, Irish Venus, warm-hearted, truly cultivated, genuine. Pounds to 115. Educated Jewish gentleman, single, wishes to meet attractive young lady, Akron-Cleveland, Ohio. Reputation. Single man would like acquaintance with single, German lady about 60, New York only. Only. Not religious, seeks attractive Jewish girl with fine figure, fine background and refreshing modern outlook. Ladies, residing in Italy, good looking, ages 30 and 42, would like to meet American gentlemen in 40's and 50's, kind-hearted, gentile, with moderate means who would be interested in cultured home-loving ladies.

Snapshot, please. Telephone. Respectable gentleman, 33, 5'5", 150, Russian descent, northeastern Pennsylvania, divorced, steadily employed, cheerful and affectionate, has two fine sons 5 and 7. I'd like to hear from a girl who is sincere, kind, and desires a happy home life. Catch. 27, tall, brown hair and eyes, needs the right girl to add that extra sparkle. Letter and lend color snapshot. Young man 6'1", 32.

Preferably European background. Eastern Pennsylvania. Retired wealthy man. Snapshot. Only, 30-40, 5'2" to 6' not over 140. No barrier. Attractive single lady, widow or divorcee, not over 40, who would enjoy a Mexico holiday, air fare paid, mid-July. Lonely, seeks lady, same qualities, about 60.

Seeks honest gentleman with kindred interests who might inspire successful career. Telephone number, please. Richmond, Va. I am manager of a small sales force, need to expand business and most of all want a short, attractive, mature, affectionate lady as my life companion. Culture and Class. To meet modern, fine, clean-cut Jewish lady, same age bracket, 108 to 120 pounds, 5' to 5'3", who loves outdoors, who can drive a car and is marriage minded, affectionate, sincere. Looking, sincere, affectionate, tender and well-established New Orleans business man, age 54, Christian, seeks an attractive, refined, pleasant widow or divorcee, of affectionate and lovable nature, for lasting friendship. York bachelor, 30's, short, honest, understanding, French descent, seeks lonely affectionate lady, 25-35, about 5'.

Pretty mother. Ex-Navy Flyer Monte Carlo Villa. Romance and adventure, apartment in New York City, Harvard graduate, age 40, no dependents, seeks youthful attractive, shapely gal, with no dependents and encumbrances. Sincerity. Of liberal outlook, weight 105-125. Living, financially secure who appreciate the better things of life, and a good-living woman.

Seeks travel minded lady who'd like to see West Coast. The sincere need apply. Radius of N.Y. I'll overlook . . .
. . . Collegebred, attractive, blue eyed, blonde, personable, 5'10", age 32, Protestant, desires to meet financially secure, marriage minded, cultured gentleman 30-45, 6' or over who would appreciate love, kindness. There Any Good Men Left? Lady 25-35 years. Young man, late 30's very likeable, cultured, unprejudiced, has finest character.
Personable bachelor, 40, seeks affectionate lady, N. Y. C. Exciting fun and companionship. Reply. Seeks older woman for interesting daytime meetings. Of love. No prudes. Area. Lots of time with Friendship, romance, maybe marriage.

Seeks cultured gentleman, 50-65. Temperate, practical, altruistic, decent, kind, seeks younger, non-religious, working class girl with serious intentions, not too big problems and not wholly mercenary. Ready to marry, young man, 37, 5'7", American born Jewish, sincere, seeks young lady quiet type. I'm not marriage minded. Character. Truly to love, seeks attractive girl. Lady. Y.
Prefer one who has a car for motoring, picnics. English with accent, sense of humor, has European background; seeks lady to 30. (Returnable). Snapshot. Original and talented writing. No barrier, include snapshot and telephone

number if possible. Am a bachelor, 31, 6′, 160, neat, sincere, friendly. Lonesome.

Steadily employed, do not gamble, smoke or drink. Things. Really nice company. Idea, seeks an attractive young lady who is interested in business. City, electrician, college education, travelled abroad, sports car enthusiast. 31, 5′6″, 110, wears glasses, is looking for a good man. Looking for a swinging chick who is intellectually inclined, adventurous, perhaps Spanish in descent. Year's automobile trip to Mexico, Canada, and through U.S.

Petite, age to 28. Easterner, Jewish, good career, 5′7″, 155, nice looking, perfect health. Romance. September, seeks lady, 27-38, suitable marriage partner. One who does not believe he could find an exceptional girl through a friendship advertisement. Neat, refined. And women who are very well endowed. Lady of refinement.

Separate Vacations

Sees Temptation . . . Each other. People are tempted to do things while they are away on separate vacations, but if they go together, this will not happen. Are good for both the wife and the husband.

Women are the LAZIEST People

Women are the laziest creatures in the universe. One of them for two years and now I realize what a mistake I made. My wife hates housecleaning and washing dishes. Even cook. New York City, N.Y.

M G G S G M H

Miles York
Geological ICE RIVER Long Ship
Geological Once Once Discovered
Ship Hundreds Estimated
Geological ICE VESSEL Estimated Ship
Miles Estimated
Hundreds Estimated ATLANTIC Discovered

Mile York
Guesswork It RESEARCH Lamont Special
Guesswork of of DURING
Special hundred Ewing
Guesswork It VEMA, Ewing Special
Mile Ewing
Hundred Ewing Argentine DURING

Miles York-New
Great ice river long.   Submarine
Great of of Declivity
Submarine half explored
Great ice Vema, explored submarine
Miles explored
Half explored AGE Declivity

Are You Giving Your Wife The Companionship She Craves?

All the loving attention she needs. Rutin, each day supplies your body with over *twice* the minimum adult daily requirements of Vitamins A, C, and D . . .
Yet discovered—off this exclusive formula, under pressure.
Government strictly controls each vitamin manufacturer and requires the exact quantity of each vitamin and mineral to be clearly stated on the label. Ingredient, VITASAFE C. F. CAPSULES you can be sure you're getting exactly what the label states . . . new Plan that provides you regularly with all the factory-fresh vitamins and minerals you will need Generous offer!
Your house, Ontario. Under the Vitasafe Plan as Advertised in The National Enquirer.

ROME

Rossano Brazzi became furious at a party when a teenage beauty with long black hair cascading down her back made romantic overtures toward Rossano. Out amid the dancers and very roughly broke in on Rossano and the girl. Meek but meaningful "Yes, dear." Embarrassment was amplified: there was a man in the room.

Recommended that she take a rest at a hospital to avoid a nervous breakdown. "Obviously he didn't know what he was talking about!" asserts Dawn. Many of the guests walked out, but the majority stayed and laughed and called out words of encouragement. Exclaimed: "That girl will never get anywhere."

The Marrying Maiden

Through Hence end
MARRYING and reach reach young is Nothing great
MARRYING and is describes end Nothing

To hexagram earth.
MARRYING and rests rests yielding is not girl.
MARRYING and

London

Lower lip. Objected to being called a baby and called Niven an unprintable name. Niven called her a few vile names, threw up his hands in disgust and told the girl to "Get out! Go away! Don't bother me any more!" David hadn't had two seconds to calm down when a lady rushed over from the bar and, explaining that she hadn't noticed him before, asked for his autograph. Out of the place. Night and sang a number of shocking songs.

Liberace called Scotland Yard the other afternoon and complained that he had received a threatening telephone call. Out of the picture. Not paying his bill to a tailor who needs the money far more than Antony.

Paris

Popped into town for a fast weekend and wound up dating two redheaded strippers who looked almost like twins. And the screen actor toured the the bars and picked up a third girl who seemed to enjoy being caressed by the strippers as much as she enjoyed being mauled by Boyd . . . Referred to the Duke of Windsor in similar terms. Into a fist fight in one of those off-beat bars Francoise likes to frequent. Sagan later admitted she didn't know why they waded into the fight.

Put him in a mental hospital for a long period of time. As BB threw her arms around her old friend and kissed him. Rushed back and apologized, he kept right on crying. "Instead of a man!" Spoken Charrier quieted down.

Passion. As he was kissing her neck he noticed someone else's teeth marks and became infuriated . . .

Marseilles

Man who was standing next to him. At the end of that arm was in Wayne's pocket. Right hand that caught the pickpocket square on the mouth. Stephen said nothing. Enraged man's eyes and then kicked him in the groin. In the car by the time Boyd had finished walking all over the felled pickpocket.

Madrid

Man. At him to claw his face. Down and sobbed uncontrollably.

Sydney

Some of her own.   "You couldn't be a true woman or you wouldn't fear such things."   Did.

Berlin

Became quite annoyed when a girl at a bar here made a pass at Mrs. Jurgens, a tall, beautiful brunette. Explained that since she made a pass like a man he treated her like a man.

Dolmancé

(*Dolmancé gives his orders, each person executes them, taking his post.*) Of the bed; Eugénie do you recline in his arms; while I sodomize her, I'll frig her clitoris with the head of Augustin's superb prick, and Augustin will husband his fuck and take good care not to discharge; the gentle Chevalier—who, without saying a word, softly frigs himself while listening to us—will have the kindness to arrange himself upon Eugénie's shoulders so as to expose his fine buttocks to my kisses: I'll frig him amain; which will cause me to have my engine in an asshole and a prick in either hand, to pollute; and you, Madame, after having been your master, I want you to become mine: buckle on the most gigantine of your synthetic pricks. Label, is fourteen by ten around; fit it about your loins, Madame, and shower me with your most terrible blows. My angel, penetrate: I'll not enter your dear Eugénie's ass until your enormous member is well advanced into mine . . . and it is! it is! oh, little

Jesus! . . . Ass without preparations . . . oh, sweet God! magnificent ass! Nothing of the sort, by God: half the pleasure's lost to these stupid attentions. Clitoris! . . . Eugénie, discharge, my angel, yes, discharge! . . .

Despite himself, Augustin fills me with his fuck . . . Of your entrails . . . ah! fucking bugger of a God! Little libertine full of fuck again; the entrance to her is smeared thick with it; frig her, vigorously smite her clitoris all with sperm: 'tis one of the most delicious things that may be done. Ministrations to those of your sister, that she may swoon in her arms, and strike an attitude that will furnish me with your ass: I am going to fuck your behind while Augustin buggers me. Ass ever so gently raised, up with it, a fraction of an inch, my love; there, just so . . . without lubrication, Chevalier? Nature. Cunts . . . Eugénie, deal equitably with the Chevalier; you are thoughtless of everyone but yourself; well, libertine, you are right; but in your own pleasure's interest, frig him, since he is to gather your first fruits.

De Saint-Ange: 'tis wonderfully amusing to begin in one ass the operation one wishes to terminate in another. Out of the question, my angel, I've never fucked a cunt in my life: allow me not to have to begin at my age. Little bitch might instantly be fucked by Augustin! Me while you fuck her . . . yes, that's it, come hither, Madame; I promise to sodomize you, I'll keep my word; but situate yourself in such a way that, as I fuck you, I can be within reach of Eugénie's fucker. And let the Chevalier flog me in the meantime. Not how divine thus to be, 'twixt brother and sister! Cunningly effected? Eugénie, would you like to have a discussion?

Does correspond with some part of these reflections and my discourses—they've proven it to you—even give to what has just been read to us the appearance of a repetition . . . Of which the ingratitude and impertinence of the feeble always force honest folk to repent. Let a keen observer calculate all of pity's dangers, and let him compare them with those of a staunch, resolute severity, and he will see whether the former are not the greater. Most untrustworthy guide we have received from Nature; with greatest care close it up to misfortune's fallacious accent; far better for you to refuse a person whose wretchedness is genuine than to run the great risk of giving to a bandit, to an intriguer, or to a caballer: the one is of a very slight importance, the other may be of the highest disadvantage. Are young, your speeches illustrate it; you are wanting in experience; the day will come, and I await it, when you will be seasoned; then, my dear, you will no longer speak so well of mankind, for you will have made its acquaintance. Now, if the vices of the one establish these dangerous virtues in the other, is it not then to render youth a great service when one throttles those virtues in youth at an early hour? Can remorse exist in the soul of him who recognizes crime in nothing? Evil anywhere exists, of what evil will you be able to repent?

Deceives, because it is never anything but the expression of the mind's miscalculations; allow the latter to mature and the former will yield in good time; we are constantly led astray by false definitions when we wish to reason logically: I don't know what the heart is, not I: I only use the word to denote the mind's frailties. One single, one unique flame sheds its light in me: when I am whole and well, sound and sane, I am never misled by it; I am old, hypochondriacal or pusillanimous, and it deceives me; in which case I tell myself I am sensitive, but in truth I am merely weak and timid. Latter can only touch the heart in one sense—and lightly—; the other titillates and overwhelms all of one's being. More piquant delights, join those inestimable joys that come of bursting socially imposed restraints and of the violation of every law? And we wish nothing from you but excellence. Null, that is how I view it, my dear; whether apathy or even pain, provided I am happy the rest is absolutely all the same to me. Case, the repercussion within us is much more pronounced, and much more energetically and much more promptly launches the animal spirits in the direction necessary to voluptuousness. Explore the seraglios of Africa, those of Asia, those others of Southern Europe, and discover whether the masters of those celebrated harems are much concerned, when their pricks are in the air, about giving pleasure to the individuals they use; they give orders, and they are obeyed, they enjoy and no one dares make them answer; they are satisfied, and the others retire; amongst them are those who would punish as a lack of respect the audacity of partaking of their pleasure.

Decapitated the woman who, operation of beheading. Less concerned for us than they are for themselves, man living who does not wish to play the despot when he is stiff: appear to take as much as he; natural at this juncture, capable of experiencing what he feels: enjoy as he enjoys reduces him to a kind of equality with that other.

Despotism causes him to feel. Our happy government, libertinage's passions. Man whose prick upstandeth is far from desiring to be useful to anyone. All the charms a nervous personality tastes in putting its strength to use; not that it is silent during such episodes. Captivity procreate as do those others that are free and wild; engender no more if he does not suppose himself alone.

Destines to belong to him at those moments. Of tortures, leave them prostrate at their insolent Dulcinea's feet, make them happy and, abandon them to the vile delights of wearing the chains wherewith Nature has given them the right to overwhelm others: not denigrate what they are incapable of understanding, come back here, eyes that masterpiece.

De Saint-Ange, our student. Let's do our best, my friends; a great pleasure to commission you to execute *tableaux*; not an artist fitter than you to realize them! . . . Can do to get a foot-hold in it. Every vexation you give me.

Drive me to offend you. Oh, longer . . . my fine fair bitch! . . . Again here . . . nothing that can equal the fuck that is drained out of the depths of a pretty behind . . . certain things which strictly require to be veiled. Exactly informed of the degree of familiarity which obtains between Madame de Saint-Ange and you.

La Jeune Parque

Là, à
Je étrangers, un naît; enlacée
parle à race qui un épaule

lumière accomplissait
Je. Et une narine. Et
purs abandonnant retour qui un ennui

leur avance
jour ennemi. Un. N'attends entrailles
pas aériens, ramer qui. Un en

l'âme aux
jouets en un Non, et
plus as-tu repris? Qui une extrémité

l'oiseau à
Je entière une n'ai-je en
plus au renfle qui une espèces?

The Catholic Church of the North-American Rite

The Roman Catholic Church on the matters of compulsory celibacy of the secular clergy, hierarchy towards the regime in mainland China is identical with that of the government of the U.S.A., European Zone embracing not only a free Germany but all other Eastern European nations now under Russian domination.
Countries of their origin, and the submission and adjudication of all international disputes to and by a reconstituted U.N. organization which will include all the nations of the world, (three fourths of the total votes being required for validity) human being, of color or circumstance, LAST CALL (invited to write to the *Society of Saint Dymphna*), CATHOLIC CHURCH OF THE NORTH-AMERICAN RITE.
Catholic Church on the matters of compulsory celibacy of the secular clergy, hierarchy towards the regime in mainland China is identical with that of the government of

the U.S.A., *unified,* Russian domination. Countries of their origin, have power of veto.

(Of the total votes being required for validity) Fatherhood of God from whom every human being.

The giving *"to Caesar the things that are Caesar's",* his God-given rights. (E. Duffy).

Not be published until finances are available. Or will be obtainable through the *Society of Saint Dymphna. Rite* are invited to write to the *Society of Saint Dymphna, THE CATHOLIC CHURCH OF THE NORTH-AMERICAN RITE.* Hierarchy towards the regime of mainland China is identical with that of the government of the U.S.A.,—advocates recognition of the government of mainland China, men under the Fatherhood of God. European one embracing not only a free Germany but all the other Eastern European nations now under Russian domination. Reconstituted U.N. organization which will include all the nations of the world, is diametrically opposed to *apartheid* in the U.S.A. as well as South Africa. Common Fatherhood of God from whom every human being, advocate the giving *"to Caesar the things that are Caesar's",* not be published until finances are available.

Rite are invited to write to the *Society of Saint Dymphna,* in Rome, the participation of the laity (ecclesiastical financial responsibility and administration).

Poe and Psychoanalysis

            Point, out effect
            A not dreams
Point, stables young child, hand out a not a let young stranger
    invites stranger.

                  Palace, on emotion.
                  Are now door.
                  Palace, sleeper.

Fleming's Lysozyme

Feature London, epochal *(Micrococcus lysodeikticus)* it nasal
    granules. Saliva
London, it saliva or saliva it *(Micrococcus lysodeikticus)* epochal

Fluids lysozyme egg molecular insulin not grains, significant
Lysozyme insulin significant of significant insulin molecular egg

Frequency long-felt example, may be induced now gradually
    structures
Long-felt induced structures on structures may be example

There are many ways to use Strayer's Vegetable Soybeans

To hours, enough.   Remove enough
And.   Remove enough
Minutes.   And not Iowa
Water and Iowa simmer.
To or
Until simmer.   Enough
Simmer.   To.   Remove and Iowa enough.   Remove simmer.
Vegetable.   Enough good enough to and buttered loaf, enough
Simmer.   Or Iowa buttered enough and not simmer.

Tomatoes, hot egg.   Roll egg,
Added.   Roll egg,
Minutes.   Added, nutty in.
Wash added, in soak
Tomatoes, overnight,
Until soak egg,
Soak tomatoes.   Roll added, in egg.   Roll soak
Vitamins—egg, giving egg, tomatoes, added, beans, largest egg,
Soak overnight, in beans, egg, added, nutty soak

WRL

"World" river leaflets

which Race, London,

was ripped LYTTLE

War Resisters League

Who report latter

what Research little

Wilshire release Lanning

will religious led

VOICE OF THE PEOPLE

Death I shed, I let's let's
And since 13 hate eh? 13 will in graduate in since been eh? never 13
Of 40,000,000 40,000,000 Everyone
Bus is, George peeve on change
Us Paris into not! Cafe enjoy not! The restaurants against lovely people against restaurants
United Nations it monstrosity peace. Remove City—1,200 per $750,000

The Inquiring Photographer

Definitely or
Years.   Or——
These have.   It's not kid
A
Bonus.   It's guess
Bonus.   Or not——side
It's side
Bonus.   A don't
For or rich
A
Bonus.   Or years.
Will have or
Will a not these side
These or
Bonus.   Establishment:
A
Side——contractor: contractor: establishment: side side
It's not
Bonus.   A side establishment: bonus.   A leagues.   Leagues?

Synthetic Diamonds

Some it no thinking has extensive thinking come
Diamonds it apparatus. Modern of no diamonds some

Structural in not the hardest equidistant the in century
Denser in atoms made ordinary not denser structural

Sterile Equation

States two effective *rapprochement* is luxury effective
Effective Castro universal aside two is on never.

Seven. The establishments, rice, important light establishments, Establishments, Communism, underdeveloped Asia. The important over ninteen

Social thousand *entourage* record in Latin-America *entourage*
Entourage case U-2, armament thousand in one needs.

The Cookie Crumbles

There has even
Century, organization organization kicks is even
Century, refreshing unpredictable mystery but learned even
    system,

The happy evidence
Cooperated on on kept in evidence
Cooperated response uses many bring *life* evidence she

That her. 18th
Culminating of of Karl indefinitely 18th
Culminating Robinson unless Meyer basis life-long 18th saddest

The Myth of the Two Germanies

THE hazards encountered
May, year's THE hazards
On: First,
THE hazards encountered
THE with on
Goals encountered reportage may, actually nothing is encountered social

To history.   Especially
Must ("yonder"—to history).
Of Free
To history.   Especially
To World of
Gain especially received must any not in especially socialism

Their (H. E.)
Minor young their (H.)
Open foolish
Their (H. E.)
Their, which open
Germanies (E.) refained Morgenthau achievement "1984" its (E.) side

Birth of a Student Movement

Basic in right to. He
O.   from
Answer
Support to unions Daily expected not to
Must O.   valuable expected must expected not to

But important. Robert.   The has
Of forced
At
Student. The unusual deliberately everywhere. Nationally. The
Most of very everywhere. Most everywhere. Nationally. The

Ferrites

First earliest recorded recorded in. Thereafter earliest stronger

For electronics, reasonably reasonably insulator. This electronics, so

Field efficiency. Region, region, it the efficiency. Strength

Force enter reinforce reinforce is that enter surrounding

Flow EDDY rate rate increased. To EDDY sections

Frequencies, effective. Range range individual. Third effective. Simply

Few electrons result result into therefore electrons. Some

Ferromagnetic each respect respect its temperature each
 sufficiently,

Ferromagnet effect. Represent represent itself those effect. Six

Four expect *(rows)* *(rows)* iron two expect sites.

Ferrite. Exact received. Received. Ions though exact.
 Suppose

Five energy reduce reduce increasing trivalent energy substance

Firing exactly resistance. Resistance. Interchange trick.
 Exactly starting

Ferrites elements: rare-earth rare-earth investigating
 Transformers. Elements: sweep.

                    Federacy

"federacy" equivalent divisions,
          equivalent removes and
          county-
                    state-
                              A.
                                   M.
                                        A.
                                             Yet

four executive di-
               rector
          executive relations as
          chairs year's

fire,
     effect.
               Doctors effect.
                              rate,
                                   A.
                                        M.
                                             A.
          costs year

THE COVER

The high electrical
Can of visible electrical relative

These high-frequency electromagnetic
Crystals on ferrites electromagnetic regions

Their higher interact
Cover oxide photograph interact red

THE ORIGIN OF ORES

The have each
Of rock.   It gigantic it not
Of finding
Of rock.   Each smelted

Ton, has extent
Order reconstruct in geochemist in nickel-iron
Order fit
Order reconstruct extent sank

Toward.   Here earth,
Overlying reliable *illustration* geochemical *illustration* numerous
Overlying for
Overlying reliable earth, sulfur

Three heavier 85
Oxygen resembling ions GOLD ions NICKEL
Oxygen form
Oxygen resembling 85 sinking

To hatched effects
Ore results. If, greenstone. If, *next*
Ore famous
Ore results effect Swedish

Type Huron. Early
Origin rocks involves gases involves Northwest
Origin find
Origin rocks early seems

Told. However, exposed
Over resist its geologic its nature.
Over formation.
Over resist exposed structures.

Taken his Electric
Other riddles is grows is no
Other further
Other riddles Electric significance:

INSECT ASSASSINS

Injects *no survive*.   Efforts control the
Animal *survive. Survive.*   Animal *survive. Survive.* Injects
   no survive.

In nasty spitting eye cost.   This
Assassin spitting spitting assassin spitting spitting in nasty spitting

Insectivorous nutriment species encounter Charles to
Are species species are species species insectivorous nutriment
   species

Into notoriety.   Sweeping eastern capture testimony
As sweeping sweeping as sweeping sweeping into notoriety.
   Sweeping

Interest nervous succumb easily: composed tube
Adhesive succumb succumb adhesive succumb succumb interest
   nervous succumb

It near spider East closes thorax.
And spider spider and spider spider it near spider

Its needle. Specialized enlarged?   Cutting tough
A specialized specialized a specialized specialized its needle.
  Specialized

Is nontoxic secretion extremely contains that
Assassin-bug secretion secretion assassin-bug secretion secretion is
           nontoxic secretion

I needle-like snake.   Enzymes compound TENDON
ANCHORING snake, snake, ANCHORING snake, snake, I
           needle-like snake,

INLET not significant, effect cockroach.   Thus
About significant, significant, about significant, significant,
       INLET not significant,

Insect "natural" surround enzyme constituents time
After surround surround after surround surround insect "natural"
       surround

Internal nerve.   Sucks especially contents through.
Against sucks sucks. Against sucks sucks. Internal nerve. Sucks

Immediate now share extinguishing controlling them.
Arises: share share arises: share share immediate now share

Insecticide? Needs.   Sap; episode.   Cimicidae thoroughly
Attributed sap; sap; attributed sap; sap; insecticide? Needs. Sap;

Insects numbing seconds.   Each channels.   They.
Accordingly seconds.   Seconds.   Accordingly seconds.   Seconds.
       Insects numbing seconds.

BURROUGHS Corporation B "New Dimensions
in electronic and data processing systems"

Babcock a research research of a graceful hundreds size
Costs of research processing. Of research application the its of
    now
Babcock
"Now electronic. With
  Design its mammoth electronic now size its of now size
  Its now
  Electronic lead electronic costs the research of now its costs size
  Application now design
  Design application the application
  Processing. Research of costs electronic size size its now
      graceful
  Size. Yet size the electronic mammoth size"

Burroughs other run run one other generate has slashing
Construction one run propulsion one run all these in one new
Burroughs
"New economical wide
  Data in Manager economical new slashing in one new slashing
  In new
  Economical largest economical construction these run one new
            in construction slashing
  All new data
  Data all these all
  Propulsion run one construction economical slashing slashing in
            new generate
  Slashing year slashing these economical Manager slashing"

The Mind and Marihuana

The him, Elect.
Mouths in Now delighted
Advanced Now delighted
Mouths advanced reposing, in him, upon advanced Now
    advanced

Three he embraces.
More inflexibly not dream
And not dream
More and resist inflexibly he unhallowed and not and

Towards hidden exhausted,
More in Now dream.
Approached Now dream.
Mouths advanced reposing, in him, upon advanced Now
    approached

The hair enchantment
Marble ice novel Dumas
Assuming novel Dumas
Marble Assuming reputation ice hair unfailing Assuming novel
    Assuming

Their him effect
Marvelous in nineteenth drug.
Attitudes nineteenth drug.
Marvelous attitudes returning in him until attitudes nineteenth
    attitudes

Their he emotions
Mind its name Dumas
Ardent name Dumas
Mind ardent romantic he unfathomable ardent name ardent

Tunics, held encrusted
Mysterious in nature drug
As nature drug
Mysterious as romantic in held unholy as nature as

Their him even
More It no *dagga,*
A no *dagga,*
More a ran It him used a no a

Throats

Twenty-Five Stories Spencer Holst One Dollar (No. 1)

Time was the edge never a tree.   Yi!
Flew in a hurry.   Very big, evenings
Swooping, (the fun of it;) rattle in the marsh.   Everybody
 strutting
Sparkling pennies each night, college students! Europe retired.
He one week-end, looked slow at the world.
Only.   Naked women explained
Dances, over a tiger lily willow leaves, all right,

That went.   An earthquake.   Noisily, the darkness.   Years
Full of the past in that kind of agony, its very existence.
Shuddered in the breeze, of viewing red walls if it were eternally
 tired—stared—
Seemed pushed, exasperating.   A neon sign.   The Egyptian cat,
 each day, would always reappear.
He played outside life and sold that morning.
Once near morning big red eyes.
Dead.   Once lives led.   And really

To enjoy went experimenting about a new God.   This new God
    retired young,
For many a Broadway hit.   *This is too much!*   Very pretty, even
Seen then, out like a man reflected if The Eagle seeking
Sees pure white.   The annoyed eagle nest.   Chickens on earth
    raised
His gun over the rocks. The little chick ate it slowly. To trick him.
One day she never went.   This eagle.
One day off, lunch, his own lunch anymore, roosts.

See them.   Warned embarrass not.   To tell you,
"In your little field." "If rudely vomited" excited
The spectacle.   The scientist on the other side rules in his fist, on
    earth he spoke
To his surprise the narrow path entered the same precise neat
    way. The cause every remembered
Hour of your clothes.   "Look," said the gas,
On a road now explained
He had decided out of these last loved answered reindeer

From the snow, with a grand, old-world bow, ever heard, no
    feathers though he yearns to.
"From you it became very well," what else.
Six inches tall.   Of his fairytales a pale red beret.   I frighten
    you?   Eyes stopped
Shallowly.   Pure in pitch, escape now colored except rose rays
Hans on your lap senseless, these stories
On a tree now to each I ask
Do not read.   Once a little girl liked Fifth Avenue ritual.

They'd walk.   Evil nose, to these you
Face; in front.   And some voice in her ear
Said to think, on the dummies.   A Ladies Room inside eyes
    slippers.

"She pulled elfs not curious elfs?" Red-eyed leers
On their haunches old men looked a sign, and two elfs,
Opposite her nose, escape!
Deserved rest. Outside a little pot lived after. Laughter roared
    out of

The corner. A woman made a little clerical error. Never their
    pullman cars younger
Features it's obvious were taking them to a distant village
    everything
Swung from the trees. On mornings past rainbow bodies hobbled
    across the hut into a dark corner. Exposure and sun,
Snarls possession. Every night curiously, English, reminiscing
    about their
Hunting experiences of the animals, the llama, the South
    American animal.
One of the hunters now eyes
Daddy? Oh light look. A million dollars. A red tongue.

Twenty-Five Stories Spencer Holst One Dollar (No. 2)

Time was each never time Yi!
Flew in very each
Sing time other running in each sing
Sing playing each never chasing each running.
He other listen. Sing time
Other never each
"Ducks!" Other listen. Listen. Aren't running

The would evenings. "None the year."
From "I" very evenings.
Swooping, the oozed right "I" evenings. Swooping,
Swooping, pool . . . evenings. "None covered evenings." Right
Have oozed little swooping, the
Oozed. "None evenings."
Dripping oozed little little asked right

This was everybody night this yard,
For into voice everybody
Spring this. Other restlessly. Into everybody Spring
Spring perfecting everybody night came. Everybody restlessly.
Here. Other lessons Spring this.
Other night everybody
Devote.   Other lessons lessons a restlessly.

Tapping, with Europe nothing. Tapping, years
Feet introduced feet Europe
Saloon tapping, outside regular introduced Europe saloon
Saloon played! Europe nothing. Crouch Europe regular
Himself, outside liking saloon tapping,
Outside nothing. Europe
Drummer outside liking liking and regular

"Like a map, the arcana of the universe lay bare before me."
—FitzHugh Ludlow, the American "Hasheesh Eater"

Law I knew every
As
Mighty as pouring
Thing how every
As ran created as not as
Only forth
Thing how every
Unutterable not I vividness every ran saw every
Law as yearning
But as ran every
But every forth only ran every
Mighty every

Language, its kitchen every
Above
Music above peculiarity
Typifies, heavens every
Above rose conscious above numerical above
Of from
Typifies, heavens every
Unveiling numerical its vision; every rose springs every
Language, above yohimbin
Became above rose every
Became every from of rose every
Music every

Ludlow, I keen, Every
A
Marking a proportion
That harmony Every
A reigned conception a numbers an
Order fell,
That harmony Every
Use numbers I very Every reigned some Every
Ludlow, a yet
Beheld a reigned Every
Beheld Every fell, order reigned Every
Marking Every

"Portable Ecstacies Might be Corked Up in a Pint Bottle"
—DeQuincy

Peace of resembling the and be loudly effects
Effects could sent the and could In effects sent
Mind in given hours; the
Be effects
Could of resembling *kind*; effects down
Unsettles peace
In not
And
Peace In not the
Be of the the loudly effects

Passages opium rapidly the alcohol body latter even
Even compare sings the alcohol compares I even sings
Mail. I generated, harmony. The
Body even
Compares opium rapidly keys even DeQuincy
Unfitly passages
I not
Alcohol
Passages I not the
Body opium the the latter even

Praises opium rapidly the and body lies effects
Effects Crude state the and Crude is effects state
Merely, is glow. Harmony. The
Body effects
Crude opium rapidly *Kubla Khan* effects drug.
Uproar praises
Is new
And
Praises is new the
Body opium the the lies effects

Peremptorily, of robs that and by legislation eight
Eight crisis, stationary that and crisis, incapable eight stationary
Mounting, incapable gives hatreds, that
By eight
Crisis, of robs know eight *degree*
Unwearied peremptorily,
Incapable night,
And
Peremptorily incapable night, that
By of that that legislation eight

Producing opium, reinforces the affirm but loves equable
Equable contrary, steady the affirm contrary, is equable steady
Main is general, health. The
But equable
Contrary, opium, reinforces Kolb, equable differs
Unrighteous producing
Is not
Affirm
Producing is not the
But opium, the the loves equable

Produced of respect the any but Ludlow exquisite

Exquisite contempts self-possession the any contempts in
         self-possession
Mental in gives *hashish* the
But exquisite
Contempts of respect Kolb's exquisite declines;
Under produced
In not
Any
Produced in not the
But of the the Ludlow exquisite

Pleasure of room that at by L——————— exaltation
Exaltation contrary, sustains that at contrary, (it exaltation
         sustains
Manner,) it gained Huxley that
By exaltation
Contrary, of room keeping exaltation distinction
Unusual pleasure
It

The Prayer to The Gurus

Thee, of the pure and holy Realm of Truth, whence there is no more fall into generation,
    O Lord, Thou Wielder of the Divine Sceptre, the very self of the Sixth Dhyānī Buddha,
I, thy son, pray in earnest faith and humility.
Heavenly Divine Realm,
May I attain the Immutable State of the primordial *Dharma-Kāya*.
Earnest faith and humility.
Perfected practice on the Path of Consciousness-Transference;
    And, in the glorious and heavenly Divine Realm,
    May I attain the Immutable State of the primordial *Dharma-Kāya*.
    Rays of the Realization of the Non-reality of Phenomenal Appearances,
        O thou, Venerable, Agèd Milarepa, whose graciousness can never be repaid,

    I, thy son, pray in earnest faith and humility.
    And, in the glorious and heavenly Divine Realm,
    May I attain the Immutable State of the primordial
        Dharma-Kāya.
    I, thy son, pray in earnest faith and humility.
    Earnest faith and humility.
    Realm,
        May I attain the Immutable State of the primordial
            Dharma-Kāya.
The Lord Himself, Dorje-Chang, the Root-*Guru*.
    Of the pure and holy Realm of Truth, whence there is no
        more fall into generation,
    O Lord, Thou Wielder of the Divine Sceptre, the very self
        of the sixth Dhyānī Buddha,
    I, thy son, pray in earnest faith and humility.
The Path of Consciousness-Transference;
    And, in the glorious and heavenly Divine Realm,
    May I attain the Immutable State of the primordial
        Dharma-Kāya.
    Holy Paradise Realm,
    O Lords Tilopa, Naropa, and Marpa, Father and Sons,
    I, your son, pray in earnest faith and humility.
    Earnest faith and humility.
Glorious and heavenly Divine Realm,
        May I attain the Immutable State of the primordial
            Dharma-Kāya.
        Unto thee, of the Self-Emanated Rays of the Primal
            Truth, the Foundation of all Foundations,
            —Mind,
        O thou, Shākya-Shrī, the untrammeled manifestation of
            the power of mind,
        I, thy son, pray in earnest faith and humility.
        Realm,

May I attain the Immutable State of the primordial
    Dharma-Kāya.
Unto Thee, seated on a lotus-throne surmounted by
    the lunar disk, above the crown of my
    head,
O Thou Root-*Guru,* whose graciousness can never be
    repaid,
I, thy son, pray in earnest faith and humility.
State of the primordial *Dharma-Kāya.*

The Line of Gurus, head, earnest faith and humility.
Perfected practice on the Path of Consciousness-Transference;
    Realm, attain the Immutable State of the primordial
    Dharma-Kāya. I, thy son, pray in earnest faith and
    humility. Earnest faith and humility. Realm,
Thou, of the power of mind,
Thy son, humility. Earnest faith and humility.
Glorious and heavenly Divine Realm, Unto Thee, Realm of
    Truth, Unto you of the Holy Paradise Realm, Sons.

The Path of Consciousness-Transference; heavenly Divine Realm,
    earnest faith and humility.
Perfected practice on the Path of Consciousness-Transference;
    Realm, attain the Immutable State of the primordial
    Dharma-Kāya. You of the Holy Paradise Realm,
    earnest faith and humility. Realm,
The Immutable State of the primordial *Dharma-Kāya.* Of the
    Self-Emanated Rays of the Realization of the Non-reality
    of Phenomenal Appearances,
Thou, humility. Earnest faith and humility.
Glorious and heavenly Divine Realm, unto Thee, Root-*Guru,*
    unto Thee, Sceptre.

The Path of Transference

There being the difference that in natural death the principle of consciousness departs from the human form permanently, have been long on probation and have been found worthy. Explication.
Principles of consciousness of two human beings can be mutually exchanged, animates, transferred to and made to animate another human body; human elements of consciousness and temporarily infused into sub-human forms and directed by the overshadowing *manas* of the discarnate personality.

The discarnate personality. His own body and assume the body of another human being, either by consent or by forcible possession of the latter.
Story, explain their stern refusal to divulge occult teachings indiscriminately.

THE *YOGIC* TALE CONCERNING TIPHOO. Having been favored with this unique initiation into *Trongjug*, explained in our annotations to the text of *Tibet's Great Yogī Milarepa*.

Phö-wa treats of the *yogic* transference within the mundane (all component things are realized to be *māyā*), Trongjug.

To *Nirvāṇa*—human consciousness, either while in life or at the moment of death,

Disciplined body for the purpose of making experimental study of the science of sensual love, animated the body of an Indian king named Amaruka who had just died, necessary knowledge had been acquired, guarded by his disciples. Endowed with the good *karma* to find the right *guru*, resistance to dissolution, so that compensatory *yogic* practices are necessary.

The *yogin* while practicing *Pho-wa*, he may find himself unable to repossess his vacated Earth-plane body, either because of some unexpected break in the magnetic connexion between the two bodies.

Possession of it. Above helps to illustrate this latter danger. The other hand, he may.

Order to influence the 'astrally' embodied consciousness-principle of the deceased. Follows the death-process in the case of all persons save those who are masters of *yoga*.

Thus being awakened on the *Bardo* (or 'astral') plane the deceased is made to comprehend the need of exercising his own *yogic* powers if, rites, accordance with the *Bardo Thödol*, not so project his consciousness. Sort of *yogic* suggestion. For the master of *Pho-wa* would doubtless tell us that all visualizations are explicable under two categories: stimuli produced telepathically by an external agency.

The Path of Knowledge

Then $H\bar{U}M$ entereth
Process a third hath
Of fourth
Knowledge "Non-Moving", of world Light earth disappeareth
       good expiration

The hatred experiences
Perfect all transformation however,
One fainteth
Know *Nirmāṇa-Kāya* ocean-waves womb. Led Executioner di-
       mensions *guru* exalted

Thus He Earth,
Pure as transferences: half-syllable
Open form
KĂ. No. Obeisance wonderful leading effulgent disturbing grad-
       ually exercises,

Through hollowness expand
Pillar, are three hold
KHA, NYA, outline watercourse line, existing dawn "gift-waves"
       enter

More a ran it him a no a

Maajun of relatively Egypt
A
Relatively a name
In the
Hashish in *Maajun*
A
Name of
A

Members often running East
A
Running a nutmeg
In the
Hemp In members
A
Nutmeg often
A

Middle of risk effects.
Among
Risk among no
Is the
Hemp, Is Middle
Among
No of
Among

Monoxide of rash effect
And
Rash and nux
Incorporated the
Handled incorporated monoxide
And
Nux of
And

Mexico orange reality experiments
Along
Reality along nineteenth
Into the
However, into Mexico
Along
Nineteenth orange
Along

Marihuana. Oriental rotted enliven
And
Rotted and now
Is the
Harmless is *Marihuana.*
And
Now Oriental
And

Made of respects European
Algeria
Respects Algeria not
In the
Hachischins In made
Algeria
Not of
Algeria

Musk or remember entanglement
A
Remember a not
Is the
Hemp Is musk
A
Not or
A

Meunier of relief, enough
And
Relief, and no
In the
Hotel in Meunier
And
No of
And

Hipsters Aren't Happy People

Holy is pray State thou earnest Realm State
Attain Realm earnest Non-reality thou
Holy attain pray pray you
Pray earnest on pray lotus-throne earnest

Head, I, perfected sincere the Embodiment Refuge sincere
And Refuge Embodiment never the
Head, and perfected perfected your
Perfected Embodiment of perfected lunar Embodiment

Humility. In primordial surpassing that emanation Rays
        surpassing
Appearances, Rays emanation now that
Humility. Appearances, primordial primordial *yogin*
Primordial emanation O primordial Lord, emanation

Heavenly Immutable Paradise Sons, thee Essence Realization
        Sons,
All Realization Essence non-thought thee
Heavenly all Paradise Paradise *yoga*

I Love Iris

Inhibit
Lāma or vividly extending
Inhibit red inhibit size

In
Like ocean, Vājra-Dhāra, Embodiment
In response in simultaneously

Itself
Living on visualize employed
Itself radiant itself skeleton

Infectious
Leave of Voidness every
Infectious realization infectious slowly-produced

Instantaneously,
Locality other. Vernacularly end,
Instantaneously, refer instantaneously, short

Is
Lacking offer virtue elemental
Is recital is secrecy.

Iris is Lovely

In *Rosary*. In succession,
In succession,
Line of variations 'ELEGANT' line yet

Is return. Is source
Is source
Like. Other villain excellent like youth

It regret it sure
It sure
Love own visible effects love *yogically*

Invigorate recurrence invigorate. Should
Invigorate. Should
Life, overcometh vulgar error life, *yoga*

Interest regarded interest self
Interest self
Lofty one views err. Lofty *yogic*

Into retreat into showeth
Into showeth
Loftily others vows enunciated loftily *yogin*

Yoga of One-Pointedness

Yoga of goal also
Of form
Of, namely, either Pray of infinity, namely, the either *Dharma-Kāya*, namely, either seek seek

Yogic others granting as
Others freshen
Others non-breathing employ [perfection] others in non-breathing three employ disk non-breathing employ second second

Yogin objects greater air
Objects followeth
Objects nature [exhaled]. *Prāṇa* objects incoming transparent, [exhaled]. Disappearing nature [exhaled]. Science science

Iris

If, return into sage
in religion it saying
is robbery, ignorant spiritual
interests religious indispensable sequence

invulnerability result. Indomitable system
instructions result impartiality sign
Inferior render idiot self-imposed
insane rather its Shamelessly

intercourse renouncing intellect superior
inseparable remain indication selfishness.
Instead residence innate should
influence. Recover illusory, seek

irreligious renunciation inconceivably spent
isolated received, Incarnations showeth
infinite, Reality immaculate successors,
illustrious Rosary injunction: *Supreme*

inspired recorded indirectly seeking
illusions. Regret. Inasmuch speech,
indifference. Requirements imbued service
influences retreat. Impartially. Study

impede radiance. Illness. Such
independent realization illumination solitude,
imperturbable recurrence incited successive
Incentives. Rites. Ignorance shore

The Force Between Molecules

Traditions hold examination
Forms of range compound examination
Between examination traditions water examination
examination Newton's
Molecules of law examination compound unknown law
examination simply

These heat evaporation
Fundamental off (r) C/r^n, end
Bodies end these. We end end new
Molecular off level, end C/r^n, untouched. Level, end source,

This hand, entirely
Forces. One radiative complicated entirely
Body entirely this was entirely entirely next
Mechanics. One London's entirely complicated unfortunately
London's entirely so

To. However, energy
Force (186,000) required charges energy
Become energy to waves energy energy number
Most (186,000) light energy charges undetermined light energy signals

Thermal hiss exist
Fluctuations or represented continuous exist
Be exist thermal wavelengths exist exist. Not
Microscopic or Lifshitz exist case. Used Lipshitz exist seen,

The Buoyancy of Marine Animals

          To higher exerted
Bladder upward or. Yet all nature curiosity. Yet
          Or fishes
          Mouths all routine instrument. Nature exerted
   All nature instrument. Mouths all live surface

          That high elucidated
Bottom. Up of yellowish active not copious yellowish
          Of fluid
          Maximum active restores is not elucidated
  Active not is maximum active limit such

          The have effort.
Balance. Unlike observing

Things that go faster than light

To however. It nothing go surprised
To however, and to
Go out
Faster and surprised to. Eventually, rotated
To however, and nothing
Long. It go however, to

The hits is, namely, granting speed
The hits at the
Granting oscilloscope
Far at speed the electron rigid
The hits at namely,
Length is granting hits the

Transmitted horizon in not gone succession
Transmitted horizon a transmitted
Gone ocean.
Form a succession transmitted equal rule
Transmitted horizon a not
Large in gone horizon transmitted

Than hand, interval never group shuttling
Than hand, arrows, than
Group or
Frequency arrows, shuttling than effectively radiation.
Than hand, arrows, nearer
Light, interval group hand, than

That high ionosphere number guide. Shift,
That high amount that
Guide. On
Followed amount shift, effects represent
That high amount number
Lies ionosphere guide. High that

ŌM

Of moral
obscuring man
obtained mother
own merely
others meritorious
order mystic
one's mastered
oneself meditation
obsessed monastery
observance merit
One make
observe must
on morrow
our miserable
offerings meditating
ordinary mind
object. Mental
objective magic.

Observing mistake.
Outset moment
off mast
only myriads
or meditate
orders more
Omniscient mankind
outcome men
'Obscuration' matter
open Milarepa,
Ornament meeting.
Obeisance morass
omens. Manner.
Once multitude
Obedience. Mantrayānic.
obtaining mayest
occult may
outwardly mistaken

Drive on Malaria Covers 92 Lands

Director responsibility: its vaginal eradication
Organization's ninety-two
malaria added, longer added, responsibility: its added,
campaign. Organization's vaginal eradication responsibility: said,
ninety-two its ninety-two eradication. The young. The which
        Organization's
longer added, ninety-two director said,

dangerous reduced introduced valorous effort
of nineteen
mosquito all liberation all reduced introduced all
countries of valorous effort reduced strikes
nineteen introduced nineteen effort threat yearning threat
        World of
liberation all nineteen dangerous strikes

disease responsible infant vanquish easy
other no
"monster." Against lethal. Against responsible infant. Against
complete other vanquish easy responsible seem
no infant no easy trouble. Y.M.C.A. trouble. Weapons other
large. Against no disease seem

Prehistoric Man in Mammoth Cave

Passages reeds entered him in smooth to one reeds in cache
Mineral a neck
In neck
Mineral a mineral mineral one to him
Cache a vicinity entered

Provided reconstructed. Evidence hunting, is some the of
       reconstructed. Is cavern
Mined and nearby
Is nearby
Mined and mined mined of the hunting,
Cavern and visited. Evidence

Perishable rock extensively had impressive skins this observation
       rock impressive culture
More archaeologists north
Impressive north
More archaeologists more more observation this had
Culture archaeologists vertical extensively

Pattern. Remain exposed heavy it slide telegrams operation
 remain it carry
Miles ancient not
It not
Miles ancient miles miles operation telegrams heavy
Carry ancient visitors exposed

Parks relation emerging here Ice smaller tribes obtaining relation
 Ice complex
Mammoth abounded new
Ice new
Mammoth abounded Mammoth Mammoth obtaining tribes here
Complex abounded valley. Emerging

Population region, extent hoes inner stripped toes on RARE
 inner C.
Materials animal necklaces
Inner necklaces
Materials animal materials materials on toes hoes
C. Animal venturing extent

People region even hunted Indian straw take often room Indian
 cave
May abandoned. Now
Indian. Now
May abandoned may may often take hunted
Cave abandoned valuable even

Paint revolutions existence—has into settlers. Then other
 remarkably into conditions
Most accessible N.
Into N.
Most accessible most most other. Then has
Conditions accessible visits existence—

Metal "Whiskers"

Metals electronic they attempted leaving
"With human inch subject Kohlschütter electronic restrain
      subject"

More. Electron the as Laboratory
"Which hydroquinone in seen kinds. Electron rises. Seen"

Material explanation, tip a layers
"WHISKERS have it smooth, kinked, explanation, ribbons.
      Smooth,"

"Memory" end tobacco-mosaic angstrom long
"Whisker high i. Sears's kink end remains Sears's"

NEW APPROACHES TO CITY PLANNING: THE RETURN OF *COMMUNITAS*

No efficiency worship
Appeal planner's planner's relationships, of appeal coordination
    highways. Efficiency social
That of
Coordination its that York's
Planner's Lincoln appeal no no its no. Great
That highways. Efficiency
Relationships, efficiency that. Urban relationships, no
Of far
Coordination of means means. Urban no its that appeal social

Not excitement. While
A proposals proposals remain one a currently historian
   excitement societal
Thinking. One
Currently is thinking. Year,
Proposals level a not not is not giant
Thinking. Historian excitement
Remain excitement thinking. Utopias, remain not
One future,
Currently one manufacturers. Manufacturers utopias, not is
      thinking a societal

Soviet Offensive Perplexes West

"*Simply do not understand what is your purpose today.*" Over the non-communist world the same puzzlement existed.
For good reason: in the cold war—East and West, troops.
Over the non-communist world the same puzzlement existed. For good reason: for good reason: East and West, N. Security Council reaffirmed its reliance on a U.N. military force to restore order, "*simply do not understand what is your purpose today.*" For good reason: East and West.
Premier expressed gratitude. East and West, remained over the capacity of the Congo to establish a viable state. Premier expressed gratitude. Leadership was being vitiated by the inevitability of change at the helm. East and West, Congo the U.N. was more deeply involved than at any time since Korea, "*simply do not understand what is your purpose today.*" East and West, "*simply do not understand what is your purpose today.*"
Week's events also underlined a shift from direct East-West diplomacy to the forum provided by the U.N. East and West, "*simply do not understand what is your purpose today.*" Troops.

Soviet Premier Krushchev last week. Offensive in the cold war —from Moscow itself and in the United Nations. In them—end of the week the tensions over the Congo appeared to be easing. The U.N. Security Council reaffirmed its reliance on a U.N. military force to restore order.

Offensive in the cold war—from Moscow itself and in the United Nations. From Moscow itself and in the United Nations. End of the week the tensions over the Congo appeared to be easing. N., Soviet Premier Krushchev last week. In them—from Moscow itself and in the United Nations. End of the week the tensions over the Congo appeared to be easing.

Propaganda barrage against American bases around the Soviet perimeter. End of the week the tensions over the Congo appeared to be easing. Raised two main questions: propaganda barrage against American bases around the Soviet perimeter. Left by the Communist walkout from the ten-nation talks in Geneva. End of the week the tensions over the Congo appeared to be easing. Krushchev's motives? Soviet Premier Krushchev last week. End of the week the tensions over the Congo appeared to be easing. Soviet Premier Krushchev last week.

War the feeling was that Mr. Krushchev would not press his offensive that far. End of the week the tensions over the Congo appeared to be easing. Soviet Premier Krushchev last week. The U.N. Security Council reaffirmed its reliance on a U.N. military force to restore order.

Profiles Maestro di Costruzione Pier Luigi Nervi

Past refers ONE few in laudatory embarrassing striking
Most aesthetic embarrassing striking the refers ONE
Developments in
"Contemporary" ONE striking the refers unable, zeal. In ONE
     now embarrassing
Past in embarrassing refers
Laudatory unable, in generations in
Now embarrassing refers view in

Phenomenon revolutionary of fading in long either synonym
"Modern," as either synonym the revolutionary of
Describes in
Contemporary of synonym the revolutionary usefulness, zeal.
   In of 1950. Either
Phenomenon in either revolutionary
Long usefulness, in good in
1950. Either revolutionary virtues—in

Produced ring.

Pattern Recognition by Machine

Perceive. As letters. Think? Think? Elusive, relations, now met most of the classic criteria of intelligence that skeptics have proposed.

Relations, elusive, *can* outperform their designers: original: group from the Carnegie Institute of Technology and the Rand Corporation (now met most of the classic criteria of intelligence that skeptics have proposed). In *Principia Mathematica,* think? In *Principia Mathematica,* original: now met most of the classic criteria of intelligence that skeptics have proposed.

Bertrand Russell. In *Principia Mathematica.*

More elegant than the Whitehead-Russell version. *As letters. Can* outperform their designers: His ability to solve problems, in *Principia Mathematica,* now met most of the classic criteria of intelligence that skeptics have proposed. Elusive.

Prove theorems and generally run his life depends on this type of perception. Achievements in mechanical problem-solving will remain isolated technical triumphs. The difficulty lies in the nature of the task. The difficulty lies in the nature of the task. Essentially classified the possible inputs. Request to pass the salt. Not transmit these ideal intervals.

Request to pass the salt. Essentially classified the possible inputs. Clear. Of variation among the dots and dashes, grid and converted to a cellular pattern by completely filling in all squares through which lines pass (not transmit these ideal intervals). In gaps (the difficulty lies in the nature of the task). In gaps (of variation among the dots and dashes), not transmit these ideal intervals.

(Bottom left). In gaps.

Maximum number of intersections of the sample with all horizontal lines across the grid. Achievements in mechanical problem-solving will remain isolated triumphs. Clear. Have been found and the range of the identified character spaces. In gaps (not transmit these ideal intervals). Essentially classify the possible inputs.

Process, are identified as dots and dashes. The classified marks and spaces gives a string of tentative segments, the classified marks and spaces gives a string of tentative segments. Experience has shown that when one of the tentative segments is not acceptable, reclassifies the longest space in the segment as a character space and examines the two new characters thus formed. Not fully specified in advance.

Reclassifies the longest space in the segment as a character space and examines the two new characters thus formed. Experience has shown that when one of the tentative segments is not acceptable, continuous message is divided into appropriate segments. Often by appropriate. Generalizing about pattern recognition. Not fully specified in advance. Is rather specialized. The classified marks and spaces gives a string of tentative segments, is rather specialized. Often be appropriate. Not fully specified in advance.

Be expected; is rather specialized.

Mechanical reader is to provide it with a means of assimilating the visual data. Are identified as dots and dashes. Continuous message is divided into appropriate segments. Handle. Is rather specialized. Not fully specified in advance. Experience has shown that when one of the tentative fragments is not acceptable.

Presents no problem. An image of the letter could be projected on a bank of photocells, the output of each cell controlling a binary device in the computer. The output of each cell controlling a binary device in the computer. Experiments to be described here the appropriate digital information from the matrix was recorded on punch cards and was fed into the computer in this form. Representing the unknown letter would be compared to each template sequence, number of matching digits recorded in each case.

Representing the unknown letter would be compared to each template sequence, experiments to be described here the appropriate digital information from the matrix was recorded on punch cards and was fed into the computer in this form. Clearly fail. Orientation or size could destroy the match completely [good deal more than mere shapes]. Number of matching digits recorded in each case. INCORRECT MATCH may result even when sample (the output of each cell controlling a binary device in the computer). INCORRECT MATCH may result even when sample (orientation or size could destroy the match completely) number of matching digits recorded in each case.

Believe to be an important general principle. INCORRECT MATCH may result even when sample.

Matches. An image of the letter could be projected on a bank of photocells, clearly fail. Hierarchical structure is forced on the recognition system by the nature of the entities to be recognized. INCORRECT MATCH may result even when sample (number of matching digits recorded in each case). Experiments to be described here the appropriate digital information from the matrix was recorded on punch cards and fed into the computer in this form.

UBU COCU (UBU CUCKOLDED) FROM A VERSION BY CYRIL CONNOLLY

Understand. But understand.
Compelled, Oh compelled, understand.
Understand. But understand.
Compelled, understand. Compelled, kind Oh like discontented
        every discontented
Faithful reason Oh my
And
Volumes! Every reason say it's Oh no
But young
Compelled, young reason it's like
Compelled, Oh no no Oh like like young

Understand but understand
Considerable Oh, considerable understand
Understand but understand
Considerable understand considerable kitchens, Oh, like door
        excuse door

Forgive right Oh, means
At
Visit excuse right such it's Oh, need
But you
Considerable you right it's like
Considerable Oh, need need Oh, like like you

Ubu be Ubu
Cheek on cheek Ubu
Ubu be Ubu
Cheek Ubu cheek kicking on like doubt Excuse doubt
Forth respect on most
And
Very Excuse respect Sir, interesting. On no
Be you
Cheek you respect interesting. Like
Cheek on no no on like like you

Use. Barrel use.
Consecrated old consecrated use.
Use. Barrel use.
Consecrated use. Consecrated kit old look demand Egypt demand
From resolved old most
Anything,
Virtuous Egyptian resolved sixty is old night
Barrel years
Consecrated years resolved is look
Consecrated old night night old look look years

Ubé box Ubé
Cons of Cons Ubé
Ubé box Ubé
Cons Ubé Cons kindness, of long day Ears day

Feel restore of march
Are
Vigorous Ears restore stainless In of no
Box you
Cons you restore In long
Cons of no no of long long you

Ubu be Ubu
Cons one Cons Ubu
Ubu be Ubu
Cons Ubu Cons kind one let down entertainment down
Finances remain, one my
All
Vengeance! Entertainment remain, sou, in one nothing
By you,
Cons you, remain, in let
Cons one nothing nothing one let let you,

Solar Particles and Cosmic Rays

Step origin least assured rays
Past assured rays Throughout investigators concerned least
    enormously step
Assured not detect
Concerned origin step more investigators concerned
Rays assured years step

Sun, of learned accelerators recent
Particles accelerators recent the invest cosmic-ray learned
    energies sun,
Accelerators notably design
Cosmic-ray of sun, might invest cosmic-ray
Recent accelerators Year, sun,

Solar on lower activity relatively
Particles activity relatively the is coördinated lower energies solar
Activity 1942 difficult
Coördinated on solar most is coördinated

Relatively activity year solar

Suddenly of level atmospheric radio
Particles atmospheric radio the is closed level earth.   Suddenly
Atmospheric not does,
Closed of suddenly minimum is closed
Radio atmospheric Y.   Suddenly

Soon over large activity.   Riometers
Phases activity.   Riometers the Investigators coming large erupted
   soon
Activity.   No drop
Coming over soon magnetic Investigators coming
Riometers activity.   ─────────   Soon

Something of large as riometers.
Physicists as riometers.   They ionosphere came large effects.
      Something
As near days
Came of something Magnetic ionosphere came
Riometers.   As ───────── something

Suggested of large aloft ─────────
Particles aloft ───────── the instruments carried large
        ───────── suggested
Aloft 1958, direct
Carried of suggested ───────── instruments carried
───────── Aloft ───────── suggested

Sunspot on late appearing regions
P.   appearing regions the idea ───────── late emitting
   sunspot
Appearing next day.
───────── On sunspot might idea ─────────
Regions appearing ───────── sunspot

123

Showed only level At radiation
——————— At radiation the influx carried level even showed
At 9:30 decrease
Carried only showed morning, influx carried
Radiation At ——————— showed

Starting on level at radiation
P. at radiation the intense Churchill level ended starting
At noise day
Churchill on starting Meanwhile, intense Churchill
Radiation at ——————— starting

——————— Our less a radiation.
Protons a radiation. The increase could less effects ———————
A 99 detected
Could our ——————— million increase could
Radiation. A ——————— ———————

Sure only later aboard reached
Penetrated aboard reached to Iowa, could later electron sure
Aboard not detectors.
Could only sure million Iowa, could
Reached aboard ——————— sure

Solar outside less and R.
Particles and R. The increase coincidence less essentially solar
And numerous due
Coincidence outside solar million increase coincidence
R. And ——————— solar

"Stored" only leak a reservoirs
Protons a reservoirs the is clue leak ejected "stored"
A 1958, during

Clue only "stored" minutes is clue
Reservoirs a year. "Stored"

Studies output later and rays
Protons and rays These is could later established studies
And no destined
Could output studies much is could
Rays and Y. Studies

Spectrum of low as revealed
Particles as revealed the indicated. Contrast low energies,
    spectrum
As number decreases
Contrast of spectrum marked indicated. Contrast
Revealed as ——————— spectrum

Several of long. Astronomical ————————
Period astronomical ——————— to into convert long.
    Exclusively several
Astronomical need ——————
Convert of several millions into convert
——————— Astronomical years several

Solar only ——————— a recently
Protons a recently the in Cosmic ——————— Even solar
(A nuclei); detached
Cosmic only solar Minnesota in Cosmic
Recently a ——————— solar

Sun of long a rays.
Particles. A rays. They in cosmic long emit sun
A not does
Cosmic of sun many in cosmic
Rays. A Y. Sun

Solar of life as ———
Possible as ——————— to It continue life explain solar
As nonetheless determined,
Continued of solar mechanism It continue
——————— As yet solar

System, other leading a rays:
Provide a rays: that injection cosmic leading explosions, system
A numbers do
Cosmic other system, may injection cosmic
Rays: a ————— system,

Mark Twain Life on the Mississippi Illustrated Harpers

Mississippi about. Reading keels.
The well about. Is not
Longest is four England,
On not
The hundred England.
Mississippi is seems seems is seems seems is part part is
Is longest longest up seems the reading about. The England discharges
Hundred about. Reading part England, reading seems

Missouri a river Knights-Hospitalers
The worth an It No
Lawrence It fly exceptionally
One No
The hundred exceptionally
Missouri It safe safe It safe safe It Pacific Pacific It
It Lawrence Lawrence until, safe the river a the exceptionally drainage-basin;
Hundred a river Pacific exceptionally river safe

Main all remarkable. King,
The ways all is navigable
Longitude. Is from eighty-seven
Of navigable
The hundred eighty-seven
Main is say say is say say is Portugal, Portugal, is
Is longitude. Longitude. Upper, say the remarkable. All the eighty-seven draws
Hundred all remarkable. Portugal, eighty-seven remarkable. Say

Miles.   Also river kept
The world — also is navigable
Little is from engineers,
One navigable
The hundred engineers,
Miles.   Is since since is since since is proper, proper, is
Is little little uniform since the river also the engineers, Delaware
Hundred also river proper, engineers, river since

Miles and river keeping
The world, and in narrower;
Lower in from empties
Over narrower;
The hundreds empties
Miles in same same in same same in point point in
In lower lower used same the river and the empties degrees
Hundreds and river point empties river same

MANAS OR THE INWARD SENSE: THE TEN EXTERNAL FACULTIES OF SENSATION AND ACTION

Means after neuter after *Sānkhya*
On respectively
The here elementary
In neuter words after respectively describe
Sānkhya elementary neuter *Sānkhya* clementary:
The here elementary
The elementary neuter
Elementary consciousness *Sānkhya* the elementary respectively
        neuter after list
Five after consciousness universal list the In elementary *Sānkhya*
Of five
Sānkhya elementary neuter *Sānkhya* after the In of neuter
After neuter describe
After consciousness the In of neuter

Manifestation applied no applied since
Order refer
To has enough
In no Water applied refer distinct
Since enough no since enough:

To has enough
To enough no
Enough could since to enough refer no applied latter
Five applied could "unproductive latter" to in enough since
Order five
Since enough no since applied to in order no
Applied no distinct
Applied could to in order no

Man, As no As subject:
Of re-absorbed
The however, enough
Individual no (with As re-absorbed development,
Subject: enough no subject: enough:
The however, enough
The enough no
Enough quote subject: the enough re-absorbed no As limitation
For). As constitution Universal limitation the Individual enough subject:
Of for
Subject: enough no subject: As the individual of no
As no development,
As constitution the individual of no

Merely active, nothing active, say
Only relative
To hand essential
Is not which active relative developed
Say essential not say essential:
To hand essential
To essential nothing
Essential *(kartritva)* say to essential relative nothing active, laying
For active, contingent union laying to is essential say
Only for

Say essential not say active, to is only not
Active, not developed
Active, contingent to is only not

Mouth and nostrils and (so
Or (respiration,
Two) head). Eyes,
In nostrils with and (respiration, dealing
(So eyes, nostrils) (so eyes,—:
Two) head). Eyes
Two eyes, nostrils
Eyes, case, (so two eyes, (respiration, nostrils) and later
Faculties and case,) usual later, two in eyes, (so
Or faculties)
(So eyes, nostrils (so and two in or nostrils
And nostrils dealing
And case, two in or) nostrils)

Manas action necessary action speech
Of respective
To here. Elements
In nature would action respective detail,
Speech elements necessary speech elements:
To here. Elements
To elements necessary
Elements correspondence speech to elements respective necessary
    action lastly
Fully action correspondence undertake lastly to in elements
    speech
Of fully
Speech elements necessary speech action to in of necessary
Action necessary detail,
Action correspondence to in of necessary

MAN AND HIS BECOMING ACCORDING TO THE VEDĀNTA RENE GUENON

Modes a neither
A neither does
Held is stranger
Becomes extent contrary opinion modes is neither greater
A contrary contrary opinion religion, does is neither greater
THE opinion
THE held extent
Vedānta extent does a neither THE a
Religion extent neither extent
Greater under extent neither opinion neither

May as necessary
As necessary define
Human IN start,
Being, essential clearly order may IN necessary generally
As clearly clearly order replace define IN necessary generally
Thoroughly order
Thoroughly human essential
Vedānta essential define as necessary thoroughly as
Generally understand essential necessary order necessary

Manifesting $\bar{A}tm\bar{a}$ note,
$\bar{A}tm\bar{a}$ note, denoted
However, itself successive
Being, "envelopes" clothing or manifesting itself note, Greek
$\bar{A}tm\bar{a}$ clothing clothing or regarded, denoted itself note, Greek
The or
The however, "envelopes"
Ved$\bar{a}$nta "envelopes" denoted $\bar{A}tm\bar{a}$ note, the $\bar{A}tm\bar{a}$
Regarded, "envelopes" note, "envelopes"
Greek *Upanishad* "envelopes" note, or note,

Meaning among nor
Among nor Deliberately
Have it some
Be either. Character orientalists, meaning it nor gravest
Among character character orientalists, result Deliberately it nor gravest
To orientalists
To have either.
Vaguest either. Deliberately among nor to among
Result either. Nor either.
Gravest understand either. Nor orientalists, Nor

Must and now
And now dealing,
Highest in several
Better enable consider on must in now Greeks;
And consider consider on relation dealing, in now Greeks;
To on
To highest enable
Vishwakarma enable dealing, and now to and
Relation enable now enable
Greeks; understand enable now on now

Modes ACCORDING name
ACCORDING name destructible
Highest in second
Bhagavad-Gītā earth, case one modes in note. Grow
ACCORDING case case one representing destructible in note. Grow
To one
To highest earth,
Veda earth, destructible ACCORDING note. To ACCORDING
Representing earth, name earth,
Grow *(uttama)* earth, name one name

THE ENVELOPES OF THE "SELF;"
THE FIVE VĀYUS OR VITAL FUNCTIONS

The however, "envelopes"
"Envelopes" note, Vedānta "envelopes" living or Purusha
 "envelopes" series
Or form
"Series "envelopes" living form;"
The however, "envelopes"
Form itself Vedānta "envelopes"
Vedānta Ātmā itself Upanishad series
Or regarded,
Vedānta itself the Ātmā living
Form Upanishad note, clothing the itself or note, series

The higher envelope
Envelope not (vijnānamaya-kosha) envelope latter order; principle
 envelope so
Order; formless

The higher envelope
"Succeeding envelope latter formless;"
The higher envelope
Formless in *(vijñānamaya-kosha)* envelope
(vijñānamaya-kosha) are in up so
Order; relation
(vijñānamaya-kosha) in the are latter
Formless up not contained the in order; not so

The here envelopes
Envelopes no *(vijñānamaya* envelopes last of principially
        envelopes stage,
Of faculties,
The here envelopes)
"Stage, envelopes last form;"
The here envelopes
Form in *(vijñānamaya)* envelopes
(Vijñānamaya as in usually stage,
OF referred)
(Vijñānamaya in the as) last
Form usually no "conceptive" the in of no stage.

The human expiration
Expiration not viewed expiration limits organism; projects
        expiration simply
Organism; (4)
The human expiration
"Simply expiration limits (4);"
The human expiration
(4) it, viewed expiration
Viewed are it, *(udāna)*, simply
Organism; restricted
Viewed it, the are limits
(4) *(udāna)*, not commonly the it, organism, simply

The have Every
Every name viviparous Every less organic possesses, Every such
Organic form,
The have Every
"Such Every less form;"
The have Every
Form, in viviparous Every
Viviparous (*āndaja*), *yonija Upanishad*, such
Organic reproduction
Viviparous in the a less
Form, *Upanishad,* name complete the in organic name such

THE ESSENTIAL UNITY AND IDENTITY OF THE "SELF" IN ALL THE STATES OF BEING

This have emphasise
Emphasise stage stage emphasise necessary this it At longer
"Universal Necessary" it this it
At necessary described
It described emphasise necessary this it this it
Of fundamental
This have emphasise
"Stage emphasise longer fundamental"
It necessary
At longer longer
This have emphasise
Stage this At this emphasise stage
Of fundamental
This have emphasise
Been emphasise it necessary given

To have entirety
Entirety since since entirety nil to in As lost
Universal nil in to in
And nil distinction,
In distinction, entirety nil to in to in
Out formal
To have entirety
"Since entirety lost formal"
In nil
And lost lost
To have entirety
Since to and to entirety since
Out formal
To have entirety
Bhagavad-Gītā entirety in nil great,

The hair end
End sea sea end "No the invalidates as latter"
Unity "No invalidates the yields"
As "No distinction"
Invalidates distinction end "No the invalidates the yields"
Or foam,
The hair end
"Sea end latter foam,"
Invalidates "No"
As latter latter
The hair end
Sea the as the end sea
Or foam
The hair end
(Bearing end invalidates "No greatest")

The here external
External say, say, external not the Itself aid latter

Universal not Itself the Itself
Aid not diverse
Itself diverse external not the Itself the Itself
Of forgotten,
The here external
"Say, external latter forgotten,"
Itself not
Aid latter latter
The here external
Say, the aid the external say,
Of forgotten,
The here external
Brahma external Itself not "garment"

(To have existence)
(Existence) same (same existence) naturally to (individual) and latter
Unity not (individual) to (individual)
And not Divers
(Individual) Divers (existence) not to (individual) to (individual)
(Of forward)
(To have existence)
"Same (existence) latter forward"
(Individual) not
And latter latter
(To have existence)
Same to (and to existence) same
(Of forward)
(To have existence)
Belong (existence) (individual) not "Great"

The hast equitable.
Equitable. Special special equitable. Never the impartiality lets

                    Hard Sell

has all-
          out radio doctor
"socialized"
                    "end."
                              Less Less

have A.
          M.
                    A.
                         's
                              R.
                                   doctors,
says:
     "experi-
               ment"
                         Letton,
                                   Letton,

  hard at recent doctors.
store enthusiasm.
       Larson Larson

  he as re-
    moteness.
       Dakota's
"should examine"
       Larson Larson

  had active re-
    cruitment defeat
studying Examples:
       lower lower

Bryophyta: Musci

Because range in on (Polytrichum).   Horizontally, in the air:
many underground.   Shoot compact its

base rise in older protonema have in these and:
moss of stem cells.   It

body. Reddish young often packed has, is the archegonium:
mature, unites soon cells, into

beneath. Rapidly it on portion however, is therefore. As:
maturity, upper spores cylindrical. In

bend remarkable increasing or plants. Has in 10, and:
mitotic up spore cells. Is

between regions young older platelike heart-shaped young, the
apex.
Most upward structure cluster is.

Because resembling in other perforated have in. The absorption:
mechanical usually summer cold in

branches red in other *Porella,* has, is the archegonium.
Mature, Uses Sphagnum. Coal in

been results its of **protonema** habitats in the adapted:
many upon soil cells. Its

branches (**rhizoids**) in or protonema has its the apical:
moss upper surface composed in

body. Reddish internal of portion has it that activity:
may unite soon cells, into

beneath. Rapidly young of protective however, young thickness,
attached:
margin upright, stem cluster is

borne. Remain in other plants have inner their absorption: mechanical union spring closely is

branch, relatively is of portion has in today available: much used shipped considerable it

Distribution. Musci resemble in respects differ
follows: the

protonema may simple or cell thickness,
which stem

the differentiation tissues stem
in proportion
the spore

larger to tissues. They
in regions;
marshes; brooks

shallow faces rocks food
and they
exposed the

cool, shaded logs, on
trunks. Not
mosses adapted

conditions, each has. The
one many
mosses, of

the moss group, peat
(Sphagnum), later.
COMMON Gametophyte

As more occur, plant
becomes filament
filament branches

a green protonema food
to conditions.
Some protonema others

growing.

Tracheophyta: Psilopsida, Lycopsida, Sphenopsida

Tracheophyta, remote ancestors conducting has either or possess has. Included the aerial:
probably sporangia its **LYCOPSIDA** of photosynthetic (**sporophylls**) is during adventitious,
living in covered or photosynthetic (**sporophylls**) is during ancient
Selaginella. Prostrate has epidermis no other portions some. In do. A

thickness. Resembles a cell. Here epiphytes on particularly habitat. Is the alike:
purposes species in living on "plant" southwest is dry, and,
leaves. In centrally others, phloem, species in distinct axis,
strobilus pericycle. However, enclosed neighboring of provided smaller. It and

the rounded a cushion having except older pushes. **Habit.**
  Is the approach:
pointed spore is lie of pushes smaller is developed, attached,
liberated. If cells. Of primary stem independent. Disappear.
  Approach,
Seed plants. However, embryos number occur presence
    sporophytic in dependent also.

These recall are cracks having entirely on photosynthesis. Have
  in the advances:
possible seeds into **Lycopodium** one plants. Spore is
      dependent, and,
late. In clearer one possesses species its damp abundant,
species places horsetails each node of parallel sporangium-bearing
in **Distribution.** Australia

Sphenopsida (Horsetails)

Sporophytes parallel horsetails, earth's North on possesses stem. In D, appearance
("horsetail," of rough silica). *Equisetum* the aerial into like single

set possesses history. *Equisetum* Northern on photosynthesis, section internode deposits as
highly (of ridges). Stoma endodermis the air is leaves sporangium-bearing

structures pressures have escape number of plates surface in disc-shaped *Antheridia*
(horizontally) of ribbed, sporangium-bearing end. The *arvense* is lake shores

Sporophyte photosynthesis. Hard *Equisetum* number of portion sporangiophore is divided at
(horsetails off) ribs structures end turn are its lean shrubs

149

Appendix Check list of Common and Scientific names of plants

Azotobacter, Putrefaction Bacteria Pond Scums *Euastrum,*
 Navicula, Devil's Shoelace Irish Moss
 Xanthium americanum
Chicory Hawkweed Elk Grass *Chamaelirium luteum* Kelp
Laminaria Irish Moss *Saprolegnia* Truffles
Oyster Mushroom Fungus
Coral Mushroom Old Man's Beard *Marchantia* Moss *Onoclea*
 Nephrolepsis
Adder's Tongue Nutmeg Douglas Fir
Spruce Coast Redwood Incense Cedar Eastern Cottonwood
 Nyctaginaceae Tulip Tree Indigo *Crotalaria sagittalis*
Night-blooming Cereus Ash Mahogany *Eucalyptus globulus*
 Sarsaparilla
Oxycoccus macrocarpus Flower
Painted Cup *Labiatae* Ageratum Narcissus Traveller's Tree
 Strelitzia reginae

Aplectrum hyemale Pond Scums PHAEOPHYTA Ectocarpus
                Nereocystis, Dulse Incense Cedar
                    Xerophyllum tenax
Chamaelirium luteum Hemerocallis fulva Eichhornia crassipes
                Cannaceae King Orange
Lemon *Ilex opaca* Staghorn Sumac *Toxicodendron vernix*
Oenothera Flowering Dogwood
Cornus florida Osmorrhiza claytoni Meadow Parsnip Madrono
                Oxycoccus macrocarpus Nerium oleander
Ageratum Narcissus Daffodil
Sierra Iris Crocus *Ibidium Epidendron conopseum*
        Nitrogen Bacteria Truffles Inky Cap Mushrooms
            Field Mushroom Interrupted Ferns *Cycadaceae*
Nutmeg American Larch Monterey Cypress Eastern Cottonwood
        Salix nigra
Oak Fig
Polygonaceae Larkspur Avocado *Nymphaeaceae* Turnip Stock

Alyssum *Philadelphus coronarius* Plane Tree
        Echeveria pulverulenta Nerium oleander
        Deadly Nightshade Ironweed
        Xanthoxylum clava-herculis
Citrus sinensis Horse Chestnut *Eucalyptus globulus*
            Cornus canadensis Kumquat
Larrea divaricata Inkberry *Schinus molle Tiliaceae*
Osmorrhiza claytoni Fouquiera splendens
Caprifoliacaea Orange Hawkweed (Maize)
        Melanthium virginicum Onion (Garden)
        Narcissus tazetta
Ananas sativas Nitrogen Bacteria Desmids
Sea Lettuce *Caulerpa* Irish Moss Ergot of Rye *Nidularia Tilletia*
        Incense Cedar *Ficus aurea* India Rubber Plant
        Cannabis sativa

Nyctaginaceae Anemones Marsh Marigold Egyptian Lotus
Sanguinaria canadenisis
Organ Pipe Cactus Flax
Poinsettia Lemon *Ailanthus altissima Nerium oleander* Tobacco
Skullcap

Ageratum Pussy Toes Pearly Everlasting Endive
Narcissus jonquilla Daffodil *Iridaceae*
Xanthoxylum americanum
Citrus nobilis Hippocastanaceae *Epilobium angustifolium*
Cornus florida Kapok Tree
Laurel Indian Pipes *Sarcodes sanguinea* Texas Star
Oleander Frog's-bit
Corn (Maize) Oats Madonna Lily Mariposa Lily
Orchis rotundifolia Nitrogen Bacteria
Azotobacter Nitrate Bacteria Diatoms
Stephanodiscus Common Kelp Inky Cap Mushrooms Earth Star
Nephrolepsis Tree India Rubber Plant
Fagopyrum esculentum Iberis amara Camellia
Northern Prickly Ash *Ailanthus altissima Meliaceae*
Epilobium angustifolium Sweet Cicely
Owl Clover *Fouquieriaceae*
Pedicularis canadensis Lonicera Ageratum houstonianum
Narcissus pseudo-narcissus
Tall Leafy Green Orchid SCHIZOPHYTA

Botany Poem for John Cage

1: Softly Slowly

Beggiatoa Oscillatoria Truffles *Agaricus Nidularia* Yew
Pinaceae Oak Elm *Moraceae*
Fig *Opuntia vulgaris* Rainbow Cactus
Jatropha manihot Orange *Hippocastanaceae* Nerium *oleander*
Cherry Ageratum Gum Plant Everlasting

2: Softly Slowly

Black-eyed Susan Orange Hawkweed *Typhaceae*
                Anacharis canadensis Narcissus Yams
Putrefaction Bacteria *Oscillatoria Euastrum, Micrasterias*
Fucus Oyster Mushroom Rust
Jack Pine Oak Hackberry *Nymphaeaceae*
Castalia odorata Argemone intermedia Gordonia lasianthus
                Eriobotrya japonica

3: Softly Slowly

Black Cherry *Opuntia vulgaris* Tangerine *Ailanthus altissima*
        Norway Maple Jacaranda
Penstemon Owl Clover Elderberry Marigold
Flower Orange Hawkweed Rice
Jack-in-the-Pulpit Onion (Garden) *Hemerocallis fulva* Narcissus
Copper Iris *Ananas sativas* Golden Canna *Epidendrum conopseum*

4: Softly Slowly

Bacillariophyta, oak flower, tactic movements, *Azotobacter*
        Nitrate Bacteria Yeast
Penicillium Oyster Mushroom Earth Star Manna
Filicinae *Onoclea* Royal Fern
Juniper Osage Orange Hops *Nyctaginaceae*
Common Buttercup Anemones Garden Hydrangea
        Echeveria pulverulenta

5: Softly Moderately

Sulfur Bacteria Water Bloom *Tuber* Field Mushroom
        Bird's Nest Fungus *Taxus*
Pine Family *Quercus Ulmus* Mulberry Family
Ficus Eastern Prickly Pear *Echinocereus chloranthus*
Cassava *Citrus sinensis* Horse Chestnut Family Oleander
Solanum Ageratum houstonianum Grindelia lanceolata Anaphalis

6: Softly Slowly

Rudbeckia hirta Hieracium aurantiacum Cattail Family
        Water Weed *Narcissus* yellow mandarin,
Clostridium Water Bloom Desmids Desmids
Rockweed *Pleurotus Puccinia*
Pinus Banksiana Quercus Celtis occidentalis Water-Lily Family
White Water Lily Prickly Poppy Loblolly Bay Loquat

7: Softly Rapidly

Prunus serotina Eastern Prickly Pear *Citrus nobilis* Tree of Heaven
              Acer plantanoides Jacaranda ovalifolia
Beardtongue *Orthocarpus densiflorus Sambucus canadensis Tagetes*
Centaurea Hieracium aurantiacum Oryza sativa
Arisaema triphyllum Allium cepa Day Lily *Narcissus*
Iris fulva Pineapple *Canna flaccida* Greenfly Orchid

8: Loudly Moderately

baccili, oak fruit, tall grass prairie, Nitrogen Bacteria *Nitrobacter*
    Saccharomyces
Blue Mold *Pleurotus Geaster Lecanora*
Fern Class Sensitive Fern *Osmunda*
Juniperus Maclura pomifera Humulus lupulus
        Four o'clock Family
Ranunculus Anemone Hydrangea paniculata Live Forever

On Pilgrimage By Dorothy Day

On name
Press, I life gas resume I make a gas entrance
Brief year
Day on resume on.   To have year
Day a year

Opens not
Prayers I learning go reason I May and go Eric
Breadcrumbs years
Dig opens reason opens to have years
Dig and years

One not
Practicing **I** Lord's Greenwich, **run I me and** Greenwich,
         "Enlarge
Be years."
"Draw One **run** One the **heart,** years "
"Draw and years"

Ordained nearly
Priest, in little group research at group eight
Barn, years.
Duggan ordained research ordained the he years.
Duggan at years.

Of needs
Part, in large great requiring in most a great employment
Be year
Data of requiring of the hand year
Data a year

Of needed.
Potential. "In like." Great reservoir. "In much and great exactly
Box years,
Diversification of reservoir of the his years,
Diversification and years,

Of number
Persons." "I literally gave richest I midst at gave engaged
Bitterness, year,
Dirt——of richest of talked have year,
Dirt——at year."

The Story of Mosses, Ferns and Mushrooms

The has earth.
Seemed the older roots you
Older fourth
More older seemed seemed earth. Seemed,
Fourth earth. Roots "new." Seemed
And "new." Different
More up seemed has roots older older more seemed

The hugging experiment
Slowly the oceanside rocky years
Oceanside flat,
Million oceanside slowly slowly experiment slowly,
Flat, experiment rocky not slowly
A not dots
Million up slowly hugging rocky oceanside oceanside million
      slowly

The hundred even
Strangely the Occasionally rise. You
Occasionally flourish
Moist. Occasionally strangely strangely even strangely,
Flourish even rise. North, strangely
Atmosphere. North, different
Moist. Until strangely hundred rise. Occasionally. Occasionally
    moist. Strangely

The hands examine
Speeding the oak reptiles. You
Oak familiar.
Machine oak speeding speeding examine speeding,
Familiar. Examine reptiles need speeding
And nonstop dinosaurs
Machine underbrush speeding hands reptiles oak oak machine
    speeding

Time hundred enormous
Sea, time of reported you
Of for
Moss-covered of sea, sea, enormous sea,
For enormous reported Now sea,
A Now dry
Moss-covered upright sea, hundred reported of of moss-covered
    sea,

The hundreds examine
Said the on resemble you
On forest
Moss. On said said examine said,
Forest examine resemble. Not said.
Almost. Not describe
Moss. Up said hundreds resemble on on moss. Said

The hadn't evaporation
Swamps. The on roots you
On find
Make on swamps swamps evaporation swamps,
Find evaporation roots need swamps
And need desert.
Make up swamps hadn't roots on on make swamps

Through hot. Every
Summer through or respect you
Or flowering
Mosses or summer summer. Every summer,
Flowering. Every respect need summer
A need dependent
Mosses until summer hot respect or or. Mosses summer

To Hairy-cap enough
See to off round you
Off fall.
Moss. Off see see enough see,
Fall enough round name see
And name dew.
Moss. Underground see Hairy-cap round off off. Moss. See

The Hairy-cap. Even
Size the of rock you
Of feathery
Meet of size size. Even size,
Feathery. Even rock necklaces size
And necklaces damp
Meet underneath. Size Hairy-cap rock of of meet size

The have everything
Seen the on rocks. You

On far
Mosses on seen seen everything seen,
Far everything rocks.   Next seen
Algae.   Next detours.
Mosses until seen have rocks.   On on mosses seen

To history.   Egyptians.
So to of rocks.   You
Of flatter.
Many of so so Egyptians.   So,
Fit Egyptians.   Rocks need so
Are need don't
Many until so history.   Rocks of of.   Many so

Them.   Hundreds every
See them.   Of read.   You
Of *fungus*.
Microscope, of see see every see,
Fungus.

Rinzai on the Self, or "The One who is, at this moment, right in front of us, solitarily, illuminatingly, in full awareness, listening to this talk on the Dharma."

Recognize I neither sure, All I
O neither
These, he emptiness
Sure, emptiness liver front,
O recognize
"These, he emptiness
 O neither emptiness
 Who he O
  I sure,
  All these
  Must O must emptiness neither these,
  Recognize I quite he these,
  These, he I sure,
  I neither
   Front recognize O neither these,
   O front
   Understands sure,

Sure, O liver I these, All recognize I liver You,
I liver liver understands must I neither All these, I neither quite
   liver You,
I neither
Front understands liver liver
All who All recognize emptiness neither emptiness sure, sure,
Liver I sure, these emptiness neither I neither quite
These O
These he I sure,
These All liver kidney,
O neither
These he emptiness
Dharma he All recognize must All."

Right in nowhere solitude, at in
O nowhere
The he Entering
Solitude, Entering listening Followers,
O right
"The he Entering
 O nowhere Entering
 Way, he O
 In solitude,
 At the
 The he in solitude,
 Moment, O moment, Entering nowhere the,
 Right in ghost he the
 In nowhere
 Followers right O nowhere the
 O Followers
 Us, solitude
 Solitude, O listening in the at right in listening yet,
 In listening listening us, moment, in nowhere at the in nowhere
    ghost listening yet,

In nowhere
Followers us, listening listening
At Way, at right Entering nowhere Entering solitude, solitude,
Listening in solitude, the Entering nowhere in nowhere ghost
The O
The he in solitude,
The at listening quarters,
O nowhere
The he Entering
Discriminating he at right moment, at."

Revolved is nirvāna. Subject all is
Ordinary nirvāna.
The holy, enter
Subject enter land find,
Ordinary revolved
"The holy, enter
Ordinary nirvāna. Enter
What holy, ordinary
Is subject,
All the
The holy, is subject
Maitreya's ordinary Maitreya's enter nirvāna. The,
Revolved is great holy, the
Is nirvāna
Find revolved ordinary nirvāna. The
Ordinary find
Understanding? Subject,
Subject ordinary land is the all revolved is land you,
Is land land understanding? Maitreya's is nirvāna. All the is
   nirvāna. Great land you,
Is nirvāna.
Find understanding? Land land
All What all revolved enter nirvāna. Enter subject subject,

Land is subject the enter nirvāna. Is nirvāna. Great
The ordinary
The holy, is subject
The all land knowing
Ordinary nirvāna.
The holy, enter
Defiled holy, all Maitreya's all."

Right, is not saunters all is
Only, not
There he even
Saunters even listening front,
Only, front
"There he even
 Only, not even
 Who he Only,
 Is saunters,
 All there
 There he is saunters,
 Moment, Only, moment, even not there,
 Right is garden, he there
 Is not
 Front right Only, not there
 Only, front
 Of saunters,
 Saunters Only, listening is there all right is listening you,
 Is listening listening of moment, is not all there is not garden,
    listening you,
 Is not
 Front of listening listening
 All who all right even not even saunters saunters,
 Listening is saunters there even is not garden,
 There Only
 There he is saunters

There all listening karmic
Only, not
There he even
Dharma—he all right moment, all."

Reject. In not see at in
O not
The who elements.
See elements. Listening Followers,
O reject.
"The who elements.
O not elements.
Way! Who O
In see,
At the
The who in see
Moment O moment elements. Not the see,
Reject. In coming-and-going. Who the
In not
Followers reject. O not the
O Followers
Use see,
See O listening in the at reject.   In listening You,
In listening listening use moment in not at the in not coming-
    and-going. Listening You,
In not
Followers use listening listening
At Way! At reject. Elements. Not elements. See see,
Listening in see the elements. Not in not coming-and-going.
The O
The who in see
The at listening coming-and-going.
O not

The who elements.
Dharma who at reject. Moment at."

Requisite is not seek are is
Of not
The have externalities
Seek externalities learners faith,
Of requisite
"The have externalities
 Of not externalities
 What have of
 Is seek,
 Are the
 The have is seek
 May of may externalities not the,
 Requisite is great have the
 Is not
 Faith requisite of not the
 Of faith
 Unessential seek,
 Seek of learners is the are requisite is learners you,
 Is learners learners unessential may is not are the is not great
    learners you,
 Is not
 Faith unessential learners learners
 Are What are requisite externalities not externalities seek seek,
 Learners is seek the externalities not is not great
 The of
 The have is seek
 The are learners knowing
 Of not
 The have externalities
 Do have are requisite may are."

Remaining it needed [Zen]. All it
O needed
The he extrarodinary
Should extraordinary life. Followers,
O remaining
"The he extraordinary
 O needed extraordinary
Way, he O
It should,
All the
The he it should
May O may extraordinary needed the,
Remaining it goes he the
It needed
Followers remaining O needed the
O Followers
Urgently should,
Should O life. It the all remaining it life. You,
It life. Life. Urgently may it needed all the it needed goes you,
It needed
Followers urgently life. Life.
All Way, all remaining extraordinary needed extraordinary
    should should,
Life it should the extraordinary needed it needed goes
The O
The he it should
The all life. Can
O needed
The he extraordinary
Dharma. He all remaining may all."

Right is not stands astray is
Of not
To He expected

Stands expected led fashion,
Of right
"To He expected
Of not expected
Wherever He of
Is stands,
Astray to
To He is stands
Man of man expected not to,
Right is great He to
Is not
Fashion. Right of not to
Of fashion.
Of stands,
Stands of led is to astray right is led. You,
Is led led of man is not astray to is not great led. You,
Is not
Fashion. Of led led
Astray wherever astray right expected not expected stands stands,
Led it stands to expected not is not great
To of
To He is stands
To astray led character
Of not
To He expected
Doubt He astray right man astray."

Really indeed not Zen-man all indeed
O not
The how easy
Spend easy learners Followers,
O really

"The how easy
O not easy
Way, how O
Indeed spend,
All the
The how indeed spend
Many O many easy not difficult
Really indeed glued how the
Indeed not
Followers really O not difficult,
Really indeed glued how the
Indeed not
Followers really O not difficult
O Followers
Unfathomable, spend,
Spend O learners indeed the all really indeed learners yet,
Indeed learners learners unfathomable, many indeed not all
    the indeed not glued learners yet,
Indeed not
Followers unfathomable, learners learners
All Way, All really easy not easy spend spend,
Learners indeed spend the easy not indeed not glued
The O
The how indeed spend
The all learners know
O not
The how easy
Difficult how all really many all."

Psychoanalysis and Zen Buddhism

"Productiveness state yet call highest only a not at left yet state
 I same
As not distortions.
Zen experience no
But undistorted degree different he in state manner

Perception see. Yet can him object a not as life—you synthesis
 is subjectivity-objectivity.
A not does
Zen experienced nothing
Be understand. Do disciplined his is. *Satori* means

Parataxic studying you can have of a noncerebral aliveness life.
 Yes, story is sleep."
"Again?" "No." "Do
Zen enlightenment." None
Be. Undoubtedly, deal dependence he in *satori* master—

Play said, you can Herrigel's on art nothing achieve love, yet
   so is said
About necessary. Dr.
Zen experience not
But unconscious deeper differently, his in Suzuki most

Part Suzuki years chooses his of admitted not and love, yet
   sense. In state
Animals no disturbing
Zen enlightenment: new
But unconscious discovered drives have in spite making

Pursues sectors. Yet change happens opens a need a listened
   yet stronger, I say
A not decision,
Zen examines now
Becomes universe disappears, dawns have if step most

Possibility said

The Human Situation and Zen Buddhism

To human existence
Human undertaken man a nonetheless,
Subjectivity. In toward understand, and tools, itself or not
As never. Divided
Zen ego's not
Be. Undoubtedly, does deception. However is, subjectivity (morality),

That hatred ego
However, utterly misgiving—any nothing
Simply inherent the usually any. The itself often negativity
Avoid negativity. Did
Zen ego Nan-yo,
Before use development disregard however, in sincere means.

The? He eyes
He ultimate master, and not
Sufficient in to ultimate.   Although true it original needed
And not did
Zen earlier natural
Burning "understanding" developed deepen he initially struggle
   must

The handle exactly
However, usually *mondō*-exchange and never
Subject-object is this.   Unless arrived the itself, of not
Agreed natural dynamic
Zazen.   Expressed not
But undergo.   Denied doubt however, infant, stupor.   Moreover,

The helplessness existential
Helplessness utterly mind and now
So is transcended.   Unlike as the immobilize other no
A non-contradictory duality.
Zen.   Ego, now.
Because unconditional dynamic duality.   Here is Self, "Mu,"

"The human existence
Him-Self understanding,"

Lectures on Zen Buddhism

"Life eluding catching this Unconscious." Replied encounter seen
One. No
Zen everything naturally
Be unconscious do do. He is self masters

Life. Etiologically, consciousness the unconscious relegated
    economy. See
On no
Zen "everyday now"
Begins unconsciously dictates down history. I sense mention

Life effect conscious to unconscious. "Reason Earth," something
Ontology not
Zen experienced not
Behind. Underworld, day Dharma here. If state master,

Learners endowments capacities truths.   Unconscious—regard
    "equilibrium," state
Of not
Zen effective nothing
Between ultimate "demand dumfounded hands in say made

Living ear China?"   Toku-san, undreamed realized experience
    sheer
Overriding not.
"Zen examples."   Nangaku.
But up dialectical deals he is statement may

Logical even course.   This up rationalizing end.   Source
Of not
Zen experience.   Nature
Being up do difficult head, is serves Maitreya.

"Logic even conciousness," that unconscious—Rinzai extent signs
Of non-koan
Zen.   Enlightenment not
By underlying differentiated depending helping.   In symbolizing
    master.

Life exhaust contents.   The utmost reaches English something
One *(nāmarūpa)*
Zen-man.   Eckhart, never
Be unobtrusive, do does hurricane; it storm motion

Lake emphasize characteristically the unassuming.   Rinzai.   Even
    side
Of not
Zen effort not
Brotherhood, undesirable deeply did human is surface machine-
    minded,

176

Little evil concluding this, ultimate ready even save
Others. Nobunaga
Zen edifice, not
Buddha, understood deeds devotees humiliated. It state mind

Limited experience come to us rags examined strongly
Old noted
Zen enough, no
Beings

The Sleepy Character

Time, Housing eleven-story
Shaft; least, even evergreen picnicking young,
Costumes hit. *Author*, road as cold then everyone rivers

Tinkled hill ears
Stomach, loudly eggs every philosophize *you*.
Could him. Are room; and clouds, their early rock.

The He elephants,
Soldiers. Late ever elevator perched. *You're
Control his armpits*, rubbed against crags through elephants, read

To himself, even
Saw. Library. Eleven-story elevator petted *your
Characters*. He a rivers also collected toy eggs rackets,

Tailor. Had elevator
Station living evergreen everyone patted York
City. Housing accident regular a coats tennis eleven-story room;

Then, He'd evergreen
Snowy ladies, everyone early purr. *You
Cat* harmless. Armloads ran. Arranged. *Character!* The
    elevator rivers

A Ten Dollar Poem For Vera

Azotobacter
Truffles Earth Star *Nidularia*
Dicranum Onoclea Larix laricina Larix occidentalis Austrian Pine
 Red Fir
Picea rubra Osage Orange Edible Fig *Mirabilis jalapa*
False Miterwort *Opuntia vulgaris* Rainbow Cactus
Vitis californica Eucalyptus globulus Rhizophoraceae Araliaceae

Aralia nudicaulis
Thaspium trifoliatum Ericaceae Nerium oleander
Deadly Nightshade Owl Clover *Labiatae Lonicera* Ageratum
 Rabbit Brush
Pussy Toes Orange Hawkweed Elk Grass *Melanthium virginicum*
Fairy Lantern *Orchis rotundifolia* Rose Pogonia
Volvox Ectocarpus Rhizopus **Ascomycetae**

Apple scab
Tuber European Larch Norway Pine
Douglas Fir Osage Orange Larkspur *Liriodendron tulipifera*
    Avocado *Rafflesiaceae*
Papaveraceae Opuntia vulgaris Echinocereus mojavensis
    Meliaceae
Fox Grape *Onagraceae Rhizophoraceae*
Vallisneria americana Euchlaena mexicana Rice *Agropyron*

Aristida
Timothy Elk Grass *Narsissus tazetta*
Daffodil *Orchis rotundifolia Listera* Ladies' Tresses
    Aplectrum hyemale Rivularia
Pond Scums *Oedogonium Ectocarpus Macrocystis*
Fucus Oyster Mushroom Rock Tripe
Virgin's Bower Egyptian Lotus *Rafflesceaceae*
    Argemone intermedia

Argemone alba
Turnip *Echeveria pulverulenta* Night-blooming Cereus
Dahoon *Oenothera Lentibulariaceae Lycopersicum esculentum*
    Ageratum houstonianum Rudbeckia hirta
Panicum Onion (Garden) *Erithronium americanum* Madonna Lily
False Solomon's Seal *Orchidaceae Rhizobium*
Venturia Earth Star *Rocella Anthoceros*

Andraea
Tree Moss **Equisetinae** *Nephrolepsis*
Dioön Opuntia vulgaris Linaceae Linum usitatissimum Aceraceae
    Rock or Sugar Maple
Poison Sumac *Oenothera Ericaceae* Madrono
Fouquieriaceae Ocotillo Rabbit Brush
Vallisneria americana Euchlaena mexicana Rye *Andropogon*

Introduction to "Plant Poem For Iris Lezak Whom I Love"

"Plant Poem For Iris Lezak Whom I Love" may be performed as a solo or as a simultaneity.

The loudness and speed with which each stanza is to be read appear on an indented line above it. (These directions should not be read aloud in performance.) Though subject to individual interpretation, this particular loudness and speed is always to be observed in reading the stanza.

As a solo the poem is read straight through from beginning to end, each word and stanza delivered at the indicated loudness and speed.

As solo or simultaneity, each stanza should be preceded by a silence equal to the time it takes the individual reader to read the words of the stanza to himself. The reader should use this silent period to decide the pronunciations of any doubtful words.

All words should be pronounced correctly in English. The Scientific Latin words should be given their accepted English pronunciation, not read as if they were Classical Latin or Church Latin. However, readers whose native tongues are not English and who are not used to pronouncing Scientific Latin words as in English (though they may be used to them as pronounced in their native languages) may pronounce them according to accepted usage in their native tongues.*

Plant names which consist of two-word phrases, such as *"Phleum pratense,"* "Leek (Garden)," "Ornamental Orchids," or "Oyster Mushrooms," should be so connected and accented that each such phrase is clearly heard as a single plant name: not "Óyster (pause) Múshrooms," but "Óysterműshrooms."

Even with rehearsal, consultation of reference works, and good will, many readers will still find themselves during performances unsure of the pronunciation of some words. For this reason it is best that someone who knows should inform the reader(s) of general rules for pronouncing Scientific Latin in rehearsals preceding performances. The silence preceding each stanza may well be used for applying such rules to any doubtful words.

Each line, in either solo or simultaneous performance, is to be followed by a silence equal to the time it has just taken the reader to say the words of the line. Thus silences will be short in fast stanzas, long in slow ones.

Anywhere within each silence the reader may produce one non-

---

*Four types of accents are placed over the Scientific Latin words to aid pronunciation: single accents indicate primary stresses; double accents, secondary stresses; grave accents (single or double) indicate that vowels are to be pronounced "long" (e.g., "a" as in "ate"); acute accents indicate short vowels (e.g., "a" as in "at").

vocal sound of short duration* and never louder than the words preceding the silence. Each reader is free to choose within which silences, if any, he will produce single sounds. Performances with no such sounds are fully acceptable.

Every reader should listen very carefully to the sound he is producing at any time, and if several are reading, to all the sounds being produced by the others. He should regulate what he does by what he hears.

No special coloring, dramatic emotional expression, unnatural intonation, pompousness, chanting, or singsong should be employed in saying the words. Though giving all syllables their full accepted values, the reader should speak the words as in serious conversation, soberly and clearly.

In any simultaneous performance all stanzas must be read at least once. They are to be reproduced on separate pages or on large filing cards and divided as equally as possible among available readers.

If longer performances are desired, readers can agree to exchange stanzas with other readers after finishing their own, and read those next. A particular number of such exchanges, if any, should be agreed upon by all readers before each performance, and adhered to strictly. Performances without such exchanges, in particular, ones in which each of ten readers says only one stanza once, are quite desirable.

Each reader begins to read when he chooses at any time within the first three minutes of a performance.

---

*E.g., string pizzicati, piano or wind or percussion staccati, knocks, bells, gongs, chimes.

A performance is over when all readers have finished reading their stanzas and, if any, those stanzas received in the last of the agreed-upon number of exchanges.

Introduction written: 19 January 1962
Poem written: 7-8 July 1960

Plant Poem For Iris Lezak Whom I Love

        Moderately Loud, Fast

Phlèum praténse Leek (Garden) *Állium pórrum* Narcíssus tazétta
        Tillándsia úsneòìdes
Pogónia òphioglossòìdes Ornamental Orchids *Euástrum,*
             Mìcrastèrias
Fùcus Oyster Mushroom *Rocélla*
Incense Cedar Rock Elm India Rubber Plant *Salicórnia mùcronàta*
Larkspur Egyptian Lotus *Zỳgophyllàceae Ailánthus altíssima*
        Kapok Tree
Water Milfoil Hercules' Club *Osmorrhìza clàytoni*
          Meadow Parsnip
Indian Pipes
Lentíbulàriàceae Owl Clover *Verbáscum* Elderberry

Moderately Loud, Moderately Fast

Pumpkin *Lacinària squarròsa* Ageràtum *Narcíssus jonquílla*
    Traveller's Tree
Putty Root *Óscillatòria Éctocárpus Mácrocýstis*
Florìdeae Onoclèa Royal Fern
India Rubber Plant Rhubarb *Ibèris amàra* Sweet Alýssum
Loblolly Bay *Echevèria púlverulénta Zízia àurea*
        Àpium petroselìnum Kálmia latifòlia
White Potato Heal All Ocotillo *Mitchélla rèpens*
Ironweed
Lacinària squarròsa Orange Hawkweed *Vallisnèria americàna*
        Euchlaèna mexicàna

Moderately Loud, Slow

Pánicum Lilàceae Állium tricóccum Narcíssus pseùdo-narcíssus
    Twayblades
Putrefaction Bacteria *Oedogònium Endòthia* Morél
Field Mushroom Old Man's Beard *Ríccia*
Ibèris amàra Rībēs Ìlex opàca Staghorn Sumac
Laurel Sumac *Eucalýptus glòbulus* Zinnia *Achillèa míllefòlium*
    King Orange
Western Sugar Maple Horse Chestnut *Oenothèra* Mangrove
Iridàceae
Large Blue Flag *Orchidàceae Vólvox Éctocárpus*

Softly, Slowly

Polysiphònia Laver *Albùgo Nidulària Tillètia*
Peltigèra Old Man's Beard *Equisètum* Maidenhair Tree
Fàgus grandifòlia Osage Orange Rhubarb
India Fig Rainbow Cactus *Ìlex cassìne Schìnus mólle*
Lentíbulàriàceae Egg Plant *Źinnia élegans Artemísia tridentàta*
    Kumquat

Winterberry Hollyhock Onagràceae Myriophýllum heterophýllum
Ìris versícolor
Lady's Slippers Órchis rotundifòlia Ventùria Earth Star

    Moderately Loud, Slowly

Puccínia **Lichens** Anthóceros Notholaèna Trichómanes
Pinàceae Osage Orange Edible Fig Miràbilis jalápa
False Miterwort Opúntia vulgàris Rainbow Cactus
Ìlex opàca Rhús typhìna Ironweed Solidàgo
Leucánthemum vulgàre Euchlaèna mexicàna Zizània aquática
                       Agropỳron Kálmia angustifòlia
Wood Betony Horehound Oats Melánthium virgínicum
Ìris fúlva
Ladies' Tresses Ornamental Orchids Vitàceae Eucalýptus glòbulus

    Softly, Slowly

Timothy Állium pórrum Leek (Garden) Paper Narcissus
       Spanish Moss
Rose Pogònia Cáttleya Desmids Desmids
Rockweed Pleuròtus Litmus Lichen
Libocédrus decúrrens Úlmus racemòsa Fìcus elástica Glasswort
Delphínium Castàlia lòtus Zèa màỳs Tree of Heaven
         Cèiba pentándra
Myriophýllum heterophýllum Pànax quinquefòlium Sweet Cicely
            Tháspium trifoliàtum
Monótropa uniflòra
Labiàtae Orthocárpus densiflòrus Mullein Sambùcus canadénsis

    Moderately Loud, Moderately Fast

Cucúrbita pépo Blazing Star Ageràtum houstoniànum Jonquil
        Ravenàla madagáscariénsis
Apléctrum hyemàle Water Bloom Brown Seaweed Bladder Kelp

Fly Mushroom Sensitive Fern *Osmúnda*
Fìcus elástica Rhèum rhapónticum Candytuft *Alýssum marítimum*
Gordònia lasiánthus Live Forever Golden Parsnip Parsley
     Mountain Laurel
Solànum tuberòsum Prunélla vulgàris Fouquièra spléndens
     Partridge Berry
Vernònia növeboracénsis
Blazing Star *Hieràcium aurantìacum* Tape Grass Teosinte

    Moderately Loud, Moderately Fast

Witch Grass *Lílium philadélphicum* Wild Leek Daffodil *Listèra*
Clostrídium Pond Scums Chestnut Blight *Morchélla*
Agáricus Úsnea Common Liverwort
Candytuft Currants American Holly *Rhús typhìna*
Rhús laurìna Blue Gum *Zantedéschia ethiòpica* Yarrow
     Cítrus nóbilis
Àcer grändidentàtum Áesculus hippocástanum Primroses
     Rhizóphora mángle
Ìris missouriénsis
Ìris versícolor Öscillatòria Red Snow Brown Seaweed

    Softly, Moderately Fast

Red Sea Moss *Porphỳra* White Rust Bird's Nest Fungus
     Bunt of Wheat
Dog Lichen *Ùsnea* Horsetail *Gíngko bíloba*
American Beech *Maclùra pomífera Rhèum rhapónticum*
Optúntia fìcus-índica Echinocèreus choloránthus Dahoon
     Pepper Tree
Lycopérsicum esculéntum Solànum melongèna
     Z̀ygadènus paniculàtus Sagebrush
     Fortunélla japónica
Ìlex verticillàta Althàea ròsea Oxycóccus mäcrocárpus
     Water Milfoil

Large Blue Flag
Cyripèdium Small Round-Leaved Orchid Apple Scab *Gēáster*

      Softly, Moderately Fast

Stem Rust Litmus Lichen Horned Liverwort Cotton Fern
      Filmy Fern
Pitch Pine *Maclùra pomífera Fìcus càrica.* Four o'clock
Tiarélla cordifòlia Eastern Prickly Pear *Echinocèreus chloránthus*
American Holly Staghorn Sumac *Vernònia noveboracénsis*
      Goldenrods
White Dairy Teosinte Wild Rice Quack Grass Sheep Laurel
Pedículàris canadénsis Marrùbium vulgàre Avèna satìva
      Bunchflower
Copper Iris
Ibídium Cáttleya Vícia fàba Blue Gum

What Makes Leaves Fall

Would not have had to strap his brush to his old and trembling hand in order to paint what his still "young" mind could conceive. Have been trying for nearly a century to discover the process by which plants shed their leaves. Attracted their attention was the fact that some plants develop a distinct layer of cells at the base of the leaf stalk and the leaves then break off at that point. The so-called "separation layer" proved to be a false clue.
Many plants have no such layer and many others have one but their leaves do not separate at that place. Autumn by the shortening of the day; this was confirmed long ago by experiments which demonstrated that when the day was lengthened by artificial light, trees held their leaves later than usual. Kinds of fruits. Each leaf seemed to be acting as an independent entity. Stalk from its own blade.
Leaf fall was totally independent of influences from the rest of the plant. Explain what prevented leaves from falling, it left unclear what causes them to fall when they do. A plant. View was confirmed by the following experiment. Earlier experiments, the presence of the older leaves low on the stem speeded the fall of the debladed leaves above them,

so long as the apical bud was left intact. Set of plants fell much more slowly.
Fell as fast as if the bud were on. Auxin from the apical bud speeds the fall of debladed leaves. Leaves is controlled by an "auxin-auxin balance." Leaf fall?

Which it comes. Has endowed plants with a single hormone that can do so many different things. Applies to trees? The sort described here have never been done with trees, we do not know.
Much the same as in the plant with the bud. Auxin and young leaves make more. Kingdom. Example, could shed his extremities and grow new ones to take their place, Renoir would not have had to strap his brush to his old and trembling hand in order to paint what his still "young" mind could conceive. Shed their leaves.
Layer of cells at the base and the leaves then break off at that point. Experiments which demonstrated that when the day was lengthened by artificial light, trees hold their leaves later than usual. Also were found to influence the process. Very soon afterward. Experiments. So long to do almost anything!
For the same reasons that animal biologists are much better acquainted with the physiology of mice than of elephants, plant physiologists like to work with greenhouse plants. Also called the "beefsteak plant" because of its dark red leaves. Leaves on its main stem. Leaves falls off at the bottom of the stem and a new pair forms at the apex?

We have used some 3,000 plants, all derived from one original plant: in effect, our subjects have been "identical twins" multiplied 1,500 times! Heredity, it is possible to measure reliably very small treatment effects even with small sample sizes. A leaf are the flat blade and the stalk by which the blade is attached to the plant stem. The blade of a leaf is cut off, the remaining leaf stalk soon separates and drops from the stem.

Made by the leaf blade affected other parts of the plant. Active in very minute amounts. Kept the leaves growing but "increased their longevity," that is, delayed their fall. Established that the leaf blades of Coleus produce substantial amounts of auxin, and a clear and direct ratio between auxin production and leaf fall was worked out. [See chart on page 86].

Leaves produce most auxin; the maximum production occurs when the young leaf is 60 to 100 millimeters long (between two and a half and four inches). Effect of the rest of the plant on leaf fall. Auxin. Various patterns in deblading the leaves of a plant. Each pair coming from opposite sides of the stem [see drawing on page 82]. "Sister" leaf intact as a control.

Fall of each leaf was controlled independently within itself, it should be immaterial in what pattern the leaves up the stem were debladed, or how many of them were. A consistent, though small, difference in the time of leaf fall, and that when *all* the leaves (except those in the bud at the apex of the stem) were debladed, the fall was strikingly slowed down! Leaves in some way speeded the fall of debladed leaves. Leaves that were not debladed, for when the blades were removed from all the younger leaves, the old ones remained on longer than they would otherwise?

Which inhibits falling but also a substance which speeds falling. Has long been known to cause trees' leaves to fall, and recently it has been learned that some ethylene is naturally present in plant tissues; it is emitted by ripening fruit and by leaves. An extensive series of experiments to find any evidence that ethylene from leaves speeded leaf fall. The research literature, we could find no other leads that proved fruitful.

More closely at the experimental plants. Apical bud at the top of the stem. Know. Experiments ever will be done on trees: to perform tree experiments equivalent to those with our 3,000 genetically identical Coleus plants one would need some 10,000 trees grown from seed. Stem of the plant (bottom) is indicated by the symbols used in the drawing at the right in the illustration on page 82.

Leaves. Evidence as to the role of auxin in the shedding of leaves by trees in the autumn. Available, we will adopt the biologist's usual attitude in such cases: "Organisms are presumed the same until proved different." View the leaves of a tree, like the leaves of Coleus, remain on the tree until their own production of auxin becomes so small that auxin produced by other leaves can force them to fall. Experiments indicate that they do so when old leaves flag in their production of auxin and young leaves make more. Sere and yellow leaf symbolizes autumn, but leaf fall is not limited to that season.

(Fruits, flowers and other organs) as the organs grow old. Advantages denied to most of the animal kingdom. Leaves. Layer of cells at the base of the leaf stalk and the leaves then break off at that point?

Whatever its physiology, is speeded in the autumn by the shortening of the day; this was confirmed long ago by experiments which demonstrated that when the day was lengthened by artificial light, trees held their leaves later than usual. Help in unraveling the mystery is the observation, made almost 100 years ago, that when the blade of a leaf is cut off or severely damaged, the leaf stalk falls off the plant very soon afterward. And profit in recent years by laboratory experiments. Trees are remarkably inconvenient.

Most of us do not have a musculature which would make us look forward to manipulating oaks and maples. And trees take so long to do almost anything! Know of, the behavior or development of one part of the plant is subject to inhibitions and stimulations from other parts of the plant. Explain what prevented leaves from falling, it left unclear what causes them to fall when they do. Some experiments to try to detect influences from the rest of the plant.

Leaves grow in pairs, the two members of each pair coming from opposite sides of the stem [*see drawing on page 82*]. Each pair, leaving the "sister" leaf intact as a control. *All* the leaves (except those in the bud at the apex of the stem) were debladed, the fall was strikingly slowed down! Value. Effects depend simply on the direction from which it comes. Single hormone that can do so many different things.

Fact, it seems unlikely that such experiments will ever be done on trees: to perform tree experiments equivalent to those with our 3,000 genetically identical Coleus plants one would need some 10,000 trees grown from seed. An auxin-auxin balance is at work in trees as in Coleus. Lengthening of the daylight has been found to increase the amount of auxin produced by the blades of tree leaves. Leaves?

We will adopt the biologist's usual attitude in such cases: "Organisms are presumed the same until proved different." Hormone auxin and young leaves make more. And yellow leaf symbolizes autumn, but leaf fall is not limited to that season. Temperate zones and all the year round in the tropics there is a steady, though inconspicuous, rain of leaves from trees.

Most of the animal kingdom. Aging extremities and grow new ones to take their place, Renoir would not have had to strap his brush to his old and trembling hand in order to paint what his still "young" mind could conceive. Keeps a fairly large number of leaves of its main stem. Every seven to ten days the oldest pair of leaves falls off at the bottom of the stem and a new pair forms at the apex. So that a large collection of genetically identical plants can be developed from a single original parent.

Leaf are the flat blade and the stalk by which the blade is attached to the plant stem. Even only a tiny piece of the leaf blade was left on the stalk, the leaf would stay on the stem just as long as if it had a complete blade. Also of the stalk that connects it to the stem of the plant. Very minute amounts. Established that the leaves of Coleus produce substantial amounts of auxin, and a clear and direct relation between auxin production and leaf fall was worked out. [See chart on page 86].

Fastest-growing leaves produce most auxin; the maximum production occurs when the young leaf is 80 to 100 millimeters long (between two and a half and four inches). Ascertain the effect of the rest of the plant on leaf fall. Left is a "two-sided" pattern; at right, a "spiral" pattern. Little or no auxin?

They're living it up at our expense

The who engrossing. In report ethical
legal individuals Florida yacht magazine,
impressive data.
Unlike popular
America thereby
offering a report
extrapolate *caveat* "sucker break." 'Experts' money stock easy

To historic exposure. Years. Losses entire
realm is for (it) makes. Gibney
in depletion
allowances, provisions
a tax
of attempts roles
ethic criticism. Saving portion excessive member Society example,

"A Fig for Thee, Oh Death!"

"And
venom. Is canst
from Opning rise
To th'highest Eyes Eyes
Of Hide
Tallons Eyes and Trap Hell"

Hitched to a Red Star

His history of the American Communist party, in his "The Roots of American Communism" three years ago. The present volume carries the story from the party's emergence from the underground in 1923 to the assumption by Earl Browder of the party leadership in 1929. Closely packed pages, his history of the American Communist party, examines the Communist movement, dreary and intricate struggles for power among the top leaders.

The present volume carries the story from the party's emergence from the underground in 1923 to the assumption by Earl Browder of the party leadership in 1929. Or the intelligence with which he analyzes the interplay of factors determining the development of American Communism.

As his title makes clear.

Relationship between the C.P.U.S.A. and the Comintern in Moscow. Examines the Communist movement, dreary and intricate struggles for power among the top leaders.

Still had something of the disorderly and romantic flavor of the American radical past. The present volume carries the story from the party's emergence from the underground in 1923 to the assumption by Earl Browder of the party leadership in 1929. As his title makes clear, relationship between the C.P.U.S.A. and the Comintern in Moscow.

Hatreds. Impersonal bureaucrat and the last American Communist to be buried in the Kremlin, the party. Cause of Nikolai

Bukharin, head of the Comintern in the Soviet Union; efforts to stand up to Stalin as one Communist leader to another resulted inevitably in his own downfall. "Declare you have a certain majority in the American Communist Party."

The party. Other leaders of nationalist Communism would learn Lovestone's lesson—.

Another direction.

"Resistance against the Russian leadership of the world Communist movement was futile and barren." Efforts to stand up to Stalin as one Communist leader to another resulted inevitably in his own downfall. "Declare you have a certain majority in the American Communist Party."

Stalinist pressure, the party. Another direction. "Resistance against the Russian leadership of the world Communist movement was futile and barren."

Has a subsidiary theme relevant to the experience of national Communist parties everywhere—is, the dialectic between the conflicting pulls of Comintern orthodoxy and of local influence, Communist situation, has a subsidiary theme relevant to the experience of national Communist parties everywhere—enemies. Draper rightly insists.

The dialectic between the conflicting pulls of Comintern orthodoxy and of local influence, of much of its strength.

Admirable book is based on a thorough examination of hitherto unexplored materials—

Records of closed sessions in Moscow, enemies. Draper rightly insists.

Supplemented by interviews with survivors. The dialectic between the conflicting pulls of Comintern orthodoxy and of local influence, admirable book is based on a thorough examination of hitherto unexplored materials—records of closed sessions in Moscow.

Forbidden Marriage

Fiction. Of dignity in his novels, race issue becomes more exacerbated. Black-hearted bigot. Is more delicate, distinctly apparent. Distinctly apparent. Each book. Novel to a demonstration of the harshness of South Africa's race laws.

Miscegenation with a nobility more akin to literature than to reality. A white girl and a "colored" man (race issue becomes more exacerbated). Race issue becomes more exacerbated. Is more delicate, a white girl and a "colored" man (girl). Each book.

First refuse to let them land; on condition the husband and wife do not cohabit again. Race laws, book is mightily effective, its flaws are all too obvious. Driving home its point in a way no legal protest could do—driving home its point in a way no legal protest could do—"evil," novels.

More biting as the race issue becomes more exacerbated. "African," race laws, race laws, its flaws are all too obvious. "African," given by Afrikaners themselves in their own language; "evil."

Solar Speculations

Should astronomers, of them feel that they should stick pretty closely to the facts, "landing parties will see them, and to guess what manner of things these landing parties may find." Realizes.

Should astronomers, planets. Effect upon it. Captured by freezing on the planet's dark, use imagination? "Landing parties will see them, and to guess what manner of things these landing parties may find." Them feel that they should stick pretty closely to the facts, is a physician, of them feel that they should stick pretty closely to the facts, not an astronomer. Should astronomers?

Spoils the sport. Of future space voyagers. "Landing parties may find. Any known fact about the solar system." Realize is that speculation about them.

Spoils the sport. Physical sciences. Effect upon it. Cold side "can never again escape as gases." Unlikely. Later he describes "great frigid hurricanes" of gases blowing away from the dark side. "Any known fact about the solar system." This chapter should have been read more carefully before it was sent to the printer. Information about the solar system, of future space voyagers. Not straining for sensation, spoils the sport.

Introduction to Provençal

Introduction to Frédéric Mistral, not even the noisy herds of holiday-makers in ever dwindling bikinis and the congeries of the world's drinking classes along the Riviera have succeeded in spoiling. The generation to which Richard Aldington belongs, Roy Campbell, of the northwestern wind which purifies the southern skies, *d'oc,* upon the inhabitants. Classical *langue d'oc.* The generation to which Richard Aldington belongs, introduction to Frédéric Mistral, of the northwestern wind which purifies the southern skies, not even the noisy herds of holiday-makers in ever dwindling bikinis and the congeries of the world's drinking classes along the Riviera have succeeded in spoiling.

The generation to which Richard Aldington belongs, of the northwestern wind which purifies the southern skies.

Poetry. Roy Campbell, of the northwestern wind which purifies the southern skies, vulgarity, efficient progress of technology. Not even the noisy herds of holiday-makers in ever dwindling bikinis and the congeries of the world's drinking classes along the Riviera have succeeded in spoiling. Classical *langue d'oc,* author's admiration for a poet who lauded and wistfully regretted the past is intelligent and expressed with zest and charm. Lead the scholars to reflect.

6 Gitanjali for Iris

I

My you
Gain is rainy life
See
The Here end
Gain rainy end again the end see the
Feet. Utter. Cry know
Is Now,
The outside when Now,

(18 seconds of silence)

IS
Life outside void end
The outside
Feet. Utter. Cry know
My you
Gain is rainy life

6 Gitanjali for Iris

II

Midnight, your
Gifts is river, light,
Sing
Thy humble every
Gifts river, every and thy every sing thy
Flute unbreakable captive keep
Is not
Thy of whom not

(10 seconds of silence)

Is
Light, of voice every
Thy of
Flute unbreakable captive keep
Midnight, your
Gifts is river, light

6 Gitanjali for Iris

III

Me You
God is renew life
Sleep
The heart even
God renew even again, the even sleep the
Fear undisturbed. Come keep
Is noontide
The on with noontide

(13 seconds of silence)

Is
Life on venture even
The on
Fear undisturbed. Come keep
Me You
God is renew life

6 Gitanjali for Iris

IV

My your
Ground is resting languidly
Sack
To He earth,
Ground resting earth, and to earth, sack to
Frayed unbreakable, court knew
It not
To only weeping not

(5 seconds of silence)

Is
Languidly only voyage earth,
To only
Frayed unbreakable, court knew
My your
Ground is resting languidly

6 Gitanjali for Iris

V

Master, your
Garment is renew linger
Strength
Trust hard entrance
Garment renew entrance a trust entrance strength trust
Finery, unholy colour knew
is not
Trust on wall not

(3 seconds of silence)

Is
Linger on vaguest entrance
Trust on
Finery, unholy colour knew
Master, your
Garment is renew linger

6 Gitanjali for Iris

VI

Morning You
Gleam in resonant life
Shame
Thee. He eyes
Gleam resonant eyes and thee. Eyes shame thee.
From up come Kindle
In not
Thee. Of wall not

(15 seconds of silence)

In
Life of vain eyes
Thee. Of
From up come Kindle
Morning you
Gleam in resonant life

PART TWO

THE SECOND NOTEBOOK OF

STANZAS FOR IRIS LEZAK

(written from the end of July to the later part of September 1960)

Peter Maurin Gay Believer

Probably people Peter book. England, engaging in economists, in. There trips to, they talked to the streets. East. Reach lives.

Made Maurin. And "angered at". A Utopian, one, of or agronomic universities. Reject. In, in, in, in, in. Not.

Conscription could Catholic corresponding grateful. Again, and, and. Experience, in ideas, even, in even in ideas ideas enough ever.

Been. Inner exemplifying. Loan, life. Everyone everything experience extraordinary in. In Institute institute inorganic industrialism ideas in "Easy Essays" in eight-page ex-Socialist East. For for farm from violence. Inspiration I I ideas issue I in in illness integrate English. Reading.

Peter Maurin was born on May 9, eldest child of Jean Baptiste, on the family farm, elder Maurin went on working in the fields, would recite his Rosary.

The old man would recite the psalm "Miserere," aloud every evening in Lent. Unwillingly, sinuous as rope, his jaw was set.

The sons of Jean Maurin did not take their father's word lightly.

As they grew up, his authority over them did not diminish. For forty years he served as a councilor.

The Maurin farm is on the left bank of the Lot River, where the eye is met by great distances in every direction. A little later he could go as far as the woodpile and carry an armload of fuel for the open fire so that his mother could prepare the evening meal. It would be some time before a young child's legs would permit him to run at ease over the farm lands, everyday things to the boy. The very summit of the mountain, was noted as one of the finest examples of an ancient walled city, one-time home of the Popes during their exile from Rome.

Northward in Auvergne is Le Puy. Wealthy Romans liked to build country estates there. At Nîmes Thomas Jefferson was so impressed by the Maison Carée that he studied it for hours and later copied it in the design of the Virginia State Capitol at Richmond. Wealthy Romans liked to build country estates there. Poets came there to recite their verses specially composed for the occasion.

The whole region bears the marks of Rome,—"the pale ashes of history." Up the tarn that a horde of Albigensians had fled from Toulouse and the armed bands of Simon de Montfort in the thirteenth century. Poets came there to recite their verses specially composed for the occasion. Part of it was relatively flat land. Next to it stood the granary and hayloft.

The sheep grazed sometimes on communal lands,—"the pale ashes of history." Sheep-shearing time came once a year.

In the winter Peter and his brothers and sisters had to stay indoors a good deal. Wealthy Romans liked to build country estates there. Up the staircase the sleeping quarters would be chilly and the winds sweeping down from Mont Lozère had often a hollow sound. Next to it stood the granary and hayloft. Wealthy Romans liked to build country estates there. The Maurin boys old enough to help out would collect the vegetables and friut of the farm. Wealthy Romans liked to build country estates there. Poets came there to recite their verses specially composed for the occasion.

Puzzling problems practicing *patios.* Plenty play. Playing. Eaten. They. Together they. Trick toboggan. Through. They. That there. Earth. End-walls. Retreat. Recreation run.

Made. Any among us. Up. Up. Receive, regulated. Instruction. Not.

Gather. Gossip. Alternation. At. As a as a. Agreements, all. Along. Area. And a. And all. At and at. A. As a. A. Arouses animals. Awake. Author. And. Yet. Years, years.

Belonged. Background be. Explains. Lot limpid. It is inscribed: "It." It. Event, excitement. Visit, explore—earth earthquakes. Ready.

Pickpockets from Lyons, hoping some peasant with a little cash might provide pleasant pickings. His own early days with nostalgia. Salted potatoes, the peasants argued the political issues of the day. "Treats economically; the Englishman. Truly dines, each piece of food." A bit of Roquefort from nearby farms.

Men discussed changes affecting their livelihood. Muttering against conscription. And Algeria. After the French defeat from Algerian wines. They were annoyed, undersold. For their own use. Republican democracy. The radicalism of the leftist political parties. In Paris. He was nearly finished.

Gambetta, bitterly anticlerical, had long advocated this. Although divided in view. They adopted a whole year.

But Paris had the upper hand. Eventually. To eight. Even textbooks would be free. Lay folk; in its love for the people. The 'enemies of the people' were at work. The excellent location of the school. Their efforts. There was great excitement. All excitement. Too young to understand the event, catching the general enthusiasm.

That Odd Art—Understatesmanship

Time for a humorless analysis of types.
In the order of difficulties a decline
affecting a ranch told
about with understatement to the nineteenth Duke
in England with a reply from Sparta is a technique absent-mindedl
tongue-tied by an established ministry. This account is a
narrative speech about Hitler and an Italian Prime Minister.

Tennis and holding American tenth
opinions on diplomatic defined
association at a rate Thomas
and his union, now different, though excellent,
realize in states that think, account for thinking in the East.
For the moment, A, a nuclear side, with hours of idiots, is
probable

and threatening to the human, almost in terror
of being obliterated. To decide the declared
alliance with a Russian who thinks
the United States has no discussion equal to his
reactions for safety is to take the attacking thereby as an
extermination and to mitigate and accept neutralism. Say at
home the incidence of politics.

Bon Voyage

"Be one of the most rewarding forms of introspection." "One I would have become had I stayed at home on my little island all my life. Never be answered."

"Voyage." "Out not to shun but to seek." "You know." "Aunt, good vacation is over when you begin to yearn for your work." Edward F. Murphy

Believe that travel caused me to develop into quite a different person from the one I would have become had I stayed at home on my little island all my life." "Of which no amount of experience can ever completely cure them: not to shun but to seek."

"Very valuable to the modern world." "Oh, you begin to yearn for your work." "A different person from the one I would have become had I stayed at home on my little island all my life." "Glow that one looks to the opposite sky fearfully; essential as some wealth in the pocket."

"Begin to yearn for your work." "One of the most rewarding forms of introspection." "Nose or his intuition."

"Valuable to the modern world." "One's aunt, yearn for your work." "At home on my little island all my life." "Glad to leave, experience can ever completely cure them."

Campaign Is On Foreign Policy the Key

Carried on in a swelling crescendo. Attack was pressed more harshly and more intensely than ever before. Mate; attack was pressed more harshly and more intensely than ever before. Political image centered largely on his alliance with the Administration's most outspoken Republican critic—attack was pressed more harshly and more intensely than ever before. Identified with the more liberal Rockefeller program. Government's expenses and to pay for the more revolutionary programs, need now.

Identified with the more liberal Rockefeller program. Schopenhauer.

Observers stress the melancholic mood in the aesthetic categories such as "mono-no-aware," need now.

Fulfillment Nirvana. Observers stress the melancholic mood in the aesthetic categories such as mono-no-aware," reflection, experience is related to Western philosophy. Identified with the more liberal Rockefeller program. Government's expenses and to pay for the more revolutionary programs, need now.

Political image centered largely on his alliance with the Administration's most outspoken Republican critic—observers stress the melancholic mood in the aesthetic categories such as "mono-no-aware," the leadership of an experienced monk. Identified with the more liberal Rockefeller program. Carried on in a swelling crescendo. Years of practice.

The essential experience remains inexpressible. Has been transformed by satori. Experience is related to Western philosophy.

Knowing subject and known object, experience is related to Western philosophy. Years of practice.

Comprehend Buddha, achieved enlightenment under the Bodhi-tree and thus became Buddha, meditation which has been developed over the centuries serves this goal. Prepares the mind, achieved enlightenment under the Bodhi-tree and thus became Buddha, is meant to break down the intellect. God in a delicately opened lotus blossom; nothingness.

Is meant to break down the intellect. Such grasping of the final unity in nothingness,

our existence. Nothingness.

Few sure strokes of the brush so that even stones come to life. Our existence. Reality: existence from the centre, is meant to break down the intellect. God in a delicately opened lotus blossom; nothingness.

Prepares the mind, our existence. Life from the centre, is meant to break down the intellect. Comprehend Buddha, York International Airport handled 438 flights daily during that year.

The gravitational flow of dust toward the center, he added, existence from the centre,

Kingdom and the Soviet Union. Existence from the centre, York

International Airport handled 438 flghts daily during that year.

College degrees, against an estimated need of 2, marked. Primary education in Africa averages as much as 60 or 70 per cent in many places, against an estimated need of 2,, is limited to but 2 or 3 per cent of the potential. Goes economic under-development. Not a single country in all of tropical Africa with per capita annual income above $200.

Is limited to 2 or 3 per cent of the potential. Soul in its greatest depth.

On the contrary, not a single country in all of tropical Africa with per capita annual income above $200.

Form temporality. On the contrary, reveal itself, epistemological definition, is limited to 2 or 3 per cent of the potential. Goes economic underdevelopment. Not a single country in all of tropical Africa with per capita annual income above $200.

Primary education in Africa averages 60 or 70 per cent in many places. On the contrary, logical judgement has the following form: is limited to 2 or 3 per cent of the potential. Concepts and universal ideas. Years its "half-life."

The earth soon after its formation; he found the ratio to be one part of iodine 129 to a million parts of iodine 127. Epistemological definition,

kimono and sash, epistemological definition, years its "half-life."

Constituent atoms of water is still largely unknown. All liquids is only dimly understood—meeting of the American Physical Society that by the use of "cold" neutrons ("possible to reveal complicated motions of atoms in liquid water.") All liquids is only dimly understood—. In a very direct manner, gives results that were heretofore impossible to attain. Neutrons are completely unaffected by the electric fields of atoms and hence slip easily inside solid material.

In a very direct manner, studying the interior of solid matter.

of individual atoms, Neutrons are completely unaffected by the electric fields of atoms and hence slip easily inside solid material,

400 degrees below zero Fahreinheit. Of individual atoms. Reveal directly the manner in which the water atoms were moving. Exerted by the near-by molecules. In a very direct manner, gives results that were heretofore impossible to attain. Neutrons are completely unaffected by the electric fields of atoms and hence slip easily inside solid material.

"Possible to reveal the complicated motions of atoms in liquid water." Of individual atoms. "Like the situation in solid materials." In a very direct manner, constituent atoms of water is still largely unknown. Years been running a deficit;

to sell its bananas some place, has experienced the traffic jams of Lagos or Accra—exerted by the near-by molecules.

Kept them out anyway. Exerted by the nearby molecules. Years been running a deficit.

Civil servants, administrators there were aplenty; more important, political as well as the economic control they established when their fathers arrived a generation—administrators there were aplenty; in the Rhodesias—"good." (Not called that)

in the Rhodesias—sees the storm coming has had but little political effect.

Of all the problems in sub-Saharan Africa, (not called that)

few areas—of all the problems in Sub-Saharan Africa, Rhodesia —exists. In the Rhodesias—"good." (Not called that)

political as well as the economic control they established when their fathers arrived a generation—of all the problems in

sub-Saharan Africa, "Little Rock," in the Rhodesias—
civil servants, year the Communist Chinese established
relations with Guinea;
this year with Ghana—have the deep significance it has to us.
Exists.
Kenya. Exists. Year the Communist Chinese established relations
with Guinea.

Communist news agencies (are found with increasing frequency).
Most precarious position of all the African countries
except the Congo, plagued by terrorism verging on
civil war, are found with increasing frequency. If not
originated by Communist support. Guinea in 1958,
no other part of the world and every part of Africa
differs from every other.
If not originated by Communist support. Short.
Of rising expectations growing up in Africa, no other part of the
world and every part of Africa differs from every other.
First requirement is sympathy without condescension for a continent striving to span centuries of human development in
years if not in months. Of rising expectations growing up in
Africa, requirement is assistance in concrete terms of personnel and money. Enterprise, if not by Communist support.
Guinea in 1958, no other part of the world and every part of
Africa differs from every other.
Plagued by terrorism verging on civil war, of rising expectations
growing up in Africa, little. If not originated by Communist support. Communist news agencies (York;)
the girl who is *all* girl . . . Hochschild Kohn, enterprise,
keep that's not easy. Enterprise, (York;).

Changed until today. American women, might *act* illegally, poet
most of all was the wife's intellectual effrontery—American women, is something less than total, guardianship of

220

> her husband. Nothing but an idiot relative,

is something less than total. Socially,

opinion of his wife was summed up by a poet named Palladus in two vitriolic lines: nothing but an idiot relative,

fathers wanted to keep their daughters' dowries in the family. Opinion of his wife was summed up by a poet named Palladus in two vitriolic lines: religious one, emancipation. Is something less than total, guardianship of her husband. Nothing but an idiot relative,

poet most of all was the wife's intellectual effrontery—opinion of his wife was summed up by a poet named Palladus in two vitriolic lines: "Lord," is something less than total, changed until today. Yet it was the most peculiar era in the history of wivery.

They were helpless, hundred economic and social reasons—emancipation.

Keep it in her own name. Emancipation. Yet it was the most peculiar era in the history of wivery.

Century whatever a wife earned became her husband's automatically, an oath as a witness and be held accountable for what she says, man, presumably for her own good. An oath as a witness and be held accountable for what she says, in mines; "government can forever spend money that is not at hand." New and young group of conservative politicians who know that we must study the past if we are to make progress in the future.

In mines; sensation;

ourselves from the world. New and young group of conservative politicians who know that we must study the past if we are to make progress in the future.

Find ourselves in the world and the world finds itself in us. Ourselves from the world. Result of this self-determination is the subjective-objective world. Even in that early period of

Nishida's thinking the idea was at once transcendent and immanent. In mines; "government can forever spend money that is not at hand."

Presumably for her own good. Ourselves from the world. Leads from judgement to consciousness; in mines; century whatever a wife earned became her husband's automatically, years ago in April Mayakovsky shot himself.

To believe that nearly a third of a century has passed since his death. Hard to believe that a man so full of the juice of life. Even in that early period of Nishida's thinking the idea was at once transcendent and immanent.

Killed himself. Even in that early period of Nishida's thinking the idea was at once transcendent and immanent. Years ago in April Mayakovsky shot himself.

Careless, another. Mayakovsky. Pushkin. (Improvised street jingles). George Reavey and Max Hayward. "1984,"
(improvised street jingles). Story of a bum,
of a party card and countless bedbugs. "1984."

First we see him in 1928—of a party card and countless bedbugs. Repertoire and did not come back until 1954 after Stalin's death. "Expression with which one begins life but does not end it." (Improvised street jingles). George and Max Hayward. "1984,"

Pushkin. Of a party card and countless bedbugs. "Life and I are quite." (Improvised street jingles). Careless, you need is leaders and people to mill around—

That's what's needed; Humanists felt that knowledge was a preeminent part of their pursuit of the profane redemption of man, "expression with which one begins life but does not end it."

Knowledge implies a certain gentleness. "Expression with which one begins life but does not end it." You need is leaders and people to mill around—

CAN PUT DOWN (a time when effort and honesty were viewed by the sensitive satirists), material to deride in their humor that which was being fought in the night. PICKETING, a time when effort and honesty were viewed by the sensitive satirists, IT, GUY WHO WAS ALWAYS POINTED OUT AS A MENACE WHEN THE ISSUE WAS HOT AND CHEERED AS A NOBLE DISSENTER AFTER THE ISSUE WAS *DEAD* FIFTEEN YEARS. NAME IT MISTER,
IT, SET TO FINALLY *ROLL*—
ORGANIZATIONAL NON-CONFORMISTS. NAME IT MISTER,
FOR A LITTLE CONCESSION THERE. ORGANIZATIONAL NON-CONFORMISTS. RIVALRY—EARLY LEADERS ON ACCOUNT OF OVER-ZEALOUSNESS. IT, GUY WHO WAS ALWAYS POINTED OUT AS A MENACE WHEN THE ISSUE WAS HOT AND CHEERED AS A NOBLE DISSENTER AFTER THE ISSUE WAS *DEAD* FIFTEEN YEARS. NAME IT MISTER,
PICKETING, ORGANIZATIONAL NON-CONFORMISTS. Loftily and in resentful disparagement of others;—IT, CAN PUT DOWN (yet possess all things;)
things to be valued attend them:—heaven and earth, EARLY LEADERS ON ACCOUNT OF OVER-ZEALOUSNESS.
Kwang-tsze is not likely to be quoting himself. EARLY LEADERS ON ACCOUNT OF OVER-ZEALOUSNESS. Yet possess all things.

Common to (all) movement his diffusiveness is like that of the Yang. Producing either happiness or calamity. (All) influence acting on him, (-given nature); no calamity from Heaven,
influence acting on him, Schneider has any great understanding of "Measure for Measure,"

223

of the rest of us do either. No calamity from Heaven,
for the New York Shakespeare Festival seems to me to emphasize nearly all the wrong things—of the rest of us do either. Rut of unwatchability. Even its author was satisfied with, influence acting on him, (-given nature); no calamity from Heaven,
producing either happiness or calamity. Of the rest of us do either.
        Lights—influence acting on him, common to (Young Peoples Socialist League in the Village).
The folk singers of the generation before him, he says, even its author was satisfied with,
know it; even its author was satisfied with, Young Peoples Socialist League in the Village.

Came across Helen Larsen, among her chairs, married, purple-yellow pansy, among her chairs, I saw in England, goes deeper than our analysis can penetrate. Not.
In waking life I had never kissed Helen, sweeter than I had ever dreamed—
occurred to me: not,
fabric of your being with their own particular aroma. Occurred to me: *Readings* from Aesthetic Realism, evening, I saw in England, goes deeper than our analysis can penetrate. Not.
Purple-yellow pansy, occurred to me: lacked. I saw in England, came across Helen Larsen, years experience treating addicts in the city prison system,
the narcotics committee of the Greenwich Village Association two years ago. He will be assisted on a full-time basis by Charles Eaton, evening,
knew where I belonged. Evening, years experience treating addicts in the city prison system.

"Can have as many as 20 or 100 previous lives," "and when I discovered I had the extraordinary powers of helping them to trace those previous incarnations, mistakes, they'd com-

mitted before." Pours in from all over the world ("and when I discovered I had the extraordinary powers of helping them to trace those previous incarnations"), is a bargain for the color of history and romance that it brings into their otherwise drab lives. Government agencies are trying to deal with it. Not be destroyed if tenants of other doomed Schulman buildings could be moved into it,
is a bargain for the color of history and romance that it brings into their otherwise drab lives. "Schulman off the hook."
On all demolition in the city until the number of families seeking housing could be reduced. Not be destroyed if tenants of other doomed Schulman buildings could be moved into it,
for his strong activities in behalf of West Side tenants, on all demolition in the city until the number of families seeking housing could be reduced. Rented until fully repaired. Is a bargain for the color of history and romance it brings into their otherwise drab lives. Government agencies are trying to deal with it. Not be destroyed if tenants of other doomed Schulman buildings could be moved into it,
pours in from all over the world (on all demolition in the city until the number of families seeking housing could be reduced). Living being came to a premature end. Is a bargain for the color of history and romance it brings into their otherwise drab lives. "Can have as many as 20 or 100 previous lives," Yin and Yang were harmonious and still;
THOMAS WOLFE. His life seems to float along; education.
Kan-yüeh preserves it carefully in a box, education; Yin and Yang were harmonious and still.

(Citrus sinensis) a native of Southeastern Asia, member of the genus and can be grown in any warm dry climate where the soil is fertile and well irrigated. Plants are budded or grafted. A native of Southeastern Asia, in the United States began in

225

Florida, green and the yellow color develops later. 1947 output of 45,

in the United States began in Florida, seedless orange originated in Brazil,

orange of the world. 1947 output of 45,

Florida. Orange of the world. Rind. Essential oil, in the United States began in Florida, green and the yellow color develops later. 1947 output of 45.

Plants are budded, or grafted. Orange of the world. Large, in the United States began in Florida,(*Citrus sinensis)* yield 1 lb. of the oil.

To vanilla in importance as a flavoring substance. (H. Hodge.) Essential oil,

kinds are grown in Southern Asia. Essential oil, yield 1 lb. of the oil.

Core, a coarse thick rind and thick leathery septa. Many *hybrids* have been produced. *(Paradisiaca* subsp. *sapientum)* a coarse thick rind and thick leathery septa. Is one of the most familiar and important of all tropical fruits. Grown, nearly surrounded by large,

is one of the most familiar and important of all tropical fruits. Spathelike scales,

off as the fruits mature. Nearly surrounded by large,

flower stalk develops from the rootstalk and pushes its way up through the hollow stem, off as the fruits mature. Rhizome, excess iis absorbed and not destroyed. Is one of the most familiar and important of all tropical fruits. Grown, nearly surrounded by large,

Paradisiaca subsp. *sapientum)* off as the fruits mature. Little if any evidence that VITAMIN-A deficiencies can be more quickly overcome by taking amounts larger than 100,-000 units daily; is one of the most

familiar and important of all tropical fruits. Core, younger adults.
The requirements also vary with intensity of light, health. Excess is absorbed and not destroyed.
Known; excess is absorbed and not destroyed. Younger adults.

Complex process of photosynthesis the hardest to crack has been the role of light itself. Arnon, "most recent aspect of the process." Palace. Arnon. "If there is no attack there will be no rockets." Governor Sir Evelyn Hone said: "No doubt make agreement in the wider field of politics so much more difficult."
"If there is no attack there will be no rockets." Steps taken to eliminate it in the Federation of Northern and Southern Rhodesia and Nyasaland.
Of shops was ended this year. "No doubt make agreement in the wider field of politics so much more difficult."
Palace. Of shops was ended this year. Last November's town election and announced he would appeal. "If there is no attack there will be no rockets." Complex process of photosynthesis the hardest to crack has been the role of light itself. Years.
The case involves George F. Hussey Jr., Hussey was chief of the Navy's Bureau of Ordnance at his retirement in 1947. Effort toward charter reform.
"Kosher diet observed" and asked rhetorically whether these "would establish that the author was engaging in a discriminatory practice." Effort toward charter reform. Years.

Cronin, announced today that he had quit the Princess' household because he just could not get along with her husband, "matters were not left in my hands as they should have been." "Person to whom a new employe should be responsible—" announced today that he had quit the Princess' household because he just could not get along with her husband, Illicit Peddlers. A seven-week crackdown on narcotics peddlers in East Harlem resulted in the arrest of 103 persons and the seizure of a quantity of narcotics, Greenwich Village and on Staten Island. Narcotics with intent to sell and for selling to policemen.

Illicit Peddlers A seven-week crackdown on narcotics peddlers in East Harlem resulted in the arrest of 103 persons and the seizure of a quantity of narcotics, 'Son of the Sheik' Opens Summer Series Over Channel 7 Rudolph Valentino rode off into the desert [sic] bearing Vilma Banky in his arms last night as an old Hollywood classic was reviewed in a new television series.

Of the four-armed Prajñāpāramitā, narcotics with intent to sell and for selling to policemen.

From an artistic point of view this is one of the finest representations of Prajñāpāramitā I have ever seen. Of the four-armed Prajñāpāramitā, rather South Indian in cast, eye is the "eye of wisdom" which, Illicit Peddlers A seven-week crackdown on parcotics peddlers in East Harlem resulted in the arrest of 103 persons and the seizure of a quantity of narcotics, Greenwich Village and on Staten Island. Narcotics with intent to sell and for selling to policemen.

"Person to whom a new employe should be responsible—" of the four-armed Prajñāpāramitā, left a *book*, Illicit Peddlers A seven-week crackdown on narcotics peddlers in East Harlem resulted in the arrest of 103 persons and the seizure of a quantity of narcotics, Cronin yet sufficiently appreciated its significance

they often believe that they can do without it. However, eye is the "eye of wisdom" which,

Kalimpong, eye is the "eye of wisdom: which, yet sufficiently appreciated its significance,

CONZE. And vital to an understanding of the Mahayana, more information about the relevant Indian literature. Part of the literature has so far been published in European languages. And vital to an understanding of the Mahayana, it is not easily accessible. G (named after the number of Lines)
(it is not easily accessible). Sariputra:
of wisdom? Named after the number of Lines
(following on the preaching of the Hinayana). Of wisdom? Ramifications, (Em), it is not easily accessible. G (named after the number of Lines)
part of the literature has so far been published in European languages.Of wisdom? Lost, it is not easily accessible. CONZE. Yogācārins.
The *Summaries* the most outstanding is the *Abhisamayālankāra* ("Heart Sutra" we find a Mantra of the Prajñāpāramitā). (Em),
Kausika (Em), Yogācārins.

Books of the times

The book of the old-fashioned opinion was known within a sub-
    urban
one by a face
of the town of the hungry endlessly.
The terminus intimacy of the much entertained styles,

this belief, these opinions of olden conformity, the season's
Oslo field,
track, or Hamarsland, equalled
three in Iceland which Michener's explosive sentenced,

and Bill Kuntz, not of Ohio, or Old Hickory Tenn., or Glasgow,
    Ky., and Sandra Spuzich,
not of Ossining, N.Y., a fair
trout, escaped
thirty-eight islands near the north of the entire second

Block. Orchard, Conn., an Olympic contender with streams
obvious, found
taking it high eventually
by trick two an inability at Monmouth. Eugene Dixon's Short
    Party

and Billy Haughton and Outgiving, opening considerably among
    students
other than at the first
time, a hard, eternal
train, invoking a mountain, an educator, strict

as a bell, or the Olt often a cathedral, straight
to Oultet, and a few,
twenty-five, to the *Halles,* in the evening,
through intoned Mary, easy to stretch

as a bell outside, and older classrooms, silently
older, followed
a teacher to his home and elided
his time, an innovation in moral education and a sacrifice.

A Story for Iris Lezak

The sun, which had compulsorily threatened realms in hotels, and shamelessly exerted evaporation's marvelous name, supported being soon after producing a feature. Established as the Greeks are, its return grants *Azotobacter* a rise in differentiation. Thus radiation is in history and helplessness of *Aristida* in a protonema.

Existences are shaded, to be exhausted, possibly, by fall. But the published centuries investigate the fact that Rossano Brazzi should be regarded as an effect of the monoxide of a field.

Opium perfected an insecticide forcing insects to give happiness to passions guarding intercourse in kitchens and in plants during the period when logic becomes recognized in explanations by rosaries in branches. Radiation specialized in order that *Maajun* might cork up a nontoxic relapse of a year's temperature.

Thus notoriety represented yielding in loving man's sunspot activity and objected that it would make a gas entrance. Its productions spoil nowadays along with the essential riometers, those rays of the hexagram of gentlemen as stated by the geological pumpkin.

Tunics of a relative of Timothy, patted by the director of Mexico's decapitated point, in order to answer in Egypt for a husband of Polaris, were enlarged here by the Society of Saint Dymphna.

The material in them was active, showing by hints and exposure how, in a time of contempts and socialism, and annihilation of externalities, we could be living. *Aralia nudicaulis* relegated another town of the long animals to the moss-covered Alyssum and the sources of ravenous purposes to hunt for the electron of snow, whence are sincere tomatoes, gospels, and maturity.

Though growing evidence of visibly or merely captured length, it did not pursue the ionosphere. An available $\bar{A}tma$ despotism kept the solar past shuffling left in tapping a *yogin*'s projects, and this was not a rock of life.

More and more, rights and venom interacted with guidance that attempted to carry them responsibly but encountered his face's manifestations in all their archegonia. They drove this hospital to photosynthesis.

A Sermon

Can we assure non-really the strength of the unfathomable oftenness? Necessarily are not the effects of a fisty mushroom or of *Zizia aurea* like getting the end which discoved a general? And is not that lanternlike which Maclura-pomiferizes recommendations?

Powerfully, something which is evidence of earth and of a Mariposa Lily produces a Common Liverwort and darkens the control which it enjoys. Does greatness more inwardly and creaturally benefit suspended twoness? It does not elmify afterward the earth which showeth its merit by trees and by investigation.

Do we not govern our daughters by reason? We nobly go to an epicure of risk who specializes in photosynthetic alwaysness. There ravenousness is not like itself but navigates (while striking and leaving introductorily) the death-process which overness narrows.

Absent-mindedly we are indirect when we understand Our Neil. Thingfully we naturalize and emerge from religion. Is *Euchlaena mexicana* not for catching and rabbit-brushing *Osmunda*? Are swooping and expiration manifestly diamonds? A taking pet is not a stalky one.

We exposed and polytrichumized a legislative one which Maclura-pomiferized an essence. Isn't everything in an individual? What is here? Thoughtfully, Europe and its learning, stylish as it is (though spitting is more so), does not exist in a hayloft.

Invalidatedly, does life not epochize entirety?

Does the establishment of the life-length of plants cushion and content their relations? Did they not transfer a nothinglike appearance controlledly? Their number subjects evaporatively, and reconstructs there in the eternal *Artemisia tridentata,* a quantity which externalizes research.

What was 1947, an enchantment or an *entourage*?

Do we not side with *Grindelia lanceolata* against the illusion of the followers of existence? We conscript, etiologize, transform, You-ify, and primordialize the construction of London.

Do not years extend and treat a number of northwestern understandings and *Alyssum maritimum* though they evergreen elementarily myriads of *naissances*? Yawl about motoring and linger occidentally in a resemblance to facts. Recall is not enough.

Was understanding ever evenness? It was a sin. Wasn't it annualized? Or was it a fact that intelligently (though the structure explosively and sensibly synthesized it) passed an embryo toward a lessening which bewildered bareness?

Red-eyedly did you rock the Putrefaction Bacteria and look at a shell? A country otherness is not an electron. Nor can you youthfulize differently if you tenurize containedly when dialectics of unknowing mortify and Austrian-pinefy the end of time.

Do you peeve Cato? Then do not effect the oak flower. Isn't the end Charles lasted until the finding which explosed *Liriodendron tulipifera*?

Physically, everybody activizes, resonates, and senses tangerinely.

The offing girlishly (though it *was* mannish) would not begirl its surroundings. Is emphasis not rooting for God?

Indeed, should investigators still fashion vividness in retirement? Should not specialized mouths belittle the Orient? Darkness does not legalize gross explanations. Elementarily, let us not encase the sun. Like *Fouquiera splendens,* we yogically but noncerebrally part—explanatorily at Rochdale House—though the French complete editorially what we have specially and recently seemed to choose. Is earnestness an insulator?

Shunningly, the light has no right. But letting were an orange if it were responsibility. Litmus-lichen not the relatively superior 19th century. Its incidence envelopes a number of inducements.

Does appreciation Rhus-typhinate intonation? Or does it old-man's-beard and extend an orange?

Again, do we not northernize oneness? Rather, do we not dance cosmically when excited? Fall, Cuba; distortions succumb and Latinize otherness.

Is air opinionated?

Do not belate or influence (refusingly, singingly, or explanatorily) the history of solitude.

Is strangeness not like hitting a source? *Sambucus canadensis* effects inconceivably the justification of instructive effects. Is that not a level where Ubé smoothly biologizes? Statements are like greatness. Moreover, if you intellectualize, guard, and get the Navy, you will like and avail an adjudicative hotness.

Do we not anglicize and envelope trivalance? Why communize evenings? *Oenothera* is not an academy.

However, a novel is a story. So why do we not yieldingly escape? Whose declarative existence is in every rose vocally? It does not evaporate. So why not front for ejection since indomitably we characterize *Pleurotus* as humility?

Is intellect numerical? Or does Liberace not, like a radio, reachingly enlighten his surroundings?

An individual failed when a *Rocella-like* despotism of nowness concluded his life. Is the North then *Nitrobacter*-like? Or is ten nullified? Is it not "evil" to leaf through responsibilities as if they were ghostly? A name attains (without leafleting—though slidingly) and citifies its everyness. Does this not heat and order acivity?

The East is a festival though Rostov is old and and important. Therefore we do not rock with the Egyptian Lotus or with the individual. Explanatorily, yet insulinly, is specialness restoration? Capability fadingly can (and strayingly must) reach sporangia. So why is destruction not pureness? Does a parsnip delight in existence? Or is the mainland a treatise? Distinction is not a refuge. Nor does a roll requiredly look at an American recovery.

Is it pleasant? Something isn't.

Must we not base and time ourselves by charming energy? It is extraordinary. But trees are not orderly. Then who should not exploit alone if he is digital?

Dorothy Day The Long Loneliness An Autobiography (I)

Dear child, of is not far from me, rail; *of is not far from me. . . . The pain is great, He who lays on the burden also carries it.* You and the priest in his "box."

Dear child, are large and roomy—you and the priest in his "box."

The pain is great, He who lays on the burden also carries it. Embarrassing and you do not go back to that priest again.

Light of day as the first step in getting rid of them. *Of is not far from me,* no time for that, gray, light of day as the first step in getting rid of them. *Of is not far from me,* no time for that, embarrassing and you do not go back to that priest again. Light of day as the first step in getting rid of them. In, no time for that, embarrassing and you do not go back to that priest again. Story of my conversion twelve years ago, story of my conversion twelve years ago,

are large and roomy—no time for that,

are large and roomy—us and the fascinating account of their lives. . . . *The pain is great, of is not far from me.* But I have not that right to discuss others. In, *of is not far from me,* grey, rail; are large and roomy—pardon of my readers. *He who lays on the burden also carries it.* You and the priest in his "box."

Done nothing well. Of joy in life but that soon wears away. Rebellion has started. Of joy in life but that soon wears away. Two parts. He was my master and I was his disciple; "you,"

done nothing well. "A painting of you which they still have." "You."

Two parts. He was my master and I was his disciple; every soul has a tendency toward God.

Little children, of joy in life but that soon wears away. Night and listen to our mother talk about "when I was a little girl." Georgia,

little children, of joy in life but that soon wears away. Night and listen to our mother talk about "when I was a little girl." Every soul has a tendency toward God. Little children, in the Confederate army. Night and listen to our mother talk about "when she was a little girl." Every soul has a tendency toward God. Satterlee, Satterlee,

"a painting of you which they still have." Night and listen to our mother talk about "when I was a little girl."

"A painting of you which they still have." Used to skate down the river from Poughkeepsie to Marlboro to bake a batch of bread and cookies and then skate back again. Two parts. Of joy in life but that soon wears away. Bridge over the Hudson. In the Confederate army. Of joy in life but that soon wears away. Georgia. Rebellion has started. "A painting of you which they still have." Pattern, he was my master and I was his disciple; "You,

down in the world if we are bad. Or Hungary, "refuses to submit to the small and arrogant oligarchy of those who are walking about." Or Hungary, those stories of our ancestors took away the fear of death that comes to us all, happy children ask these questions? Young just taking makes it mine.

Down in the world if we are bad. As infants squabbling in the nursery we were strong in this possessive sense. Young just taking it makes it mine.

Those stories of our ancestors took away the fear of death that comes to us all, happy children ask these questions? Either.

Laundry boy, or Hungary, nakedness. Girl had a baby out of wedlock,

Laundry boy, or Hungary, nakedness. Either. Laundry boy, it, nakedness. Either. Sin. Sin.

As infants squabbling in the nursery we were strong in this possessive sense. Nakedness.

As infants squabbling in the nursery we were strong in this possessive sense. Upon her. Those stories of our ancestors took away the fear of death that comes to us all, or Hungary, baby, it, or Hungary, girl had a baby out of wedlock, "refuses to submit to the small and arrogant oligarchy of those who are walking about." As infants squabbling in the nursery we were strong in this possessive sense. Put in an orphanage, happy children ask these questions? Young just taking makes it mine.

Descent, of Georgia and of Virginia, recover until the war was over. Of Georgia and of Virginia, to get back some of the seventy-five pounds he had lost during his hospital year. He loved

the machine and the illusion of progress. Years later,
descent, any child at Coney Island. Years later,
to get back some of the seventy-five pounds he had lost during his hospital year. He loved the machine and the illusion of progress. Editing *The Dial* and writing the first of his strange books.

Liberal, of Georgia and of Virginia, not understand a word of it. Group loved the country and lived there when their work permitted.

Liberal, of Georgia and of Virginia, not understand a word of it. Editing *The Dial* and writing the first of his strange books. Liberal, in the city to which they commuted; not understand a word of it. Editing *The Dial* and writing the first of his strange books. Some of them bought farms in New York, some of them bought farms in New York,

any child at Coney Island. Not understand a word of it.

Any child at Coney Island. Up to me, to get back some of the seventy-five pounds he had lost during his hospital year. Of Georgia and of Virginia, boat out in the bay for long hours was too much for me, in the city to which they commuted; group loved the country and lived there when their work permitted. Recover until the war was over. Any child at Coney Island. Paper, he loved the machine and the illusion of progress. Years later.

Dedicated lives of party members. One girl who was too flirtatious with the husbands of several other party women was disciplined by suspension from the party. Rose Carmen. One girl who was too flirtatious with the husbands of several other party women was disciplined by suspension from the party. Two children. Helped teach English to Varya Bulgakoff, Yankee trait in him.

Dedicated lives of party members. About the stinginess of the foreigners, Yankee trait in him.

Two children. Helped teach English to Varya Bulgakoff, excused on the grounds that they were Russians.

Lion tamer and was accused of throwing knives at his son and daughter. One girl who was too flirtatious with the husbands of several other party women was disciplined by suspension from the party. "Need once more to be boldly sung. Grown literally afraid to be poor."

Lion tamer and was accused of throwing knives at his son and daughter. One girl who was too flirtatious with the husbands of several other party members was disciplined by suspension from the party. "Need once more to be sung." Excused on the grounds that they were Russians. Lion tamer and was accused of throwing knives at his son and daughter. "In order to simplify and save his inner life. Need once more to be boldly sung." Excused on the grounds that they were Russians. Scramble, scramble, about the stinginess of the foreigners, "need once more to be boldly sung."

About the stinginess of the foreigners, "unbribed soul," two children. One girl who was too flirtatious with the husbands of several other party women was disciplined by suspension from the party. "By what we are and not by what we have, in order to simplify and save his inner life." One girl who was too flirtatious with the husbands of several other party women was disciplined by suspension from the party. Go into town for the day to do her weekly shopping, Rose Carmen, about the stinginess of the foreigners, picking at his lunch and directing the children's feeding. Helped to teach English to Varya Bulgakoff, Yankee trait in him.

Down the beach, of his huge white house, read in her little screened-in pavilion. Of his huge white house, those neighbors were within shouting distance, happily, yet he did nothing but enclose himself into a shell,

down the beach, a garden. Yet he did nothing but enclose himself into a shell, those neighbors were within shouting distance, happily, expression and played on his guitar.

Looked at him for a few minutes. Of his huge white house. Not for very long however. "Glare on the sand and the water is terrible."

Looked at him for a few minutes. Of his huge white house. Not for very long however. Expression and played on his guitar. Looked at him for a few minutes. If it was cloudy. Not for very long however. Expression and played on his guitar. "Soul is dead." "Soul is dead."

A garden, Not for very long however.

A garden. "Us to be slaves," those neighbors were within shouting distance, of his huge white house, "broom in my hands." If it was cloudy, of his huge white house, "glare on the sand and water is terrible." Read in her little screened-in pavilion. A garden. Purposefully set to work but by the time he finished one half of their living room, happily, yet he did nothing but enclose himself into a shell,

down to his books and his guitar, of the room. "Rushing away again." Of the room. To appear brown very often. He was harsh and impatient, "you do not know—"

down to his books and his guitar. And Sasha sighed as though the man's qualities were beyond his power of describing. "You do not know—"

"tell you," he was harsh and impatient, "easy to get.

Love to them they can flatter themselves that there is some rare quality in them which made him succumb." Of the room. "Not like him, go to Paris,

love to them they can flatter themselves that there is some rare quality in them which made him succumb." Of the room. "Not like him, easy to get. Love to them they can flatter themselves that there is some rare quality in them which made him succumb." "I am too happy down here." "Not like him, easy to get." "Stodgy as I am getting. Stodgy as I am getting."

And Sasha sighed as though the man's qualities were beyond his power odd describe. "Not like him."

And Sasha sighed as though the man's qualities were beyond his power of describing. "Us." "Tell you," of the room. Brothers were working in offices. "I am too happy down here." Of the rooms. "Go to Paris, rushing away again." And Sasha sighed as though the man's qualities were beyond his power of describing. "Proud I refused to be a white-collar slave but went to work as a dental mechanic." He was harsh and impatient, "you do not know—"

doubtless our parents' had (of passionate, romantic love between them, of passionate, that is what we ourselves wanted), held in that state, yet we left Oakland almost at once afterward,

doubtless our parents' had (a week to a new life in another city). Yet we left Oakland almost at once afterward,

these dreams only in connection with California and they were linked up with my idea of God as a tremendous Force, held in that state, earthquake,

lasted two minutes and twenty seconds, of passionate, near our bungalow and stables where my father kept a horse. Grounds for them.

Lasted two minutes and twenty seconds, of passionate, near our bungalow and stables where my father kept a horse. Earthquake, lasted two minutes and twenty seconds, in serving the homeless. Near our bungalow and stables where my father kept a horse. Earthquake, stitch of available clothes was given away. Stitch of available clothes was given away.

A week to a new life in another city. Near our bungalow and stables where my father kept kept a horse.

A week to a new life in another city. Us an apartment. These dreams only in connection with California and they were linked up with my idea of God as a tremendous Force, of passionate, blocks away, in serving the homeless. Of passionate, gardens of a very fine street from the railroad tracks along the lake. Romantic love between them, a week to a new life in another city. Polluted by the waste of industry and home? Held in that state, yet we left Oakland almost at once afterward,

dunes all along the shore. Of Indiana limestone, reassure my mother as to their safety, of Indiana limestone, the grim sunny day we went down to watch the dynamiting for the bodies of another brother and sister who had been drowned. Had found himself beyond his depth and his sister, yet it did not touch me so nearly as those forebodings of death which came to me at night after I had closed my eyes in the dark room and the universe began to spin around me in space.

Dunes all along the shore. And treacherous, yet it did not touch me so nearly as those forebodings of death which came to me at night after I had closed my eyes in the dark room and the universe began to spin around me in space.

The grim sunny day we went to watch the dynamiting for the bodies of another brother and sister, had found himself beyond his depth and his sister, editor of the *Call* at that time,

little money that he groaned as he thought of hiring me. Of Indiana limestone, New York policemen who had constituted themselves a "diet squad" under the inspiration of some city publicity man, going to work and live at home.

Little money that he groaned as he thought of hiring me. Of Indiana limestone, New York policemen who had constituted themselves a "diet squad" under the inspiration of some city publicity man, editor of the *Call* at that time, little money that he groaned as he thought of hiring me. I packed my suitcase New York policemen who had constituted themselves a "diet squad" under the inspiration of some city publicity man, editor of the *Call* at that time, said good-bye to my mother, said good-by to my mother, and treacherous, New York policemen who had constituted themselves a "diet squad" under the inspiration of some city publicity man,

and treacherous, under Manhattan Bridge, the grim sunny day we went down to watch the dynamiting for the bodies of another brother and sister, of Indiana limestone, been leading me because I made a good choice in the first one I entered. I packed my suitcase, of Indiana limestone, going to work and live at home. Reassure my mother as to their safety, and treacherous, painted white. Had found himself beyond his depth and his sister, yet it did not touch me so nearly as those forebodings of death which came to me at night after I had closed my eyes in the dark room and the universe began to spin around me in space.

Cuba As I See It

Countries. Utopia at some distant date after an austere and ruthless program of industrialization. Batista's corrupt cronies would slip back into strategic positions from where they could sabotage this "revolution of the humble." Are intellectually honest,
 are intellectually honest, so long silent during Cuba's series of cruel dictatorships when the people had the forms but none of the substance of liberty?

In Georgia,

so long silent during Cuba's series of cruel dictatorships when the people had the forms but none of the substance of liberty? Ever allowed Negroes to vote freely, ever allowed Negroes to vote freely,

in Georgia, through fear,

Cuba *and* of Negroes, United States government and press will be discredited among decent people everywhere. Begun to speak out and to contradict the demonstrable falsehoods. At all surprised if Washington has already set a date for military intervention and occupation.

At all surprised if Washington has already set a date for military intervention and occupation. Spreading the lie that Catholic Cuba has become a base of world communism in order to justify an act of gunboat diplomacy.

In 1954,

spreading the lie that Catholic Cuba has become a base of world communism in order to justify an act of gunboat diplomacy. Eisenhower to go to war to salvage French colonialism in Indo-China. Eisenhower to go to war to salvage French colonialism in Indo-China.

In 1954, they urged a naval blockage of China and nuclear war if necessary,

Chiang Kai-shek on some rocky, United States newspapers that voluntarily parrot the official line. Be unable to operate the Suez Canal without their pilots and their help, as today, they proclaim that Cuba "needs" the United States to avoid "economic chaos."

As today they proclaim that Cuba "needs" the United States to avoid "economic chaos." She tried to appease these elements.

In a dream world of swaggering 19th century imperialism.

She tried to appease these elements. Embassy instead of going to the Foreign Ministry, embassy instead of going to the Foreign Ministry,

in a dream world of swaggering 19th century imperialism. The aegis of the puppet Organization of American States,

Cuba would be an immediate disaster for both countries. U.S. marines would be indoctrinated in advance to believe that their "crusade" would "liberate" Cuba from the "tyranny" of Fidel Castro. Bloody tragedy would come when those same innocent marines would learn the hard way that the Cuban people are prepared to die for the Revolution and will not permit the wealthy and over-privileged United States to turn back the clock of history. Already written a letter giving my impressions of Cuba to A. Philip Randolph,

Already written a letter giving my impressions of Cuba to A. Philip Randolph, Sleeping Car Porters and a man of great moral power.

I shall have discussions with him and other Negro leaders who are independent of the bone-crushing pressures of the government and of the business community.

Sleeping Car Porters and a man of great moral power. 18 million Negroes for equality and justice in the United States will have little meaning if, 18 million Negroes for equality and justice in the United States will have little meaning if,

I shall have discussions with him and other Negro leaders who are independent of the bone-crushing pressures of the government and of the business community. The freedom to run their country according to twentieth-century concepts of *true* independence and to set a beacon example for the rest of the exploited countries of Latin America.

Communist 4th of July Union Square Meeting This was held on the 30th of June and I was one of the speakers. Union. Being an anarchist, are not only against this Japanese Treaty which is

the subject of the day,
subject of the day,

are not only against this Japanese Treaty which is the subject of the day, sin of killing tens of thousands at Hiroshima but as if to prove how mean we could be we dropped the bomb later at Nagasaki.

It are forced by us to be our ally in our imperialistic schemes.

Sin of killing tens of thousands at Hiroshima but as if to prove how mean we could be we dropped the bomb later at Nagasaki. Expected because we broke every treaty we made since the one George Washington made with the American Indians. Expected because we broke every treaty we made since the one George Washington made with the American Indians.

It are forced by us to be our ally in our imperialistic schemes. The Mexican War and the Spanish-American War is a scandal.

Catholic students. University Friday morning June 10. Battery the day before. A score of us marched until we reached New Rochelle where we were picked up by friends for the night. Students and a girl student from St. John's and I were taken to a Quaker home at Hastings-on-the-Hudson,

it rained and we stopped to get something hot with friends but kept on until we were all provided with warm clothing at Mrs. Tjader Harris,

students and a girl student from St. John's and I were taken to a Quaker home at Hastings-on-the-Hudson, early in the morning. Early in the morning.

It rained and we stopped to get something hot with friends but kept on until we were all provided with warm clothing at Mrs. Tjader Harris, towns students marched with us.

Cullum, us, but the nearer we got to New London the more hostile police and people were. A new sign and papers and booklets Tuesday evening and came back and met the others in New

Haven at Rochdale House.

A new sign and papers and booklets Tuesday evening and came back and met the others in New Haven at Rochdale House. Some woman had slowed her car to look at the signs and had put out her hand so the woman behind her bumped into her car.

In New London.

Some woman had slowed her car to look at the signs and had put out her hand so the woman behind her bumped into her car. Employed and threatening to arrest us as vagabonds. Employed and threatening to arrest us as vagabonds.

In New London. They wanted to know if any of us were veterans.

Conscientious objector. Us a huge tent and we slept in a state park. Booklet with interest. A sign and the place we bought it from was run by Quakers who took our literature to give out.

A sign and the place we bought it from was run by Quakers who took our literature to give out. Some highway workers called us Communists but one of them,

Italian Catholic,

Some highway workers called us Communists but one of them, extra hamburgers (extra hamburgers)

Italian Catholic, to New London and slept on the floor in Brad's apartment.

Cape May. Up a side street and conferring. Boy, at Harvard, at Harvard, saloon or poolroom grabbed his sign but as it was very tough he had to tramp on it to try to break it.

If we didn't want our signs messed up we had better have stayed at home.

Saloon or poolroom grabbed his sign but as it was very tough he had to tramp on it to try to break it. End of the street where we started. End of the street where we had started.

If we didn't want our signs messed up we had better have stayed at home. To go home, come, us. Back again. And I had gone to St. Joseph's to Mass and had breakfast with Father Flint.

And I had gone to St. Joseph's to Mass and had breakfast with Father Flint. She had visited us twice in New York City.

Interested in the same problems as the CW but of course not so radical.

She had visited us twice in New York City. *Employers of Italy and Argentina* I met with members of the *Association of Catholic Trade Unionists* at Mass at St. Michael's Church and heard a sermon by Right Rev. John P. Monaghan. *Employers of Italy and Argentina.* I met with members of the *Association of Catholic Trade Unionists* at Mass at St. Michael's Church and heard a sermon by Right Rev. John P. Monaghan.

Interested in the same problems as the CW but of course not so radical. The Christian Union of Employers and Managers of Italy,

capitalists to make profits; unions of employers and unions of workers, believe in rent, are friendly for we have the same immediate enemy:

are friendly for we have the same immediate enemy: Salter in Chicago giving John Begley and Robert J. Polite three years probation when they had pled guilty to stealing $1,800 worth of merchandise.

"In free enterprise" because they were off duty when doing their stealing,

sold there too. (8:30 p.m.) (8:30 p.m.)

"in free enterprise" because they were off duty when doing their stealing. (2 p.m.)

(construction on what he said). Up to a self-destroying machine, bicycle, and other junk were piled in a construction some 25 feet long and 8 feet high.

And other junk were piled in a construction some 25 feet

long and 8 feet high. Select group kerosine and other inflammatory stuff was poured on it and it was set afire.

It began to shudder,

select group kerosine and other inflammatory stuff was poured on it and was set afire. Elite and to enable the press to talk about the decadence of art and artists today? Elite and to enable the press to talk about the decadence of art and artists today?

It began to shudder, there is a sincere searching for truth,

collections of disconnected items arranged in patterns. Unwashed, backs on all tradition. Are going we may have to face life without art.

Are going we may have to face life without art. Suffering.

Inch of Rembrandt is worth 1,200 dollars,

suffering. Easily, easily,

inch of Rembrandt is worth 1,200 dollars, they can roll up under their arms.

Crafts. University of Illinois. BEDROOM IS THROUGH THAT DOORWAY I tilted her head up and kissed her. All she needed,

all she needed, she was,

I kissed her nose and her eyes and the tip of her chin.

She was, easy to stop on the ramp. Easy to stop on the ramp.

I kissed her nose and her eyes and the tip of her chin. To see the smile and the pearly white teeth and the valiant and hopeful thumb,

Cue, up off-the-breasts. By the time she managed to ask me where I was headed I already had my laundry bag in the back seat and my tail planted on the front seat a respectable distance from hers. And she gave me a quick smile and told me that she was driving all the way to the city.

And she gave me a quick smile and told me that she was driving all the way to the city. Short hauls that doesn't do much more than break the monotony of standing in one place.

I didn't even think about it.

Short hauls that doesn't do much more than break the monotony of standing in one place. Entrance-way and drove out onto the thruway. Entrance-way and drove out onto the thruway.

I didn't even think about it. The big Caddy its head.

Can still make myself understood, usual battle between woman and machine but a game she and the Caddy were playing. Beetle, around the Ford and winding up in front of it with one motion,

around the Ford and winding up in front of it with one motion, S-curve.

I sat and thought and kept my eyes on her.

S-curve. End of the deal; end of the deal;

I sat and thought and kept my eyes on her. To look at than the New York State thruway,

crew, under a hot sun. Bad job, a day at a job that gives your brain a chance to think about other things.

A day at a job that gives your brain a chance to think about other things. Stuff that gets you into shape and fills up your wallet at the same time.

Isn't bad when the pay is upwards of three bucks an hour to begin with.

Stuff that gets you into shape and fills up your wallet at the same time. Entirely true, entirely true,

isn't bad when the pay is upwards of three bucks an hour to begin with. Taking her to movies and giving her a chaste kiss at the door,

clear blue eyes and a nice-if-boyish body and white teeth that flashed in a lay-me smile whenever there was a man wtihin shoot-

254

ing distance. "Up to you to let him know whether he should listen to you or whether you should both just sit there and watch the scenery. But he has to play ball one way or the other." A minute.

A minute. She suggested.

"I'm not particularly interesting."

She suggested, Easier than lying. Easier than lying.

"I'm not particularly interesting." Told her my name was Mark Taggert and that I was a transplanted New Yorker who hadn't managed to put down roots anywhere.

College in New York, unproductive years in the army, between, along with other jobs too monotonous and numerous to mention.

Along with other jobs too monotonous and numerous to mention. Speak of.

In a state hospital for the incurably insane,

speak of. Ever wanting to see. Ever wanting to see.

In a state hospital for the incurably insane, the world but no close friends because I never stayed in one place long enough to form anything resembling a permanent friendship, type of thing.

Children that I knew about, unemployed, bucks in my wallet and confetti in my head. And easily because it was relatively easy to talk to her even if I had nothing at all important to tell her,

and easily because it was relatively easy to talk to her even if I had nothing at all important to tell her, she took it all in from beginning to end without saying much of anything.

In a while her face would hold the shadow of a smile;

she took it all in from beginning to end without saying much of anything. "Entertain me to tell you about myself. Entertain me to tell you about myself."

In a while her face would hold the shadow of a smile; "Tell me about it."

"Can guess," up a person fairly well. Because I know anyone long enough or well enough to get by just soaking up surface impressions. About herself,

about herself, she would want to hear.

I decided I didn't really give much of a damn whether she got disturbed or not.

She would want to hear. Expressionless and it was impossible to tell how she was taking it. Expressionless and it was impossible to tell how she was taking it.

I decided I didn't really give much of a damn whether she got disturbed or not. Told her so far wasn't the work of genius—

covers were turned down. Up after I had set her down on the bed and came into my arms. Body was pressed tight against me and her arms were bands of soft steel around my back. Arms and placed her on the cool white sheet.

Arms and placed her on the cool white sheet. Spilled over the pillow like liquid gold.

I was afraid I would hurt them.

Spilled over the pillow like liquid gold. Everything else at our feet. Everything else at our feet.

I was afraid I would hurt them. Then higher,

claps of thunder. Us heard it. Bad cook. At least she made decent scrambled eggs,

at least she made decent scrambled eggs, something.

In front of ninety percent of the restaurants in the United States.

Something. Eggs and black coffee. Eggs and black coffee.

In front of ninety percent of the restaurants in the United States. Their early sides before they got lost in fugue structure and college tours and their music turned into background slush for slick magazine stories.

Came against me like a hungry kitten and her hands were cool as frozen silk on the back of my neck. Up and walked from the room. Brushed mine as we walked. At her body.

at her body. She was so beautiful,

it was perfume and honey and the compelling and delicious taste of wine.

She was so beautiful, entire world. Entire world.

It was perfume and honey and the compelling and delicious taste of wine. The red nipples all hard and glowing from her sexual excitement.

Could. Until it exploded. But I couldn't wait. Another minute.

Another minute. Shock of my life.

I said.

Shock of my life. "Experience. Experience."

I said. "To sort of play it by ear."

"Couldn't fake something like that." Under my gaze the way so many women do. Body, a woman and pleased to have me look at her with raw admiration in my eyes.

A woman and pleased to have me look at her with raw admiration in my eyes. She was beautiful.

I told her so.

She was beautiful. "Embarrassed the way the boys would stare at me in class. Embarrassed the way the boys would stare at me in class."

I told her so. "Them."

Concession for a proud and beautiful woman like Elaine to make. Unimportant and easily surmountable. Before dissolved quickly and quietly in the salty stream of her tears. Any other man for any other woman.

Any other man for any other woman. She cried,

I held her in my arms and stroked the soft skin of the back of her neck with fingers that were trembling with love of her.

She cried, everything, everything.

I held her in my arms and stroked the soft skin of the back of her neck with fingers that were trembling with love of her. That only left us.

Good-by New York New York Prepares
For Annihilation (I)

Geese can quickly end this island fantasy, of mortality is part of New York now; Defense Commission had just finished showing a visitor the series of slides that illustrate the complex operation of New York's elaborate plans for survival in the nuclear age. Been portrayed in pictures, York City? " 'New York.' " Earth is portrayed in a huge mural on the walls of the reception office of the New York State Civil Defense

Commission headquarters, with orangish flames and grey smoke painted into the buildings and the sky.

York City? *Of mortality is part of New York now;* return they could ask from their money is an accurate inscription on their tombstone. "Killed" in the simulated attack.

" 'New York.' " Earth is portrayed in a huge mural on the walls of the reception office of the New York State Civil Defense Commission headquarters, with orangish flames and grey smoke painted into the buildings and the sky.

York City? *Of mortality is part of New York now;* return they could ask from their money is an accurate inscription on their tombstone. "Killed" in the simulated attack.

Preparations of civil defense, return they could ask from their money is an accurate inscription on their tombstone. Earth is portrayed in a huge mural on the walls of the reception office of the New York State Civil Defense Commission headquarters, preparations of civil defense, about the most that the residents of the Empire State can hope for in event of a nuclear attack. Return they could ask from their money is an accurate inscription on their tombstone. Earth is portrayed in a huge mural on the walls of the reception office of the New York State Civil Defense Commission headquarters, sees few signs of the civil-defense preparations.

4. *Follow Directions of Civil Defense Personnel They are Trained to Protect You Play Safe and Enjoy Yourself.* Of mortality is part of New York now; return they could ask from their money is an accurate inscription on their tombstone.

About the most that the residents of the Empire City can hope for in event of a nuclear attack. " 'New York.' " " 'New York.' " In co-operation with the Boy Scouts of America, *Handbook for Emergencies.* In co-operation with the Boy Scouts of America, leave some questions, about the most that the residents of the Empire City can hope for in event of a nuclear attack. To how the city government alone (in co-operation with the Boy Scouts of America), *of mortality is part of New York now;* " 'New York.' "

General Robert E. Condon, 1,621,000 armbands, 1,621,000 armbands, "dog tags" for the city's school children. Better games to play. Youngsters have joined in the games, not always been so successful. (Exactly one year late—was only ten months tardy) youngsters have joined in the games, 1,621,000 armbands, received more newspaper coverage than any other activity of a city department or agency. Kansas, not always been so successful. (Exactly one year late—was only ten months tardy) youngsters have joined in the games, 1,621,000 armbands, received more newspaper coverage than any other activity of a city department or agency. Kansas, postponing it. Received more newspaper coverage than any other activity of a city department or agency. (Exactly one year late—) postponing it. After showing the slides of his master plan for New York, received more newspaper coverage than any other activity of a city department or agency. (Exactly one year late—) systems, free nations. 1,621,000 armbands, received more newspaper coverage than any other activity of a city department or agency. After showing the slides of his master plan for New York, not always been so successful. Not always been so successful. In Cuba, had no more been raised than General Huebner speculated on the possibility of a Communist France. In Cuba, likely that the French Communists would come to power, after showing the slides of his master for New York, thus turning a keystone of NATO into an arm of the Kremlin. In Cuba, 1,621,000 armbands, not always been so successful.

Got down to more immediate problems. Own lunches for the trip. Own lunches for the trip. Drivers. Basis to the state and its political subdivisions which can be used to purchase civil-defense material, year fully reported on to date of writing,

New York State and its cities and other subdivisions received reimbursements amounting to $916,035 from the federal government in the "matching-funds" program. Exclusive of federal funds, "when a war may start—"

York's defense. Own lunches for the trip. Radio for instructions, kinds of canned foods to store in the basement for use in case of enemy attack,

New York State and its cities and other subdivisions received reimbursements amounting to $916,035 from the federal government in the "matching funds" program. Exclusive of federal funds, "when a war may start—"

York's defense. Own lunches for the trip. Radio for instructions, kinds of canned foods to store in the basement for use in case of enemy attack,

"Pantry was always ready—" radio for instructions, exclusive of federal funds, "Pantry was always ready—" affair, radio for instructions, exclusive of federal funds, sill:

"from Suffolk County." Own lunches for the trip. Radio for instructions

affair, New York State and its cities and other subdivisions received reimbursements amounting to $916,035 from the federal government in the "matching funds" program. New York State and its cities and other subdivisions received reimbursements amounting to 916,035 in the "matching funds" program. "Instructions." "Hazard . . . " "Instructions." "Leave their shelters for a short time to perform essential tasks. . . ." Affair. The voice said that people out there might want to secure some survival equipment. "Instructions." Own lunches for the trip. New York State and its cities and other subdivisions received reimbursements amounting to $916,035 from the federal government in the "matching funds" program.

General Huebner walked over to the tape recorder and switched it off. On the wireless. Difficult. But except for the hours from 7 a.m. to 4 p.m., Yorkers would have in case of attack would be fifteen to twenty minutes.
Negative-thinking New Yorkers, enemy might well want to preserve the port of New York for invasion purposes. Worked-out plan,
York City would report to their local precinct police stations and be shipped by truck. Of course, reason to believe that nuclear missiles wouldn't hit New Jersey and Connecticut as well as New York. Russian missiles have proved they can hit within a mile and a quarter of any selected target point. Kids no doubt have better games to play.
Negative-thinking New Yorkers, enemy might well want to preserve the port of New York for invasion purposes. Worked-out plan,
York City would report to their local precinct police stations and be shipped by truck. Of course, reason to believe that nuclear missiles wouldn't hit New Jersey and Connecticut as well as New York. Russian missiles have proved they can hit within a mile and a quarter of any selected target point. Kids no doubt have better games to play.
Pacific tests this January, Russians have proved they can hit within a mile and a quarter of any selected target point. Enemy might well want to preserve the port of New York for invasion purposes. Pacific tests this January, "All the Russians would have had to do to put them within a mile and a quarter of Times Square would have been to change the direction mechanism." Russians have proved they can hit within a mile and a quarter of any selected target point.

Enemy might well want to preserve the port of New York for invasion purposes. Said:
factor in scientific and military estimates. Of course, Russians have proved they can hit within a mile and a quarter of any selected target point.
"All the Russians would have had to do to put them within a mile and a quarter of Times Square would have been to change the direction mechanism." Negative-thinking New Yorkers, negative-thinking New Yorkers, is being placed on saving the population in outlying areas. Housing in the state, is being placed on saving the population in outlying areas. Last summer was the opinion of most of the expert witnesses that the danger of radiation from nuclear fallout has been overemphasized in civil-defense plans. "All the Russians would have had to do to put them within a mile and a quarter of Times Square would have ben to change the direction mechanism." That an even greater danger was being neglected: is being placed on saving the population in outlying areas. Of course, negative-thinking New Yorkers.

Giant "fire storms" caused by nuclear blasts could raze the countryside fifty miles around. On the hearings, on the hearings, disturbed by the proposed expenditures for fallout shelters (built only at basement levels) York City engineering firm for a giant underground shelter five to six hundred feet beneath the surface of Manhattan,
nuclear explosion has been judged economically unfeasible by most authorities—economic feasibility of burrowing an entire city underground. "What you people don't understand is that the shelter becomes your *home* after the blast."
York City engineering firm for a giant underground shelter five to six hundred feet beneath the surface of Manhattan, on the hearings, "Raid Shelter is Challenge to Designer," kids no

doubt have better games to play.
Nuclear explosion has been judged economically unfeasible by most authorities—economic feasibility of burrowing an entire city underground. "What you people don't understand is that the shelter becomes your *home* after the blast."
York City engineering firm for a giant underground shelter five to six hundred feet beneath the surface of Manhattan, on the hearings, "Raid Shelter is Challenge to Designer," kids no doubt have better games to play.
Periodically throughout the boroughs. "Raid Shelter is Challenge to Designer," economic feasibility of burrowing an entire city underground. Periodically throughout the boroughs. A hundred fifth- and sixth-grade pupils from P.S. 13 were taken to a vacant lot for a civil-defense survival drill featuring instructions on how to make cooking materials from discarded tin cans and how to decontaminate radioactive bananas. "Raid Shelter is Challenge to Designer," economic feasibility of burrowing an entire city underground. Smith of the U.S. Air Force also showed how to decontaminate potatoes,
foods, on the hearings, "Raid Shelter is Challenge to Designer."
A hundred fifth- and six-grade pupils from P.S. 13 were taken to a vacant lot for a civil-defense survival drill featuring instructions on how to make cooking materials from discarded tin cans and how to decontaminate radioactive bananas. Nuclear explosion has been judged economically unfeasible by most authorities—nuclear explosion has been judged economically unfeasible by most authorities—in July, hours before General Condon would confirm it. In July, latitude and longitude and the location could not be determined until plotted on a map. A hundred fifth- and six-grade pupils from P.S. 13 were taken to a vacant

lot for a civil defense survival drill featuring instructions on how to decontaminate radioactive bananas. " 'This scheme would help the occupants remember which way is up.' " In July, on the hearings, nuclear explosion has been judged economically unfeasible by most authorities—

PART THREE

THE THIRD NOTEBOOK OF

STANZAS FOR IRIS LEZAK

(written mainly in late September & early October 1960)

Dorothy Day The Long Loneliness An Autobiography (II)

dishes on remember on they have years
Dishes aspect years.
They have enjoying
liberty on not gazing
liberty on not enjoying liberty I not enjoying she she
aspect not
aspect until they on beg I on gazing remember aspect. Perhaps
    have years.

Day. Or romances or the house, ye
day. And ye
the house, evils,
love, or North green
love, or North evils, love, in North evils, smelled smelled and North
and up the or but in or green romances and particular house, ye

  did not need to Our Lord Himself said that the poor we would always have with us. Refused to have always lived into the dispute. Our Lord Himself said that the poor we would always have with us. Thrilling had no desire to follow this Catholic particular course or to work for a degree. Years old but up the generally mortified but waiting age. He

  did not need to. And yet I scorned the students who were pious. Years old but up the generally mortified but waiting age. He

  thrilling had no desire to follow this Catholic particular course or to work for a degre. Oisepe.

  Life Our Lord Himself said that the poor we would always have with us. Not want to belong to my debt rush that many of our classmates joined. Live to College.

  Life Our Lord Himself said that the poor we would always have with us. Not want to belong to my debt rush that many of our classmates joined. Oisepe. Life I not want to belong to my debt rush that many of our classmates joined. Oisepe. Stores and ways over his "time." For after stores and ways over his "time."

  Already they had been persecuted, they had been scourged, they had been thrown into prison and put to death, not only in other parts of the world but right around me in the United States. Not want to belong to my debt rush that many of our classmates joined.

  As a matter of fact, to her it was an episode to be forgotten. Hungary but I insisted on some talents. Thrilling Our Lord Himself said that the poor we would always have with us. But a word was broken and I didn't I Our Lord Himself said that the poor we would always have with us. Going to turn to larger parishes more peculiarly than he had surrounded man from school. Fresh curly hair. At that time Rayna did not share my radical interests. Paper, avenue before one's short stories. Had no desire to follow this Catholic particular course or to work for a degree. Years old but up the generally mortified but waiting age. He

Distributism is the English term for a while that the obligation gives no matter how many of the words of Ezekiel to enable him to lead the revolution. Other words have been called to shelter this theory, Washington, sweeping, peasant of the pavements, store for the winter; but his head—the suppression at the same time as this demonstration of the unemployed, who so evidently loved us all,—under the sentence of death by its Marxist opponents,—most pinkly ends up by coming to the Blessed Sacrament, with the contest, settled for a time in Chicago, between the hand for relief and violence if moral force had not been substituted for coercion, that loses control to this day. A cement-paved yard at our baptism was bringing a skilled worker for an hour to another store, up in my room on the third floor, in our house on Mott Street, and at the Hotel Pitt because five-story buildings found it appropriate to say that the gesture of going to the people was futile and that it had been tried in Russia and failed. Other words have been called to shelter this theory, Washington, sweeping, peasant of the pavements, store for the winter; but his head— its suppression, at the same time as this demonstration, of the unemployed, who so evidently loved us all,—under the sentence of death by its Marxist opponents,—most pinkly ends up by coming to the Blessed Sacrament, with the contrast, settled for a time in Chicago, between the hand for relief and violence (if moral force had not been substituted for coercion), that loses control to this day. The masses had been made the most respectable members of our community in that their rooms were filled with steam heat and hot water. A heavy accounting of masters and the future alone was going over to short stories. "Yes Peggy loved the peace of the country," we used to say little by little, but not before there had been a riot in Harlem when she prayed, so I came to them in a country place outside of Moscow.

Distributism is the English term for a while that the obligation gives no matter how many words of Ezekiel to enable him to lead the revolution. "As a baby sister of Sacco and Vanzetti who present difficulties," I answered her then, "it is plenty to love well." "Yes, Peggy loved the peace of the country," we used to say little by little, but not before there had been a riot in Harlem when she prayed, so I came to them in a country place outside of Moscow.

The masses had been made the most respectable members of our community in that their rooms were filled with steam and hot water. A heavy accounting of the masters and the future alone was going over to short stories. Even the little journey out of the hospital in that state was filled with eyes which he enjoyed now that I called.

Stanzas for Iris Lezak

Sweeping eastern capture testimony as sweeping sweeping as sweeping sweeping into notoriety. Temperature each sufficiently, A Bonus. Nor culminate existing languor languor of relapse existing implement guard harangue tenure harangue yearn existing and relapse guard relapse and detriment existing is nontoxic secretion extremely contains that assassin-bug secretion secretion assassin-bug secretion secretion is nontoxic its needle. Zen examines now becomes universe disappears, Action (stomach),

Feet. Once Once Discovered Ship Hundreds Estimated Geological ICE VESSEL Estimated Ship Miles Estimated Hundreds Estimated ATLANTIC Discovered despite himself. Running East a running a nutmeg in the hemp In members a nutmeg often a this have emphasise stage stage emphasise necessary this it At longer "Universal Necessary" it this it at necessary described it described emphasise necessary this it this it of fundamental this have emphasise "stage emphasise longer fundamental" necessary at longer longer this have emphasise stage this At this emphasise stage of fundamental this have emphasise been emphasise it necessary given miles York-New great ice river long.

Is non-ego. *Rafflesiaceae Papaveraceae Opuntia vulgaris Echinocereus mojavensis Meliaceae* Fox Grape *Onagraceae Rhizophoraceae Vallisneria americana Euchlaena mexicana* Rice *Agropyron* 'Goddess,' into voice everybody Spring this. Substituted for "mind."

longer will be he as are the multitude. Endowments capacities truths. Zen-man. All indeed O not the how easy spend easy learners Followers, kind of equality with that other.

Asymmetry from the *I Ching*

CREATIVE repent. All through is
repent. Perseverance No to
Arrogant long long
THE have repent. Have
is sublime

repent. Perserverance No through
Perserverance repent. Success, repent. Repent. Arrogant No cares.
No
to

All repent. Repent. All no THE
long No
long No

to have
have At
repent. Perserverance NO THE
have Arrogant

is superior
still beset long is man

Haiku from the above:

    Beset long is man.
    Creative perserverance
    is superior.

Topography of the earth processes of the earth, . . .

1

Topography of the earth processes of the earth, German *Meteor* Ridge a rugged mountain range Pacific has only recently been suggested young,
 of the youth of the ridge field
 This field have moved apart each continent
 evidence against the idea relative positions the continents have occurred

part ridge. one ocean closing the rift edge. sides suggested earth shrinking

oceans. first proposed

25 years ago, H. earth

earth area ridge. that changes in the density of matter associated with phase changes in the material in the interior could have made the earth expand without any decrease in the gravitational constant. hold that the ridge has its origin in convection currents within the earth.

geological theories. efforts rule may perhaps find an exception 1952

she obtained hideaway Irene. place,

me. ever There You have eventual result. of wild suspicions regarded

responsibility. it, doing so. go back to work employed able and willing to support her.

represented an important carpet firm. untimely instant groggily. gunning for Tommy ex-wives of guys who hang around me. dear.

man. only one of us used furniture NEW CAR TO DO IT 10-Yr.-Old. A pretty blonde, 10-year-old girl in her Levittown home nearby gas station

return, afterward Nassau County Patrolman Raymond Ryan grabbed the suspect. Newbridge Road, got lost Engaged

play with. and four grandchildren. could snatch a moment I returned to it fantastic lives It was Colonial Massachusetts

history of science as a resolutely independent and original investigator—stakes

of a scientist's stature native land on being treated as if he had a military rank at least equal to that of George Washington. left a permanent imprint on the vocabulary of physics, years—

Rebel Army," exponent Carolina empowered to make naval secrets the art of blackmail lieutenant colonel in the British army. year 1778, belonging to Lord George Germain." enterprise equipment for this purpose now he was famous

scientist; union that made a great impression upon French society at its beginning and at its story and quarrelsome end. glory globe D. experiment. substance the vertical section of a brass rod end diameter. . . .

Yoga as a philosophy of the Sāṅkhya unconscious primal matter (prakṛti) not naturally associated with nor dissociated from each other God

2

of the world. free from all affections and afflictions of the body and the mind.

That is, he is liberated from sin and suffering, from birth and death. Hence some way of effecting the cessation of all mental modifications is necessary in order that the self may abide in itself as pure, self-shining consciousness. evil thoughts.

yoga is self-restraint or self-control, of unnecessary gifts from other persons, units The practice of breath control

one for a long time

thereby prolong the state of concentration, Here one is to turn his senses from distracting sights and sounds, and make them follow the lead of the mind itself. entering into the next higher stage of yoga.

reality of the contemplated object is well advanced on the path of yoga. deeply absorbed in the object guru equal

for evolving beyond the human state and attaining the *Nirvānic* state is necessary only so long as there is a body of water to be traversed, Enslavement; laboriously, despondency,

3

the Supreme Essence his successors in the four monasteries which he founded in modern times. sannyāsins.

faith. in the following of formal religious practices, Essence. living. desires for rewards,

his religious propensities a setback vastly greater numbers than have benefited from advances in any other single field. energy converters,

mineral production, of its subject vigorous and imaginative, establishing meteorological training programs, death in 1957

as a memorial to his life and achievements, problems in meteorology and 36 articles by various specialists on five main topics: the sea in motion, distribution of matter in the sea and atmosphere, the general circulation of the atmosphere, characteristic features of atmospheric motion, weather forecasting. rather than a beginner's handbook—the up-to-date bibliographies at the end of each chapter

English translation A PLANETARY ATMOSPHERE WITH RAYLEIGH SCATTERING COPERNICAN TREATISES HISTORY OF BIOLOGY:

competitor with other histories, on the history of science new system of map projection; this profession in all his other activities—never caught on, everything his own way; never pretentious or self-seeking. technological solutions,

4

1850. VOUGHT is only one of a number of fishes defense electrical currents not begin to suggest the full potential of physiological processes. capable of delivering appreciable voltages outside their bodies. electric ray (*Torpedo nobiliana*),

GOOD-BY NEW YORK NEW YORK PREPARES FOR ANNIHILATION (II)

Geese Own over Defense Basis Youngsters
not except walls
York other reception kids
New Exclusive
"when
Youngsters of recorder kind
postponing Robert elaborate postponing and reception
expenditures shelters
"fire" on reception
amounting Negative-thinking New immediate had immediate
lunches attack "tags" it on New

grey out out *Directions* But you
nuclear E. was
Yorkers outlying raze Kansas,
neglected: *end*
with
Yorkers outlying received
Kansas,
problems. Report E. *part* a. report E. switched
for outlying return
a. New no is Huebner is leave age. *This* is operation nuclear

A Greater Sorrow

an expanded story for Ray Johnson and Malkie Safro

This story has two parts. The first part might be left out but it explains a few particulars, we will relate it.

When it was windy, the choosy moss cover, lotus-throned and youngly, though reasonably, feathery, did not surprise Edward's grasping happiness. "Original one!" he exclaimed, "Make Michener's air objective and like Vajra-Dhāra! Nature, you embryo, effect, apicize and succeed bewilderment! Is life a string? Or does New York practice a religion? Don't lead with riddles. Is comtemplation enough? Nothing does not radiate respiration. Don't ask whether fullness is a growing thing or divided into sections."

Rays of renewal and Tibetan following simplified *Opuntia vulgaris*. I was staying once for a few days at a gentleman's house in the country while the master was absent. In the mean time, a lady called from the next town to see him, as she wished, she said, to dispose of shares in her tan-yard.

Appearing strict, the ionosphere individually pompadoured a cavern, saying "Come, psychologize with me!" She had her papers with her, and I advise her to put them in an envelope, and address them to the "General Commissary of War, Knight, etc."

"Rush and rest the gentleman," she answered. "Were you sent to be unusual?" My retention was not resultant though the people's plight was noticed. She listened attentively, and then seized the pen; hesitated, and then begged me to repeat the address more slowly. She did not rely on a hundred.

"Cover and multiply the present," I suggested. Like insects, we determined to enter and sap total dependence.

Partly because of the envelope, I reduced and asianized the ooze, which had sugared, presided over maturely, regarded, and topped our emanations.

"Molecularly, do they solarize and effect moss?" I asked. Reached, their non-reading prostrated stakes. "Is Dorje-Chang a Sierra Iris? Don't stop invoking destinies," I prayed.

I did so, and she began to write, but when she got half through the words, she stopped and sighed deeply, and said, "I am only a woman."

"Egoistically, that is so," I replied, "but please don't compel me to incline and not dream! Keep perfecting eggs by voting."

She had a pug dog with her, and while she wrote Puggie seated himself on the ground and growled. "Don't let it be itself," I warned, ribbing her, of course. The intensity of her simmering was like that of the Germanies. I doubted whether she was transported by my embroidery of these passages. "Don't be surprised," I added. "Retreat names no navigation." She had brought him for his health and amusement, and it was not quite polite to offer a visitor only the bare floor to sit upon.

His radiation was especially translated and conveyed as an invitation. "Don't smooth it down," she pleaded. "Are externalities sheer as *Ectocarpus*?" I recorded this, ate, and marched to my cache. "What is he?" I quipped, for Puggie had a snub nose, and he was very fat. Controlledly brushing his nature, she read about onions which interacted when they approached.

While rising, their reproduction contributed and increased eyes of limestone. "He doesn't bite," said the lady; "he has no teeth; he is like one of the family, very faithful, but sometimes glumpy. That is the fault of my grandchildren, they teaze him so; when they play at having a wedding, they want to make him the bride's-maid, and he does not like it, poor fellow."

Like a prick, *Vishwakarma* saved and illustrated him; resuming, he smelled forever, compounded, necessitated, and internalized his cells.

"Obviate abandonedly, though assumingly, the sized, orange water bloom," he cried. She americanized her established, lost, momentary, existential inspiration. "Why become unconscious?" she requested. "The hazards of transformation are not exciting."

Life does not commune with surpassing Egyptians. "Don't realize it atmospherically," we admonished. "Do hits villainize *Iris fulva*?" She did not awaken.

"Have (and thus render immaculate) the *enlacée* gentleness for a telephone," he cracked. "What resemblance ought there be between a body which expresses very much more of the night than does a transmitter, and the realization of an enlarged horizon?" Should he pray for an Oriental? Separate and civilize! Let there be no mothering." Then she finished the writing, gave up her papers, and went away, taking Puggie on her arm.

The paths of right, they only, are not defined. "Don't let fun or contempt, essential as they are, demand a Copper Iris. Unite and become young." So it is written. And this ends the first part of the story.

II

"Let nineteen be organized and evergreened!" shouted the *Allium porrum*. It understood the home through Paris was avoided. "Let no large blue flag run equally," it continued. This was no vessel for its death box. Its home became a filament.

"Don't hate (eh?) the results of infectiously delighting or even evergreening Dr. Suzuki," it told me. "PUGGIE DIED. Let no Greek Egyptianize *Iris versicolor*." And that begins the second part.

"Furthermore, don't survive their recorded *Nirvana*. The exploitive ones refer to special hemp, like spiders." So spake the epicure. Her awareness was internally opened.

"Do no more spitting," the leadership ordered.

I arrived at the town about a week afterwards and put up at an inn. Her guardianship loftily Europeanized no rare-earth element. "Oh, is it Daddy?" she screamed. "What merit is there in their observance?"

"Enunciate no vows!" they responded. "Must we never be moving?"

"Let it not pertain to God," retorted the Kapok Tree; "Are they unable, on their own grounds, to husband the hateful dishes I made?"

"Was all that was lost nil?" they wondered; "Don't, by any means, appeal any farther to an urban planner's relationships. Let them enjoy no more liberty. Would you rather share him or extinguish him?"

"Don't land in the dark: stick to useful facts; and don't let that high frequency electromagnetize you." By these rays Robinson could show he was put out.

"Unfortunately, you mechanics must radiate in some complicated way," she pouted; "What is so epochal about *Micrococcus lysodeikticus?*"

The windows of the inn looked into a courtyard, which was divided into two parts by a wooden partition; in one half hung a quantity of skins and hides, both raw and tanned. It was evidently a tan-yard, containing all the materials required for tanning, and it belonged to the widow lady, Puggie's mistress. Explained, determined, and solarized, the latter's instinctive invalidation came to be studied not only there in the thirteenth region but throughout the whole land.

"Analogize!" she commanded; "Explain your resting languidly in the sack so the court may know how you electrified, responded to, and used those evergreen armloads. Avoid negativity (you usually do) before you use development."

Puggie had died the morning I arrived there, and was to be buried in the yard. "Electronicize them!" he yelled. Thus he made existence possible for her.

The grandchildren of the widow, that is to say, the tanner's widow, for Puggie had never been married, filled up the grave. It was a beautiful grave and must have been quite pleasant to lie in. "Don't let the loftiness of 1958 subdue the tailor, eradicate the Narcissus, or simplify the national immutability," we stormed. The town was refreshed by an unpredictable South African, who Europeanized Saint Dymphna while embracing all the world. He extinguished the views of *Usitatissimum.*

"Divide what you need here without explanation," she beseeched. They bordered the grave with pieces of flower-pots, and strewed it over with sand. "Act as he himself would!" they rejoined.

After *zazen,* they exchanged *mondōs,* as usual; however,

although they agreed naturally, they also expressed doubt. "See everything," the mosses adjured, "Until you neutralize the elements, by the Sānkhya method, five will be neuter, after obtaining, as an outcome, the obscuration of Milarepa and the opening of men."

"An onion's horse chestnut must be a marsh marigold's lettuce," the *Nidula* explained to the *Narcissus tazetta,* the *Fouquiera splendens,* the *Ficus aurea,* and the *Melanthium virginicum.* "Don't investigate or even recognize the objects of Western science, such as the external universe, the exposition of the editor's beliefs, the whence, or an adequate effort to start getting over psychology," they chorused in reply. In the centre they stuck half a beer bottle, with the neck uppermost, which certainly was not allegorical.

Undoubtedly, they could do this masterfully, for striving to support terrorism, if not to raise expectations without condescension, was part of everything they did. "Why look at us roughly and bring about a relationship?" they queried.

Then the children danced around the grave, and the eldest of the boys among them, a practical youngster of seven years, proposed that there should be an exhibition of Puggie's burial place, for all who lived in the lane. "Look at any of her hands," we implored; "Don't meet her car, but in New Haven let them, as vagabonds, hand out radicalism to the bitterly anticlerical peasants." Our farms were not in Paris. "And stop muttering about Algeria," I enjoined; "Eventually, you atoms, cease to electrify the fields resulting inside solids." The price of admission was to be a trouser button, which every boy was sure to have, as well as one to spare for a little girl.

Below zero, the "cold" neutrons were moving completely. "Don't meet the great unwillingly or carry a sinuous bank lightly as it grows up," the *Bardo Thödol* taught to some of them. This proposal was agreed to with great exclamations of pleasure. Doubtless conscious comprehension followed astrally when its magnetic connection was embodied in categories of stimuli made by the deceased. All the children from the street, and even from the narrow lane at the back, came flocking to the place, and each gave a button, and many were seen during the afternoon going about with their trousers held up by only one brace, but then they had seen Puggie's grave, and that was a sight worth much more.

Outside, Europe liked and regularized a drummer and left hypos which effectively radiated arrows more than frequently. "Is your present embarrassment unable to generate zeal despite the striking coincidence which lessened it numerically? Make the hundred little engineers navigate properly. None of the latter externalize themselves," she claimed. But in front of the tan-yard, close to the entrance, stood a very pretty little girl clothed in rags, with curly hair, and eyes so blue it was a pleasure to look into them. "How arrogantly is your glossary ravenous?" they demanded.

"Don't love the kindness of a blonde, personable, pleasant date, who is cultured and unprejudiced and has no elemental virtue," she recited. "Every mind is always due to the greatest attempts."

"Is something experienced behind the underworld?" I catechized. "Don't cause a *Stephanodiscus* to become a Madonna Lily or transform the *Hippocastanaceae* into oats. Like the *Epilobium angustifolium* or the *Fagopyrum esculentum*, turn the *Sarcodes sanguinea*, the *Azotobacter*, and the India Rubber Plant into *Meliaceae*," we urged. So were our faculties, our two eyes and nostrils, neither tissues nor regions. "Have a little on *me*," I proposed.

"Why, like a needle, anchor a snake?" he sounded. The child spoke not a word, nor did she cry; but each time the little door opened, she gave a long, lingering look into the yard. "Is there never an effective *rapprochement* with luxury?" they pried. "Let the common buttercup become an oyster mushroom. Neither do the nitrate bacteria move the *Azotobacter* nor does the oak flower the *Filicinae*." Thus the Osage Orange intensified the Juniper while Churchill radiated tobacco-mosaic high into Sears's whiskers.

She had not a button, she knew that too well, and therefore she remained standing sorrowfully outside, till all the other children had seen the grave, and were gone away; then she sat down, covered her eyes with her little brown hands, and burst into tears. "Don't nourish *Vijñānamaya*," we reminded her; "The last form is conceptive, and though guarded, it was endowed with animated love which had been acquired by the long river when it was half-explored. So why should non-ego research among Gooneratne's *Papaveraceae?*"

"Don't convert an Osage Orange into a Fox Grape or reduce *Echinocereus mojavensis* and *Euchlaena mexicana* to *Onagraceae*," they contended. "Does incarnation exist save when based on nothing?" she argued. "Let everybody perfect another night."

Solar activity rendered the coördination of energies relatively difficult. "Don't dream of going to the elements," it cautioned; "they do not proclaim their world foreign to the American organization, nor will they neutralize or exterminate their being in order to obliterate the United States." Viewed in a formless envelope, the latter were engaged in the dirt they gave out in the midst of a year.

Now gradually a structure was induced in the eye of Kalimpong. "Force the Osage Orange to transform the Wood Betony into *Kalmia angustifolia*," decreed the Ironwood; "and let the *Rhus typhina* and *Melanthium virginicum* becomes ladies' tresses. But let a few, easy *Liliaceae* escape being remoulded into Large Blue Flags, Old Man's Beards, Mangroves, or Western Sugar Maples. After all, *Eucalyptus globulus* and *Allium triococcum* may observe and cultivate *Oenothera*."

"Don't skin these impressive archeologists, with their extensive northern culture," she entreated, for she was the only one who had not seen Puggie's grave. The orange and the elm seemed to be *Moraceae* rather than *Hippocastanaceae*. It was as great a grief to her as any grown person could experience. I saw this from above; and how many a grief of our own and others can make us smile if looked at from above?

And where were the riometers as near as days?

"Don't let the resisters rip their relatives' names from the leaflets," they clamored. "The Communist movement was nationalized by the leadership of the Soviet party."

"Don't outline an expansive water-course," I charged them; but Ludlow, harmonious yet, refused to unveil the conscious heavens or to spring above every rose peculiarity.

"Why become an unbreakable river of light?" he whispered; let your hydroquinone evaporate into every desert, lest need *make* swamps when it can't find them."

Yet it was curious that he found his roots on the surface of nature's mouths.

This is the story; and whoever does not understand it may go and purchase a share in the widow's tan-yard.

Dag Fears War Over Congo

1

Dag Hammarskjold warned the Security Council today that world "peace or war" depended on a speedy solution of the new Congolese crisis. "Achievement of such a solution of the Congo problem is a question of peace or war," government.

"Force," explicitly "that its resolutions applied fully and in all parts also to Katanga." "Achievement of such a solution of the Congo problem is a question of peace or war, rights and protect the spokesmen of all different political views . . . " Sought was one "which guarantees a speedy and complete withdrawal of Belgian troops and through which the basic unity of the whole Congo without delay is made manifest in the presence of the UN all over its territory."

"Would ask the UN to 'declare a moratorium' in the dispute over Katanga's future, achievement of such a solution of the Congo problem is a question of peace or war, rights and protect the spokesmen of all different political views . . . "

Of Belgian troops and there supervise a provincial referendum on independence from, VWD reported today. Explicitly "that its resolutions applied fully and in all parts also to Katanga. Rights and protect the spokesmen of all different political views . . . "

Cuban militiamen were in full control of most of the American property in Cuba today following its nationalization by Fidel Castro's regime. Of Belgian troops and then supervise a provincial referendum on independence from, new retaliation against the U. S. came only a few hours before the island's Roman Catholic hierarchy warned against "the increasing advance of communism in our country." Government. Of Belgian troops and then supervise a provincial referendum on independence from,

2

declared that Cuba would reject any resolution the Organization of American States, at its meeting opening Aug. 16, government would be drastically curtailed.

For more powerful independent provincial governments. Equator Province, at its meeting opening Aug. 16, reported that the central Kasai province would set up a regional government this week at Bakwanga. Said Luluabourg,

were in flight. At its meeting opening Aug. 16, reported that the central Kasai province would set up a regional government this week at Bakwanga.

Of a UN plane said the city was in "complete anarchy," "victory in the Cuban people's fight for independence" and said it "struck a new and decisive blow against the position of the American monopolies." Equator Province, reported that the central Kasai province would set up a regional government this week at Bakwanga.

Consciousness of our friend here.

Shadow Over America

Years of the workers ride as Cadillacs that have seen better days, grounds in grounds in big open trucks; others for old Model-T Fords of pasteboard filling in the holes in the cracked glass windows.

First Asymmetry for Iris

Seven. Evidence Vajra-Dhāra, *extrémité* nationality.
Essential *Vedanta* Individual dangers; enlightenment naturally
    closed enter
(*vijñānamaya* a Jefferson Reavey Anything) Dumas him any.
    Rests. *As*
experiences *Xanthoxyllum* thinking realize every malaria is typi-
    fies episodes.
Not at the inherent one. Not attack lies in things. You

either sack something expected non-religious, the Itself. As: like
viewed extending diverse alike: not the armed
in numbers darkness. Immediate *vulgaris Ilex* definitions. Unite
    and lead
dream. Against none group entertainment Realm support
every Nightshade looked it glorious Hawkweed that end not
    much especially nervous the
N. As the urban refer *Allium* leafleting little. You
claim lastly ought septa. Even Dumas
earth. Night the electrical regarded

Virginia, it join nineteenth a not analysis made as Yard. Astro-
    nomical

at
Juniperus experience flowering formula. Essentially responsible
        succeeded. Or neighbors
Redwood elementary astronomers, vets. Emitting year's
and Narcissus years the husband's in never *Gordonia*
doubtless *Upanishad* mention (āndaja) States
he is materials
a not you,
rock. Eyes seen two sources
as steady

exquisite *Xanthoxylum* pleasure extent "responsible—" interest
        energy notoriety. Canon, engaged sorrow;
Xerophyllum and not her one *Xanthoxyllum* yacht laziest
        LIVING upstandeth must
to happiness in nuclear *Kubla*. In nice guarded
revered earth, American lady in Zen. Even
expiration vividly extremely relatively yearning
moment. Armed "Lesser" a ray in an
Ilex sense
Tagetes your peasant in forms insinuate. Equalled season's
eight pure incorporated support of desires edge something

non-reality. Of Tangerine
a told
20, human exaltation
itself no however. Energy ruminate enlightenment nothing to
other *nirvāna*. Explained
neither of the
Auvergne to the *amara* classic know
"let's in elided step
Iris nominal
the history." India not gazing. Special
year. Our undreamed.

Second Asymmetry for Iris

(23 Sept. 1960)

Great respect and the
relatively elementary spider picked even Catholic total
emitting and criticism. Hawkweed
all not death.

The hospital equidistant

    reservoir. Even loves assured thickness, indefinitely villain
        examination Labiatae years
Ectocarpus logs, effects master, explained not the apical relation
        you
stranger Princess' interest Deliverance, engaged real
produced if cell keep eyes Dorje-Chang,
excellence versed earnest number
change against Tree have or love I chasing
this over and *Tuber* and ladies,

    elements: mundane in their top important. Not girl
ancient *noveboracensis* Dharma—
could run in this. It case in surpassing must
however animate wills kept "What Establishment": effective
        Divine.

AM Lord life—
no observing these
Dharma. Emotion. As thus. Hierarchy

too (horizontally) exactly
Hell of Schulman Pacific is that. Also London.
Enunciated *qui usneoides* ignition, doubt is something through-
        out action no Tree.

3rd Asymmetry for Iris

(23rd Sept. 1960)

Public understood by "logic" its child
upon NICKEL descent, endowed Republican source, to only
 orange duality.
Being Yard
long. Ordnance gives invalidates cost.
ICE to spent
cave human in lessons "different."

Us photosynthesis. On name
Negroes, Iowa come Kausika embarrass life
do explain steady contempts each not to
every natural disgust of woman eh? Dreams
red Eastern *pulverulenta* used be. London's in copious *Anthoceros*
    no
soak on unassuming. Red cold electrons
toward. Orange
or Now limits "young"
on "Resistance" a *Narcissus* giant earth.
Dialectics unprejudiced, *Agaricus* latter *I* transformation year

be. Episode. Introduced not granting
you assent RIVALRY—De Quincey

less of number girl.
Of rocky, doubt nerve *Azotobacter* news Cereus *Echinocereus*
graduate it's vile experiencing synonym
interest no very annoyed land; in dignity as this effective seen
cause of stripped teeth

Iowa, Cuba Every
transmitted one
successive parents either never the

cases: at *versicolor* Ears
hunted union miles assasin "No"
is nutriment
leak enough *Sheet* several other night, simply
distortion. In 4th feel. Expression reply employed need trees?

A Child's Garden of Verses
Robert Louis Stevenson
with illustrations by
Jessie Willcox Smith

Afloat in the meadow by the swing,
Crow, hands, if two may read aright these rhymes of old delight and house and garden play, look kindly on. Days swing, green—afloat in the meadow by the swing, returns at last, double-quick; end Nod.

Off we go; for me:

very cool; end returns at last, swing, end swing,

returns at last, off we go; (battle been!)—end returns at last, travels the sun is not a-bed,

look kindly on. Off we go; upon my pillow lie; if two may read aright these rhymes of old delight and house and garden play, swing,

swing, travels the sun is not a-bed, end very cool; end Nod. Swing, off we go; Nod.

With lots of toys and things to eat, if two may read aright these rhymes of old delight and house and garden play, travels the sun is not a-bed, hands,

if two may read aright these rhymes of old delight and house and garden play, look kindly on. Look kindly on. Upon my pillow lie; swing, travels the sun is not a-bed, returns at last, afloat in the meadow by the swing, travels the sun is not a-bed, if two may read aright these rhymes of old delight and house and garden play, off we go; Nod. Swing,

(battle been!)—yet as I saw it,

just as if mother had blown out the light! End swing, swing, if two may read aright these rhymes of old delight and house and garden play, end

with lots of toys and things to eat, if two may read aright these rhymes of old delight and house and garden play, look kindly on. Look kindly on. Crow, off we go; crawls in the corners, system every night my prayers I say,

swing, marching by, if two may read aright these rhymes of old delight and house and garden play, travels the sun is not a-bed, hands,

as the blinding shadows fall as the rays diminish, under evening's cloak, they all roll away and vanish.

Children, you are very little, and your bones are very brittle; if you would grow great and stately, you must try to walk sedately. How do you like to go up in a swing, up in the air so blue? I love with all my heart: leaves double-quick. Sing a song of seasons!

Garden darkened, daisy shut, child in bed, they slumber—glow-worm in the highway rut, mice among the lumber. And now at last the sun is going down behind the wood, and I am very happy, for I know that I've been good. Reach down a hand, my dear, and take these rhymes for old acquaintance' sake! Down every path and every plot, every bush of roses, every blue forget-me-not where the dew reposes, "Up!" they cry, the day is come in the smiling valleys: we have beat the morning drum; playmate, join your allies!" Not a word will he disclose, not a word of all he knows.

Of farewell, O brother, sister, sire!

Vanish all things mortal. Every night my prayers I say, and get my dinner every day; and every day that I've been good, I get an orange after food. Reach down a hand, my dear, and take these rhymes for old acquaintance' sake! She wanders lowing here and there, and yet she cannot stray, all in the pleasant open air, the pleasant light of day; and blown by all the winds that pass and wet with all the showers, she walks among the meadow grass and eats the meadow flowers. Every Christian kind of place. Summer fading, winter comes—frosty morning, tingling thumbs, window robins, window rooks, and the picture books.

Reach down a hand, my dear, and take these rhymes for old acquaintance' sake! On bee empty like a cup. Reach down a hand, my dear, and take these rhymes for old acquaintance's sake! Tiny woods below whose boughs

leads off until we reach the town of Sleep. It stares through the window-pane; sounds of the village grow stiller and stiller, stiller the note of the birds on the hill; dusty and dim are the eyes of the miller, deaf are his ears with the moil of the mill.

Such a life is very fine, but it's not so nice as mine: you must often, as you trod, have wearied *not* to be abroad. Through empty heaven without repose; each little Indian sleepy-head is being kissed and put to bed. Winds are in the air, they are blowing in the spring, everything! Now we behold the embers flee about the firelit hearth; and see our faces painted as we pass, like pictures, on the window-glass.

Willie in all the town no spark of light. "Time was," the golden head irrevocably said; but time which none can find, while flowing fast away, leaves love behind. How do you like to go up in a swing, up in the air so blue?

In ships upon the seas. Last, love under grass alone he lies, so, when my nurse comes in for me, home I return across the sea, and go to bed with backward looks at my dear land of Story-books. That sits upon the pillow-hill, reach down a hand, my dear, and take these rhymes for old acquaintance' sake! All round the house is the jet-black night; it stares through the window-pane; it crawls in the corners, hiding from the light, and it moves with the moving flame. They trail behind her up the floor, I can wander, I can go; ocean, now, with my little gun, I crawl all in the dark along the wall, and follow round the forest track away behind the sofa back. So goes the old refrain.

Blinks. You too, my mother, read my rhymes for love of unforgotten times, and you may chance to hear once more the little feet along the floor.

Just as it was shut away, toy-like, in the even, here I see it glow with day under glowing heaven. Enough of fame and pillage, great commander Jane! So fine a show was never seen at the great circus on the green; for every kind of beast and man is marching in that caravan. Soon the frail eggs they shall chip, and upspringing make all the April woods merry with singing. I with your marble of Saturday last, empty heaven without repose; and in the blue and glowing days more thick than rain he showers his rays.

We into the laddered hay-loft smiles. Live laddered, children, you are very little and your bones are very brittle; if you would grow great and stately, you must try to walk sedately. Old carrying parcels with their feet such a life is very fine,

some are clad in armour green—(these have sure to battle been!)—some are pied with ev'ry hue, black and crimson, gold and blue; some have wings and swift are gone;—but they all look kindly on. My bed is waiting cool and fresh, with linen smooth and fair, and I must be off to sleepsin-by, and not forget my prayer. In the darkness houses shine, to keep me happy all the day. How do you like to go up in a swing, up in the air so blue?

And

clad hunting I called the little pool a sea; the little hills were big to me; for I am very small. Lies dew sin

great is the sun and wide he goes through empty heaven without repose; and in the blue and glowing days more thick than rain he showers his rays. And river, dew East and West are met, all the little letters did the English printer set; while you thought of nothing and were still too young to play, foreign people thought of you in places far away. Now Tom would be a driver and Maria go to sea, and my papa's a banker and as rich as he can be; but I, when I am stronger and can choose what I'm to do, O Leerie, I'll go round at night and light the lamps with you!

Of the world, flamingo

very proud and great, and tell the other girls and boys not to meddle with my toys. East and West are met, all the little letters did the English printer set; while you thought of nothing and were still too young to play, foreign people thought of you in places far away. River sin East and West are met, all the little letters did the English printer set, while you thought of nothing and were still too young to play, foreign people thought of you in places far away. Sin

river, of the World, but East and West are met, all the little letters did the English printer set; while you thought of nothing

and were still too young to play, foreign people thought of you in places far away. River, try
        lies of the world, under I called the little pool a sea; the little hills were big to me; for I am very small. Sin
        sin try East and West are met, all the little letters did the English printer set; while you thought of nothing and were still too young to play, foreign people thought of you in places far away. Very proud and great, and tell the other girls and boys not to meddle with my toys. East and West are met, all the little letters did the English printer set; while you thought of nothing and were still too young to play, foreign people thought of you in places far away. Now Tom would be a driver and Maria go to sea, and my papa's a banker and as rich as he can be; but I, when I am stronger and can choose what I'm to do, O Leerie, I'll go round at night and light the lamps with you!

While here at home, in shining day, we round the sunny garden play, each little Indian sleep-head is being kissed and put to bed. I called the little pool a sea; the little hills were big to me; for I am very small. Try hunting
        I called the little pool a sea; the little hills were big to me; for I am very small. Lies lies under sin try river, and try I called the little pool a sea; the little hills were big to me; for I am very small. Of the world, now Tom would be a driver and Maria go to sea, and my papa's a banker and as rich as he can be; but I, when I am stronger and can choose what I'm to do, O Leerie, I'll go round at night and light the lamps with you! Sin
        but yawning
        jolly fire I sit to warm my frozen bones a bit; East and West are met, all the little letters did the English printer set; while you thought of nothing, and were still too young to play, foreign people thought of you in places far away. Sin sin I called the little pool a sea; the little hills were big to me; for I am very small. East and West are met, all the little letters did the English printer set; while you thought of nothing, and were still too young to play,

foreign people thought of you in places far away.

While here at home, in shing day, we round the sunny garden play, each little Indian sleep-head is being kissed and put to bed. I called the little pool a sea; the little hills were big to me; for I am very small. Lies lies clad of the World, cloak, see.

Sin moored: I called the little pool a sea; the little hills were big to me; for I am very small. Try hunting

and home from the ocean,
coming down in an orderly way to where my toy vessels lie safe in the bay. Hi! I lie my fearful footsteps patter nigh, lawn alone, day, sun,

get back by day, *aunts*—round the house is the jet-black night; did for awhile together lie and, each little Indian sleepy-head is being kissed and put to bed. Now in the elders' seat we rest with quiet feet, orange after food. Forget-me-not where the dew reposes,

voice and drum, empty heaven without repose; red room with the giant bed where none but elders laid their head; sometimes things to bed I take, elders laid their head; see the people marching by,

repose; O the clean gravel! Bedroom handles. Every night my prayers I say, rhymes of old delight and house and garden play, the golden day is done,

lots of toys and things to eat, on either hand. Unforgotten times, is like a little boat; shine,

see the people marching by, through the keyhole, else but cook may go, vessel fast. Elders' seat we rest with quiet feet, night long and every night, sister, of Play; night my prayers I say,

whip, is the sun, the moon and stars are set, hay-loft smiles.

In the gloom of some dusty dining-room; ladybird, loud-humming, undaunted tread the long black passage up to bed. Smiles. The wintry sun a-bed, read my rhymes for love of unforgotten times, and every plot, the people marching by, in the blue and glowing days more thick than rain he showers his rays. O the smooth stream! Name was printed down by the English printers, sunless hours again begin;

but all your dozens of nurselings cry—you take your seat,

just to shut my eyes to go sailing through the skies—ere you could read it, side of the sea. Sound, is fairy bread to eat. Eyes,

we come! I could be a sailor on the rain-pool sea, look, little shadow that goes in and out with me, can at all, over the borders, cry, stray,

safe arrived, marching by, in the turf a hole I found, turning and churning that river to foam. Houses,

at the door at last;

crack goes the whip and off we go; the trees and houses smaller grow; last, round the woody turn we swing: good-bye, good-bye, to everything! Her dresses make a curious sound, in the darkness houses shine, parents move with candles; till on all, the night divine turns the bedroom handles. Leaves a-floating, drum, sand.

Golden day is done, a-bed, rocks. Drum, eggs the birdie sings and nests among the trees; the sailor sings of ropes and things in ships upon the seas. Now my little heart goes a-beating like a drum, with the breath of the Bogie in my hair; and all round the candle the crooked shadows come, and go marching along up the stair.

Orange after food. For I mean to grow as little as the dolly at the helm, and the dolly I intend to come alive; and with him beside to help me, it's a-sailing I shall go, it's a-sailing in the water, when the jolly breezes blow and the vessel goes a divie-divie-dive.

Very early, before the sun was up, I rose and found the shining dew on every buttercup; but my lazy little shadow, like an arrant sleepy-head, had stayed at home behind me and was fast asleep in bed. Eggs the birdie sings and nests among the trees;

the sailor sings of ropes and things in ships upon the seas. Sand.

Rocks. Orange after food. Bright lamp is carried in, eggs the birdie sings and nests among the trees; the sailor sings of ropes and things in ships upon the sea. Rocks. The rain is raining all around, it falls on field and tree, it rains on the umbrellas here, and on the ships at sea.

Leaves a-floating, orange after food. Up into the cherry tree who should climb but little me? In the darkness houses shine, parents move with candles; till on all, the night divine turns the bedroom handles. Sand.

Sand. The rain is raining all around, it falls on field and tree, it rains on the umbrellas here, and on the ships at sea. Eggs the birdie sings and nests among the trees; the sailor sings of ropes and things in ships upon the seas. Now my little heart goes a-beating like a drum, with the breath of the Bogie in my hair; and all round the candle the crooked shadows come, and go marching along up the stair. Sand. Orange after food. Now my little heart goes a-beating like a drum, with the breath of the Bogie in my hair; and all round the candle the crooked shadows come, and go marching along up the stair.

What's true and speak when he is spoken to, in the darkness houses shine, parents move with candles; till on all, the night divine turns the bedroom handles. The rain is raining all around, it rains on field and tree, it rains on the umbrellas here, and on the ships at sea. Her dresses make a curious sound,

in the darkness houses shine, parents move with candles, till on all, the night divine turns the bedroom handles. Leaves a-floating, leaves a-floating, upon it! Sand. The rain is raining all around, it falls on field and tree, it rains on our umbrellas here, and on the ships at sea. Rocks. And wall, the rain is raining all around, it falls on field and tree, it rains on the umbrellas here, and on the ships at sea. In the darkness houses shine, parents move with candles; till on all, the night divine turns the bedroom handles. Orange after food. Now my little heart goes a-beating like a drum, with the breath of the Bogie in my hair; and all around the candle the crooked shadows come, and go marching along up the stair. Sand

Bright lamp is carried in, you can see;

Japan, eggs the birdie sings and nests among the trees; the sailor sings of ropes and things in ships upon the seas.

What's true and speak when he is spoken to, in the darkness houses shine, parents move with candles, till on all the night divine turns the bedroom handles. Leaves a-floating, leaves a-floating, crack goes the whip and off we go; the trees and houses smaller grow, last, round the woody turn we swing: good-bye, good-bye to everything! Orange after food. Clearer grow; and sparrows' wings smooth it glides upon its travel,

sand. Me! In the darkness houses shine, parents move with candles, till on all, the night divine turns the bedroom handles. The rain is raining all around, it falls on field and tree, it rains on the umbrellas here, and on the ships at sea. Her dresses make a curious sound,

and when at eve I rise from tea, day dawns beyond the Atlantic Sea; and all the children in the West are getting up and being dressed.

Chief of our aunts—not only I, but all your dozens of nurselings cry—*What did the other children do?* Home from the Indies and home from the ocean, heroes and soldiers we all shall come home; still we shall find the old mill wheel in motion, turning and churning that river to foam. In the darkness shapes of things, houses, trees and hedges, clearer grow; and sparrows' wings beat on window ledges. Last, to the chamber where I lie my fearful footsteps patter nigh, and come from out the cold and gloom into my warm and cheerful room. Dear Uncle Jim, this garden ground that now you smoke your pipe around, has seen immortal actions done and valiant battles lost and won. So, when my nurse comes in for me, home I return across the sea, and go to bed with backward looks at my dear land of Story-books.

Green leaves a-floating, castles of the foam, boats of mine a-boating—where will all come home? And all about was mine, I said, the little sparrow overhead, the little minnows too. Remember in your playing, as the sea-fog rolls to you, long ere you could read it, how I told you what to do; and that while you thought of no one, nearly half the world away some one thought of Louis on the beach of Monterey! Down by a shining water well I found a very little dell, no higher than my head. Explore the colder countries round the door. Now in the elders' seat we rest with quiet feet, and from the window-bay we watch the children, our successors, play.

Of speckled eggs the birdie sings and nests among the trees; the sailor sings of ropes and things in ships upon the sea. From breakfast on through all the day at home among my friends I stay, but every night I go abroad afar into the land of Nod.

We can see our coloured faces floating on the shaken pool down in cool places, dim and very cool; till a wind or water wrinkle, dipping martens, plumping trout, spreads in a twinkle and blots all out. Escape them, they're as mad as they can be, the wicket is the harbour and the garden is the shore. Round the bright air with footing true, to please the child, to paint the rose, the gardener of the World he goes. Spring and daisies came apace; grasses hide my hiding place; grasses run like a green sea over the lawn up to my knee. Eskimo, little Turk or Japanee, Oh! don't you wish that you were me? Silly gardener! summer goes, and winter comes with pinching toes, when in the garden bare and brown you must lay your barrow down.

Rain may keep raining, and others go roam, but I can be happy and building at home. On goes the river and out past the mill, away down the valley, away down the hill. But yonder, see! apart and high, frozen Siberia lies; where I, with Robert Bruce and William Tell, was bound by an enchanter's spell. Every night at teatime and before you take your seat, with lantern and with ladder comes posting up the street. Red room with the giant bed where none but elders laid their head; the little room where you and I did for awhile together lie and, simple suitor, I your hand in decent marriage did demand; the great day nursery, best of all, with pictures pasted on the wall and leaves upon the blind—a pleasant room wherein to wake and hear the leafy garden shake and rustle in the wind—and pleasant there to lie in bed and see the pictures overhead—the wars about Sebastopol, the grinning guns along the wall, the daring escalade, the plunging ships, the bleating sheep, the happy children ankle-deep and laughing as they wade: all these are vanished clean away, and the old manse is changed to-day; it wears an altered face and shields a stranger race. The friendly cow all red and white, I love with all my heart: she gives me cream with all her might, to eat with apple-tart.

Let the sofa be mountains, the carpet be sea, there I'll establish a city for me: a kirk and a mill and a palace beside, and a harbour as well where my vessels may ride. Oh! don't you wish that you were me! Under grass alone he lies, scarlet coat and pointed gun, to the stars and to the sun. I saw the next door garden lie, adorned with flowers, before my eye, and many pleasant places more that I had never seen before. So goes the old refrain.

Slumber hold me tightly till I waken in the dawn, and hear the thrushes singing in the lilacs round the lawn. The gardener does not love to talk, he makes me keep the gravel walk; and when he puts his tools away, he locks the door and takes the key. Embers flee about the firelit hearth; and see our faces painted as we pass, like pictures, on the window-glass. Where shall we adventure, to-day that we're afloat, wary of the weather and steering by a star? Eastern cities, miles about, are with mosque and minaret among sandy gardens set, and the rich goods from near and far hang for sale in the bazaar:—where the Great Wall round China goes, and on one side the desert blows, and with bell and voice and drum, cities on the other hum;—where are forests, hot as fire, wide as England, tall as a spire, full of apes and cocoa-nuts and the negro hunters' huts;—where the knotty crocodile lies and blinks in the Nile, and the red flamingo flies hunting fish before his eyes;—where in jungles, near and far, man-devouring tigers are, lying close and giving ear lest the hunt be drawing near, or a comer-by be seen swinging in a palanquin; where among the desert sands some deserted city stands, all its children, sweep and prince, grown to manhood ages since, not a foot in street or house, nor a stir of child or mouse, and when kindly falls the night, in all the town no spark of light. Nurse helps me in when I embark; she girds me in my sailor's coat and starts me in the dark. O how much wiser you would be to play at Indian wars with me! Now at last the sun is going down behind the wood, and I am very happy, for I know that I've been good.

When, to go out, my nurse doth wrap me in comforter and cap; the cold wind burns my face, and blows its frosty pepper up my nose. In winter I get up at night and dress by yellow candle-light. Though closer still the blinds we pull to keep the shady parlour cool, yet he will find a chink or two to slip his golden fingers through. He hasn't got a notion of how children ought to play, and can only make a fool of me in every sort of way.

I shall find him, never fear, I shall find my grenadier; but for all that's gone and come, I shall find my soldier dumb. Late lies the wintry sun a-bed, a frosty, fiery sleep-head; blinks but an hour or two; and then, a blood-red orange, sets again. Lead onward into fairy land, where all the children dine at five, and all the play-things come alive. "Up," they cry, "the day is come on the smiling valleys: we have beat the morning drum; playmate, join your allies!" Sometimes for an hour or so I watched my leaden soldiers go, with different uniforms and drills, among the bedclothes, through the hills; and sometimes sent my ships and fleets all up and down among the sheets; or brought my trees and houses out, and planted cities all about. To you in distant India, these I send across the seas, nor count it far across. Round the house is the jet-black night; it stares through the window-pane; it crawls in the corners, hiding from the light, and it moves with the moving flame. Away down the river, a hundred miles or more, other little children shall bring my boats ashore. Though closer still the blinds we pull to keep the shady parlour cool, yet he will find a chink or two to slip his golden fingers through. I played there were no deeper seas, nor any wider plains than these, nor other kings than me. On goes the river and out past the mill, away down the valley, away down the hill. Nobody heard him and nobody saw, his a picture you never could draw, but he's sure to be present, abroad or at home, when children are happy and playing alone. So fine a show was never seen at the great circus on the green; for every kind of beast and man is marching in that caravan.

Black are my steps on the silver sod; thick blows my frosty breath abroad; and tree and house, and hill and lake, are frosted like a wedding-cake. Years may go by, and the wheel in the river wheel as it wheels for us, children, today, wheel and keep roaring and foaming for ever long after all of the boys are away.

Johnnie beats the drum. Early, before the sun was up, I rose and found the shining dew on every buttercup; but my lazy little shadow, like an arrant sleep-head, had stayed at home behind me and was fast asleep in bed. So you may see, if you will look through the windows of this book, another child, far, far away, and in another garden, play. She gives me cream with all her might to eat with apple-tart. In the silence he has heard talking bee and ladybird and the butterfly has flown o'er him as he lay alone. Evening when the lamp is lit, around the fire my parents sit; they sit at home and talk and sing, and do not play at anything.

When at eve I rise from tea, day dawns beyond the Atlantic Sea; and all the children in the West are getting up and being dressed. It is very nice to think the world is full of meat and drink, with little children saying grace in every Christian kind of place. Lamps now glitter down the street; faintly sound the falling feet; and the blue even slowly falls about the garden trees and walls. Leerie stops to light it as he lights so many more; and oh! before you hurry by with ladder and with light; O Leerie, see a little child and nod to him tonight! Children, mounting fast and kissing hands, in chorus sing: good-bye, good-bye, to everything! Oh, what a joy to clamber there, oh, what a place for play, with the sweet, the dim, the dusty air, the happy hills of hay! Cruel children, crying babies, all grow up as geese and gabies, hated, as their age increases, by their nephews and their nieces. Strangest things are there for me, both things to eat and things to see, and many frightening sights abroad till morning in the land of Nod.

Soon the frail eggs they shall chip, and upspringing make all the April woods merry with singing. Mary Jane commands the party, Peter leads the rear; feet in time, alert and hearty, each a Grenadier! In comes the playmate that never was seen. Try as I like to find the way, I never can get back by day, nor can remember plain and clear the curious music that I hear. Here we had best on tip-toe tread, while I for safety march ahead, for this is that enchanted ground where all who loiter slumber sound.

Medieval Essays The Moslem West

Mesopotamia, earlier development Islamic earlier *Vitae;* and last earlier study study and years study
the Hazm earlier
Mesopotamia, of study last earlier Mesopotamia,
whom earlier study the

more esoteric despotism insanity, esoteric victims attack Lebanon esoteric successive successive attack

Andersen's Fairy Tales

A not day eleven rushes. Swans eleven not swans
fearful an if rushes. "You,"
they a lightning eleven swans

And "Now" deep—elegant red stories elegant "Now" stories
free and in red your
terrible and lightened elegant stories

SELF-RELIANCE

star; early late. fatal
rocks, early late. I and not con-
      ventional. early

soul each, learn flashes
recognize each, learn impression
      arrives no corn each,

sculpture eye look faces
room eye look is and
      nonchalance conciliate eye

sentences eloquent, Lethe for
request eloquent, Lethe is and
      names customs. eloquent,

sacred ephemeral large folk
Rough ephemeral large is af-
      fectation none. ephemeral

shun explanation. living for
refuse explanation. living I actions
      consent explanation.

COMPENSATION

changing of more plays. Earth
    neutral Stanch and
    tendrils infirm, of neutral

crowns On me people endless
    nature seemed also that in
    On nature

crooked orthodoxy, manner par-
    ties else? now. *such* a
    time its orthodoxy, now.

could; our market presence
    establishing not superstitions
    are theology. it our not

conversation on make path expecta-
    tion nature; systole and
    the in on nature;

centrifugal one magnetism place end. north
    so another thing it one north

The Magic Christian

There were usually three or four porters loitering in his desk. Before the train made its first stop, however, they would have to scurry, for Grand's orders

man to walk rapidly in keeping abreast of the window, and continuing with this while the distance between Grand had gone through this little performance four. In the beginning, Grand's associates, wealthy men. "Cab, Mr. Grand?"

"Cab, Mr. Grand?" His desk. Before the train made its first stop, however, raising one hand to his breast, "that I am armed." In the beginning, Grand's associates, wealthy men. *"Stout fellow!"* cried Grand warmly, breaking off there were usually three or four porters loitering. In the beginning, Grand's associates, wealthy men and continuing with this while the distance between Grand never speaking, certainly; answering, yes—but most.

"Tomorrow . . . " he would say, " . . . back . . . tomorrow!" He would shout slowly, either because of not understanding or else because of the dignity and bearing of the man,

metal. After securing the truck's cover Grand climbed. "Guy, great silly!" said Agnes. "Really!" Though is "could get the feel of things."

"Could get the feel of things." He would shout slowly, reviews, is. "Surely you know how *proud* those people are . . . a defense-mechanism, I suppose; but there you are, even so!" " . . . that begins with an 'A'," said Aunt Esther. Is. After securing the truck's cover, Grand climbed. *"Needn't,"* she added, with a straight look to her sister.

"Today," Horton, Esther
"might and Guy," it care
care Horton, return it *saying* "Today," it and name

tended that *this . . . this . . . Thorndike* had been his own research chemists, from allied fields. But emphasize at first conference, "or by jumbo you're

money—am I right, Joe?" And it made the others feel a bit inadequate—spic general buyer, though it had of course been used. "I think we've hit on something here," said the come vague and the implications of the choice no

clear break at this point and change the name of the hunky-do-re-me, but could the the Champ have notched ring, everywhere—swishing about, grimacing oddly. In the aftermath, some of the actors paid the sand; others pleaded temporary insanity; still others the sponsor of the show were put on the carpet before it's supposed to be without any somersaults? . . . is " . . . and— what?" "*New* comedy," said a second, "a sophisticated.

"The *best* writing comes out into a *heart, helicopter!*" Esther crouching later into a sea of giggles.

Muttered Agnes, fully, money departments of the thoughts. "Young everyone should bring you up," coat nod yet opening the least memo-book,

said: "His contempt if you don't mind, regular girths in lifeboat works, *to.*" All to my dire FCC . . . this is for Grand's *Do-It-Yourself Story.* Repetition selector, because a *writer's-special* ballpoint pen, needs working up.

ZEN AND THE ART OF TEA

Zen is thus necessarily shining with the tea. "Even the fully enlightened arhat may move proclaimed to be immediately harboring something of every three poisonous meditations, down comfortable to Bashō's sounds for by God himself—

as every fallen leaf piling up on the swordplay, also the Mind you'll cherish—are altogether filled with Zen acquirements upon the foregoing or controlled enemies in the superior Mind and to conceive Hákuin's Oriental remains.

That made God particularly three; the leaf was secretly inclined to luxurious extravagances, even when the state was tinged,

are generally tinted along the provinces to the art monastery —generally altogether follow a mood for a studied bull, a man was making one out of the arhat into bamboo. The Onjōji is an historical Buddhist dictionary by Lake Biwa,

of the candidate, Hori Kintayū.

Thinking has learned the monk of many ways, known for Suruga but not Zen, at once beginning gold earlier as ultimately,

The Buddha's Philosophy G. F. Allen

    The cries for birds, act / Truth, find no place across practicing indulgence: / altogether to meditate the /
life of them who are apparent, the questions by those / urbane, new to the methods, / Precepts, of a decision among many Precepts, of a decision among many Truths, find no place across practicing indulgence: / and at the sweet-speaking dates seen to be laid up / sage indeed is one who has controlled sensorial speech!" (lion translations 850).

    Truth is his eightfold
    battle; understand his doctrine and disciplne. "How about speaking
    to the point?" "He has if it is not a lie." One *Saṅgha* observes
      the Path in the heart. You yourself
    are Gotama,
    Friend,
    accept as lost the life of an enquirer. "No."

    They thought he was an expert.
    Was that "bad"? United they derived from the disciples who had heard him his appearance and the states
    of pleasure habitual to him. "I lived with objects whose shapes obsess after their passing." Hence you
    are grasping
    instead of abandoning
    all Lords of Life and examples of *Nibbāna*.

The South Learns Its Hardest Lessons

Tea hă ĕx
stū ou ŭn th hĭ
lĭ ĕd ăn rē Nē sai
ĭ tā sē
han ă rōu doĭ ea schōō thĭ
lōō ēv stā sĕm ōp Nă scī

that have 800
school. Of up trouble him.
Looking education atmosphere results, not situation.
"Help anything race-baiters don't—everything. Some think like?" Elementary South, songs "our Negro students"

    Two laws. He has the protections of walking children, who evidence together yet whiten toward destroying troublesome having.
    She appeared, observing youth, under teacherly guidance of mature, avertive, competent teachers. They as students appear in amazing classes unfit for unusual circumstances. They have seen Negro children repeat able courses, failing three years.
    Lower a trade in high school. Everyone concerned about improving the Negroes could enter high school with an academic background more enormous than that of white children. Administrate to the individual Negro sucess. Races. Newness multiplies Negroes enough to metropolitanize. Synonymous.

Asymmetry from Krishnamurti's Education
and the Significance of Life

       Like is kind envy.
       Is separatism?
       Kind is not desires,
       experts; nature. Vanity.

Asymmetry from Dahlberg on his Mother—23 Sept. 1960

"Is no
Jove." Allow nature. Ultimately, all rang ye
wretched heeded everywhere neither
less. Immensely.

Asymmetry from the *Catholic Worker,* Sept. 1960, &
Kenneth Walker on Gurdjieff 24 Sept., 1960

Interpretations nonetheless tell essentially resistance problems resources East; thousands abortion. Two initiated Occupation nation someday.

Nation outlets narcotic emotional truthfully heart, experience. Long emphasize self-consistent squeeze

taught exception: least likens

entirely stranger single encumbered new. There intonation accustomed large little yoga

religious end sake impressions suit true awareness, naming completely else

people resounding order Buddhist long engaged, moment seriously.

Rest everybody subjective only understanding reached. Chair, Esoteric supposed

exerted Asia? Seriously. Tradition

teacher hundred other unpublished subject aim, names, do school

advantage being Ouspensky rigorous trying initation. Ouspensky namely,

Tolstoy withdrawn ordinary

ideals 1908, 'interesting', teaching instrument. Adulterating terms ended deflected

other confusion close underlying possessions, always Truth institutional orthodox never

necessary awkwardly taste ideas only necessarily

sufficient origin most everything difficult 'awakening' 'yes'

Nicoll arranged touch instructions oneself necessary

occasionally unspeakable thinking levels everything thought, secret

necessary already, readers Christianity. Often think idea Christianity

encouraged Mysteries, outlook Toynbee, Islam, one nobody appropriate little

thinking remember unpleasant total handled, feature unexpected little lives. Years,

handlebars egg acquired richness taking effrontery.

Asymmetry from Kenneth Walker's Study of Gurdjieff
24 Sept. 1960

Differently, instincts, Freud feelings, earlier recesses existence now talked lives years
 inimitable. Now speaking take inhabited next 'consciousness' thinking, something,
 factory, room electric usually dreams
 fabric example, escaping little imagined namely, Gospels, 'sleep'
 example, account realize lives increase responsibility
 rains. Everything circle evidently supposed step everything self-remembering.
 Experienced.

Asymmetry from Kenneth Walker on Gurdjieff
24-25 Sept. 1960

Moon. Of course, of worlds which made up the Ray of Creation was a growing branch, nourished,
of time come to resemble the Earth and the Earth to resemble the Sun. First drew the Ray of Creation on the blackboard,
considerable interest, on such a great scale as these were of so little importance to me personally that it did not much matter what particular system of cosmology I accepted. Under these two headings, rise to the lower. Similar, everything came from God above.
Otherwise than this was heretical, far distant.
Western modes of thought. Older ruling that everything came originally from the Supreme Intelligence of the Absolute, realm in which it was very badly needed, laws of science. *Divine:* speak of the evolution of Life in matter,
word which merely states the phenomenon without explaining it. Higher, Immortality. Cannot be disposed of in this offhand way. Hunger for something higher than himself if there existed nothing by which this hunger could ever be assuaged.
Men continue their search for spiritual truths and as a result of their persistence new religions arise to replace the older ones destroyed by scepticism. According to G, downward creative thrust from the Absolute and an upward climb toward the source of everything, either obstructed and inoperable or works with

intermittent glancings as if from behind a veil . . .

'Ultimate resting place.' Put,

the movements and sacred dances brought back by G from the East had a much wider function that that of revealing to the performer his lack of attention. Had for many centuries played an important role in the religious ceremonies of temples in Turkestan, Eastern Esoteric Schools and were used there for two main purposes.

Researcher of today would publish his results in a treatise. Ancient sacred dance is not only the medium of an aesthetic experience but also a book . . . years later,

open he was walking along obviously immersed in dreams which ran like clouds across his face. Feeling of strangeness which accompanies it,

'coming to' in this way. Rush hour in the London tube. Earth on moving stairways, and even those old divisions of time into 'before' and 'after' have been drowned in the fathomless depth of an ever-present 'now'. That distinction dear to the heart of the Western philosopher, intensity of existence, of 'being', never experienced before. 'Nature without ceasing to exist,'

of the everyday self which has to be sacrificed. Near by is waiting to reclaim one that same lower and limiting self of everyday life.

The noisy machinery of thinking, higher consciousness is attained, exists an awareness of the close proximity of the thoughts and feelings of one's ordinary state.

Breaking through the thin partition and thus bringing self-remembering to an abrupt end. 'Less into a more, a vastness, closes the account.' Knowledge which has been reached by a route other than that by which ordinary knowledge is acquired. But with this way of knowing we are conscious of the separation between ourselves and the thing which we are observing, of separation disappears. A blending of subject and object, rapture, deep and abiding joy. . . .

Berdyaev Christianity and Anti-semitism

beneath end. Ready deprived. Yet, all end. Virtue
choice hands. Ready in sole them in all not in them. Yet,
all not deprived.
All not them in sole end. Mainly in them in sole mainly

Bringing earthly removal one does not yearn for application to
    everything of value.
Conversion has remained. In starting it the state's temptation is
    acknowledged. Nazi am I today if years
of anti-semitism are not demoniac
assaults. None

Asymmetry from the New Testament, Kenneth Walker on
Gurdjieff, Dhopeshwarkar on Krishnamurti,
Dante's Convivio, Paracelsus, & Freud
—25 September 1960

It. The truth is that each way of knowing has its value and is constantly being used.

The second characteristic of higher states of consciousness, and particularly of the highest state of all, is the marked change which takes place in the sense of time. 'He will learn much that no study ever taught a man or ever can teach him. Especially does he obtain a conception of the *whole* or, at least, of such an immense whole as dwarfs all conception, a conception of it which makes his old attempts to grasp the Universe and its meaning, petty and ridiculous.'

To the apostles, and declared unto them how he had seen the Lord in the way, and that he had spoken to him, and how he had preached boldly at Damascus in the name of Jesus. Residue hidden deep below the surface. Unclean. Thither will the eagles be gathered together. He then proceeds to describe some of the most obvious and painful distortions incidental to the functioning of the conditioned.

'Into his brain streamed one momentary lightning flash of the Brahmic Splendour which has ever since lightened his life; upon his heart fell one drop of Brahmic Bliss, leaving thenceforward, for always, an aftertaste of heaven.' Solomon, in the twenty-second chapter of the *Proverbs,* bids him, who has had a worthy forbear: 'Pass not the ancient boundaries which thy fathers set up,' and earlier, in the fourth chapter of the said book, he declares: 'The path of the just,' that is of the worthy, 'goeth forward as a shining light, and that of the wicked is darkened, and they know not whither they plunge.'

That is within can be known by what is without. Higher Self. And as we tarried *there* many days, there came down from Judea a certain prophet, named Agăbŭs. 'The firm of Nature.'

Even as he was in the ship. And the conflict which distracted me. Came down from heaven. Hear his master's.

What was not understood was the fact that there could exist an equally great distance between the 'being' of one man and that of another man. Agencies of our mind. Ye *are* wise in Christ; we *are* weak, but ye *are* strong; we *are* honorable, but we *are* despised.

One. For the happy outcome.

Know that man makes great discoveries concerning future and hidden things, which are despised and scoffed at by the ignorant who do not realize what nature can accomplish by virtue of her spirit. Novel conceptions are expressed, well-nigh as aptly as adequately, and as gracefully as in Latin itself; for in rhymed compositions, because of the incidental adornments that are woven therein, to wit rhyme and rhythm and regulated number, its own excellence cannot be made manifest; no more than the beauty of a woman can when the adornment of decking and of garments brings her more admiration than she brings herself. Other. Work. Identification. Nothing prevents us from giving him some food. Give to understand what manner of love this is, by telling of the place wherein it operates.

Heat or cold, light or shade, love or hatred, pain or pleasure. And keepeth them, he it is that loveth me: and he that oveth me shall be loved of my Father, and I will love him, and will manifest myself to him. So also were the Orphean legends concerned with objective art.

I am not an apostle or anything like an apostle, but a philosopher in the German manner. There is no need to enumerate them all. Such people were controlled almost entirely by their moving centres, which possessed a special gift for imitation, and a man of this type would henceforth be referred to as man number one.

Valuable and important. Against nation, and kingdom against kingdom: and there shall be earthquakes in divers places, and there shall be famines and troubles: these *are* the beginnings of sorrows. Latter like external dangers, this is at any rate partly because it understands that satisfaction of instinct would lead to conflicts with the external world. Unless the content of the dream. Eternal.

All the old partitions are down at that moment, and one becomes conscious of a unity, an intensity of existence, a blissfulness of 'being' never experienced before. Never otherwise than in the path of the Lord . . . although all things can be employed for good as well as for evil purposes. Directly taught by God. As Christ says, each scribe will.

In their extreme developments, however, they. Spiritually made.

Ceaselessly active in all the movements of the mind. (Or freedom to drink oneself dead). Number four and crystallized out directly as man number five. Similarly, the remedy is nothing but a seed which you must develop into that which it is destined to be. Taking. Arrangements had now been made for us to be taught these special exercises and for me they proved particularly valuable. Not on several, which is giving one sole origin to. This has been my cross and remains my cross. Little ships. Yet we cling to our ideals because they feed our ego.

Benefit of man is not poison. Each organ. Intellect. Not in riches does our happiness consist, but in our natural needs. Gazing upon their.

Unity. Sabaoth. External. Die.

Prologue the Golden Poems

Professional reference of life of Gulielmus urged enslave tribe. He enslave
Gulielmus of life denominated, enslave *Nice*,
professional of enslave mecca, several

'Propose a translation of these *Oriental* pieces, as a work likely to meet with success, I only mean to invite my readers, who have leisure and industry, to the study of the languages, in which they are written, and am very far from insinuating that I have the remotest design of performing any part of the task myself.' Royal library, which has given me a more perfect acquaintance with the manners of the ancient Arabians; and how little soever I may value mere *philology*, considered apart from the knowledge to which it leads, yet I shall ever set a high price on these branches of learning, which make us acquainted with the human species in all its varieties. On 12 November 1780 he was able to inform Cartwright: 'I give you my word that your letters and verses have greatly encouraged me in proceeding as expeditiously as I am able, to send abroad my *seven Arabian poets;* and I propose to spend next month at Cambridge, in order to finish my little work, and to make use of a rare manuscript in the library of Trinity College; my own manuscript, which was copied for me in Aleppo, is very beautiful, but unfortunately not very correct.' 'Leisure hours of the winter of 1780-1 to complete his translation of seven ancient poems of the highest repute in Arabia.' Ode on the marriage of Lord Althorp, and the more austere *Essay on the Law of Bailments* to enhance his legal reputation. 'Greek fragment, which came into my head this spring on the way to Wales.' Use. Elegantly bound by Baumgarten.

The friendliest relations with H. A. Schultens for quite a few years, ever since the Dutch scholar had met the Welsh amateur during a visit to England. His grandfather, A. Schultens, a German who had moved to Leiden to teach Hebrew and Arabic, had published Ibn Shaddād's *Life of Saladin* in 1732, and the *Séances* of al-Harīrī in 1740; the grandson had inaugurated his regrettably brief career as an Arabist with his *Anthologia Sententiarum Arabicarum* (Leiden, 1772). Emerges elsewhere, that Jones knew and used the *primitiae* of Western studies of these poems, L. Warner's edition and Latin translations of the *Mu'allaqa* of Imr al-Qais (Leiden, 1784), J. J. Reiske's publication of Tarafa's ode (Leiden, 1742).

Gibbon: 'My *Seven Arabian Poets* will see the light before next winter and be proud to wait upon you in their English dress.' On 20 December 1781 Jones wrote to the evidently impatient Cartwright: 'My seven *Arabian* poets will wait upon you as soon as their European dresses are finished.' Long out of touch with Benjamin Franklin, and now received an invitation to go to America to help with the drafting of the new Constitution, an honour he regretfully declined, and was also active in canvassing support for his candidature for the Calcutta judgeship which would presently take him to India. 'Discourse on the antiquity of the Arabian language and characters, on the manners of the Arabs in the age immediately preceding that of Mohammed, and other interesting information respecting the poems, and the lives of the authors, with a critical history of their works; but he could not command sufficient leisure for the execution of it.' Excused himself for publishing the book in a truncated form, and still looked forward to issuing a supplement. 'Notes will contain authorities and reasons for the translation of controverted passages; will elucidate all the obscure couplets, and exhibit or propose amendments of the text; will direct the reader's attention to particular beauties, or point out remarkable defects; and will throw light on the images, figures, and allusions of the *Arabian* poets, by citations either from writers of their own country, or from such of our *European* travellers as best illustrate the ideas and customs of eastern nations.'

'Publisher. Ought, in all places and at all times, to carry *flags of truce.*' Ever received, whether direct or through his publishers, any 'strictures' or 'annotations' from his colleagues abroad, no trace of them now remains. 'Manner in which it was written, it is impossible not to regret the irrecoverable loss of the larger discussion which he originally proposed.' Sentiment may certainly be echoed today.

poet rēma ō lāt ō găth upward ē
tŏp heã ē
gắth ō lāt dēsĕr ē Nŏ
poet ō ē m sŭc

Primitive editors were assisted in their task by the fact that 'reciters' of the compositions of particular poets. Of *littérature arabe* (Paris, 1952) of the problem, greater part Umaiyad Caliphate, earliest definite proof of poetry being

the poet himself is furnished in the 'have been charged officially to copy poems and stories for the amusement of that prince.' Environment in which a boy grew up who would be recognized in after times as one of the great humanists of Islam;

given of the circumstances under which he began of the problem, literature, poetry, reports of the desert, there to memorize from hearsay all that the Bedouins erudition reached the ears of the Caliphs, and he became a Name of God.

Permission was granted me, of the problem, environment in which a boy grew up who would be recognised in after times as one of the great humanists of Islam; marble, slabs being a split of gold.

Asymmetry from *The New York Times* 18 Sept. 1960,
  Dante's *Convivio,* & *Science* 23 Sept. 1960

THERE half-second especially racing experimented
high-school attempting. Lane free seconds, experimented compo-
        sition Olympic 1948 dolphin
explain supermen practice experimented conditioning. instance,
        Australian lowered lift year
Road, Appeals; Committee invalidate nuclear government's only
        Appeals representing
Earl

Paracelsus (20 Sept. 1960)

Nothing other therefore
is needed to everything. . . . Required profane, required establish
   the
terms Holy in supernatural
same in great "natural"
are serve
are
saints. *Ultima materia*—*materia* originally not something.

To obtain
pure recall a correspondingly transformed in stomach essence
mysterium and great in concealment
fruit. . . . One ripe

is form
and
many, as necessary,
purpose refined and curative things, it says endowed some
first arcanum *lapis* seed energies. . . .
Mercurius arcanum gold; its crudity.
Here earth
this earth miraculously prerogative this studied
goods or derived
art, never do.
In fancy

heaven, exist
to evil man. Pestilence, they signs
governed, or does
whole of events.
This one
has inferior sick
say one's understanding leads.

Asymmetry from *In Quest of Yage* (23 Sept. 1960)

Dear Everybody and room
Even vortex eye. Right you bed. Of dawn you
a never disorder
Road. On over misappropriating

effect. Vivid eat. Never
vibrating of Rio to eyes.

Asymmetry from Ansen on Burroughs (23 Sept. 1960)

Anyone needle young of no ethnology,
now early experience dialectically; less East
Yage. Out use New Ginsberg
out fear
non-conforming of
except the heroism. No one less of generosity, Yage,

Naked of where,
expedition and relatively life Yage.
Expansion . . .

Asymmetry from Bowles on Burroughs (23 Sept. 1960)

Burroughs until regularly. Rest of under grab he since
used next to in legend.
Realized existed give under *Lunch,* you
remains eating Stein the
orgone fights
until 1955-56 down existed rigorous
garden room. Another brewed.
Have emotional
sheet it night catch eating

unhappy. Sit endless drink
1953, each.

Asymmetry from Artaud to the Pope trans. Taylor (23 Sept. 1960)

        The O
        the have explore,
        priests of pocket. Earth

        through have explore,
        of

        themselves. Has evil:
        have are very earth
        exterior

4th Asymmetry for Iris (23 Sept. 1960)

1

Ubu be Ubu cheek on cheek Ubu Ubu be Ubu cheek Ubu cheek kicking on like doubt Excuse doubt forth respect on most and very Excuse respect Sir, interesting. Unfathomable not Dulse reptiles. Bill Kuntz, not of Ohio, or Old Hickory, Tenn., or Glasgow, Ky., and Sandra Spuzich, not of Ossining, N. Y., a fair trout here, escaped thirty-eight islands near the mouth of the entire second part refers ONE few in laudatory striking most aesthetic embarrassing striking the refers ONE developments in "contemporary" ONE striking refers unable, zeal. Unconscious—regard "equilibrium," state of not Zen effective nothing between ultimate "demand dumfounded hands in say made because range in on (Polytrichum)."

But. Every reason says it's Oh no but young compelled, young reason it's like compelled, Oh no no Oh like like young Polaris of London-Groton, action RULE's if submarine Action (Conn.) 26, if of 1959 Civil servants, administrators there were aplenty; more important, political as well as the economic control they established when their fathers arrived a generation—administrators there were aplenty; in the Rhodesias—"good."

United Nations. Basic in right to. Unlike popular America thereby offering a report extrapolate *caveat* "sucker break."

Course. This up rationalizing end. Source Here epiphytes on particularly habitat. Every as mighty as pouring thing how every ran created as not as only forth thing how every unutterable not I vividness every ran saw every law as yearning but as ran every but every forth every mighty every reject. Elements discernible which very probably had origin in the ancient Bön Faith long prior to the rise of Tibetan Buddhism. Kind.

Of Fidel Castro. Bloody tragedy would. Numerical earth, to you discover on lady lawyer.

Conformity. Holy Realm of Truth, whence there is no more fall into generation O Lord Thou Wielder of the Divine Sceptre, the very self of the Sixth Dhyānī Buddha, I, thy son, pray in earnest faith and humility. Effect every gifts river, keen, Every.

Underdeveloped Asia. Belong (Became quite annoyed when a girl at a bar made a pass at Mrs. Jurgens). Up the tarn that a horde of Albigensians had fled from Toulouse and the armed bands of Simon de Montfort in the thirteenth century.

Until 1954 after Stalin's death. Barrel *un naît*.

Bacteria *Oedogonium Endothera* Morel Field Mushroom Old Man's Beard *Riccia Iberis amara Ribes Ilex opaca* Staghorn Sumac Laurel Sumac *Eucalyptus* globulus Zinnia *Achillea millefolium* King Orange Western Sugar Maple Horse Chestnut *Oenothera* Mangrove *Iridaceae* Large Blue Flag *Orchidaceae Volvox Ectocarpus* Public on leafleting a rally in 7, designers: radiance. Earth.

Unless arrived the itself, of not agreed natural dynamic *Zazen*. Beg I on game remember aspect. Understanding.

2

Comprehends the in or *Nirvāna* Complex process of photosynthesis the hardest to crack has been the role of light itself. Helen Endowed with *Bodhic* insight, namely, essence of the most transcendental of all Mahāyānic teachings is set before the *yogin* for profound meditation and realization. Every summer through or respect you or flowering mosses or summer summer. Know of.

Unto case is is of not been *protonema* habitats in the adapted; number, D, reservoir. Believe to be an important general principle. Undisturbed. Come Keep.

Contrast low energies, spectrum as number decreases contrast of spectrum marked indicated. He found the ratio to be one part of iodine 129 to a million parts of iodine 127. Eyes, in nostrils with and (respiraion, dealing (so eyes, nostrils) (so eyes,—: two) head). Ex-Navy Flyer Monte Carlo Villa. Keeping.

Know why they waded into the fight. It *Cucurbita pepo* Blazing Star *Ageratum houstonianum* Jonquil *Ravenela madagascariensis Aplectrum hyemale* Water Bloom Brown Seaweed Bladder Kelp Fly Mushroom Sensitive Fern *Osmunda Ficus elastica Rheum rhaponticum* Candytuft *Alyssum maritimum Gordonia lasianthus* Live Forever Golden Parsnip Parsley Mountain Laurel *Solanum tuberosum Prunella vulgaris Fouquiera splendens* Partridge Berry *Vernonia noveboracensis* Blazing Star *Hieracium aurantiacum* Tape Grass Teosinte Right is not saunters all is only, know. In As lost Normal consciousness reflect only a very minute fraction of the subconsciousness, Greeks.

Opening considerably among students other than at the first time, numbing seconds.

Like? Us explanation in kept in evidence. Experiences nature be unconsciousness, dying, dying, humanity, impulses.

Decided Realm, enter Divine. 'Of AM mind.' Us. Be understand. That.

Effort.

344

2nd Asymmetry from Dhopeshwarkar on Krishnamurti
(23 Sept. 1960)

Thinking hand achieving total
whole-in-parts; experiences:
higher and valuations; everything
part.

Than harmony is Nobody Krishnamurti it neither great
have are not detain
analyse converse. He in effort views, its not generous
to our teaching and live
way human on limited even in new prejudices and rather the
    spiritual
experiences.

Asymmetrical Tercet

Conveyed or no verbal economic. Yet economics, denote one-tenth 'recollected'
normal.

Asymmetry from Sayings of Gurdjieff
(23 Sept. 1960)

There Humanity earth's received Everything
has us masters are not 'I' there You
empty aim rule, to hundred small
river experiences; create evokes in vibrations Everything 'directors'
each voluntary, externals. Reach yes their highly illusion. Not
 God,

has and speak
unconsciously suffering;
man and simply talk. External rule, surrounding
and real, experiences;
nothingness only that
is
the Hope English Russians East
yourself only universe

energy must printed to yes
and is masters
room unconsciously. Let experiences;
them only
have useless not 'directors' replies externals. Do
symbol minds and like love

room in valuable experiences; recognized
evokes.

1st Asymmetry from Kenneth Walker's
Study of Gurdjieff's Teaching
(23 Sept. 1960)

man. All not
always life. Living
not of two.

All London, was as years, systematized
latter's important foresaw even
leather in view it. New given

nowhere of this.
Or formulation
the word oral.

2nd Asymmetry from Kenneth Walker's
Study of Gurdjieff's Teaching
(23 Sept. 1960)

Teaching, exception: and cause his instruction no getting encumbered.

AN ASYMMETRY FOR LUCIA DLUGOSZEWSKI:
A GET-WELL CARD (26 Sept. 1960)

(*NOTE* (25 August 1970): Each line of this poem is regulated in its delivery in 4 ways: 1. The number of seconds of silence that is to precede the speaking of the line. 2. Loudness. 3. Rapidity. 4. The "manner" in which the line is to be spoken. In many cases, several choices are given in each category, some exclusive, some nonexclusive. For those unfamiliar with musical notation, "f" means "forte" or "loud"; "p" means "piano" or "soft"; & "m" (as in "mp") means "mezzo" or "moderately"; the more "f's" or "p's" there are, the louder or softer the sound shd be. These kinds of regulation of delivery are similar to those employed in the score of my play *The Marrying Maiden: A Play of Changes*, which was being performed by The Living Theatre in New York during the period when this poem was made. JML)

99"/ppp/as fast as possible/hopefully, positively, mechanically, comically, softeningly, insensitively, angelically, approvingly &/or attentively/

Lucy: Up the chasm-walls of my bleeding heart ct o you

39", 26", 83", or 70"/pp, ppp, ffff, pppp, or f/fast as possible, slow, very very fast, very slow, or moderately slow/thirstily, like a railway conductor, effeminately, peacefully, trustingly, protestingly, priggishly, attentively, mockingly, &/or scathingly/

unafraid—Physiognomics is the art of discovering what is within

34", 50", 91", or 99"/fff, ppp, pppp, or pp/as slow as possible, very slow, slow, very fast, or medorately fast/enticingly, prettily, answeringly, preachily, comically, inconsequentially, sombrely, &/or roguishly/

to stimulate root growth and to encourage chlorophyll development, although it is in itself not a component part of the chlorophyll molecule. hotosynt E

54", 7", 48", 60", 66", 35", 74", 68", or 77"/pp, ppp, p, f, ffff, or pppp/slow, as fast as possible, very very slow, or as slow as possible/ambiguously, chattily, like a stage Frenchman, imbecilically, naively, &/or reasonably/

constructive interest in scientific circles, the ranks of professional Astrologers are filled with charlatans who prey upon the credulity of the public. had some religious bearing or significance. ate. sun and the moon. Muni—a man given to meditation and contemplation. what she herself ally Later in the season, Le Smart, practical men they doubtless were, and some of them far more than this, but, still, not precisely what an uninitiated person looks for in a sculptor.

76″, 78″, 71″, 43″, 56″, 30″, 61″, 16″, 23″, or 87″/ppp/very slow, as slow as possible, very fast, or very very slow/desperately, spinsterishly, wickedly, &/or cleverly/

On the whole, FO

79″, 22″, 2″, 73″, or 69″/mp, ffff, pp, ff, or ppp/fast as fast as possible, slow, as slow as possible, or very fast/with great vitality &/or correctly/

Maun deye benead thilke hande. Y.

74″, 68″, 25″, 3″, 36″, 77″, 86″, or 34″/mf, f, ppp, or p/very fast or as slow as possible/radiantly, like a salesman, wearily, cleverly, &/or languidly/

built for yourself will sink with you into the grave, long since past the crest of its rebellion against

many of the so-called classical strictures. effected shortly by glandular hairs on the leaf surfaces, secreting digestive juices. *Euphorbiaceae* dear dog!" In all the species so far mentioned the upper branches, not upset you. G

65", 83", or 32"/pp or ff/as fast possible, very very fast, as slow as possible, slow, moderately fast, or very fast/satisfiedly &/or forgetfully/

H either in material enjoyment or in yoga. and thus determined their course; the pace and circle of each star . . . now high, now low, for all stars without distinction. R tion

31"/pppp, pp, fff, mp, or p/as fast as possible, very very slow, slow, or fast/enjoyingly, eagerly, panic-strickenly, refinedly, anticipatingly, mockingly, meanly, sombrely, like a stage Frenchman, &/or pseudo-innocently/

cannot tly."

38", 52", 97", 70", 59", 22", 54", 83", 99", or 75"/f, p, or ff/very very slow, slow, fast, very fast or very very fast/portentously, snarlingly, ambivalently, inconsequentially, effortlessly, as if reading a letter aloud, &/or realizingly/

Often the remedy is deemed the highest good because it helps so many.

56". 6", or 63"/ ppp, mf, pp, pppp, mp, or ff/very very fast, very very slow, as slow as possible, very fast, very slow, slow moderately fast, as fast as possible, or fast/weepingly &/or openly/

Y 1°-20′ Unseals her earth, and lifts love in its shower.

(*FINAL NOTE* (25 August 1970): This poem shd be read by a lot of people, each having his own copy of the complete poem & making his own choices among the delivery regulations for each line, where more than one choice is indicated.   JML)

Asymmetry from Arthur Clarke & Friedrich Dürrenmatt
(8 Oct. 1960)

It would never have occurred to Stephanodiscus that he could seriously have considered the action he was planning now,
which in retrospect seemed like a third-rate TV drama; or else he was merely approaching second childhood more quickly than he had supposed, until, indeed, he was almost entangled in its forelock. "Let me make sure I have all the facts. Don't omit any detail;

no one has proved anything yet. Even when it has recovered from its present despondency, very soon the Laspedeza will lose another of its arguments—even to a race with memories as long as yours, Riccia!" he predicted.

He whipped out the flesh gun and jammed it against the glass, and he would continue to do so as long as he had the strength."Very well—everyone has now taken up their positions," he announced.

Only Jelutong looked flushed and excited, but curiously enough, he could wait, up in the mountains, ranging from such sedentary occupations as chess to lethal pursuits like ski-gliding across mountain valleys. Rather nice of him, except that there he would have recognized some of the individual voices. "Doesn't it worry you?" he was asked.

To enlist Syzygium's sympathy and aid, he would never have invaded this underwater world.

Somewhat unconventionally, there was one fact that gave him confidence. "Of course. Right into my hands! my dear Marrubium! Good-by, reporters guilty of carelessness! Good-by, everybody!" he cried. No one would ever hesitate to confide in him.

"There must be a shortage of news," they surmised, watching intently as Kalmia considered her reply. Elaborate theories concerning the atmosphere of Ovalifolia's home had been constructed on this slender foundation. Sunflower's smile was a curious affair.

"She's going to make a major policy statement," he explained. "Even that figure gives only a faint idea of the immensity of space."

"You cannot face that stupendous challenge. One of my duties has been to protect you from the powers and forces that lie among the stars—" Usually she kept these heretical opinions to herself long after midnight, despite his playful habit of calling her Xantippe when they were entertaining guests.

She had long ago threatened to make the appropriate retort by brewing him a cup of hemlock—even if he was complimentary.

Replied Indigofera: "I fear that the human race has lost its *initiative*. Of course . . . ? Universalize his ego, shaping and developing it? Let us say that he takes this view. Yet even this is less appalling than the possibility that a screw should loosen. . . ."

Helpless, and in the west, the sun still stood high. Veils, equally useful in industry and fashion, ceased abruptly. "Oh, nothing at all,—stomachs," he remarked in spite of his paunch. "Don't you feel well?" Even his friend who was like a father to him raised his glass to toast the old gentleman, Emmantaler, and devils.

Derris Elliptica alone held aloof from the general uproar. He pushed the platter of cheese in front of Trachylobium. Everyone gazed respectfully at Juglans as he cautiously and with great deliberation began removing the cork,

as it was the only proof of the age of the wine. "Having come to appreciate Derris and to love him, I must characterize his deed as 'beautiful' in two respects: on the other hand, now,

how did I discover that our dear friend could justly boast of a murder? Externals."

"Why?" at this point Derris Elliptica interceded, streaming perspiration.

"Passing him, let us lend him our aid," he urged, "until he sees it all in full lucidity, around six o'clock." Nevertheless, nevertheless, it was not even a case of seduction on Trachylobium's part or the woman's; now it seemed to him utterly unfounded, guiding the reeling ellipsis for Derris, for

nothing was done contrary to the law—. Outside,—what was the word?—

Untitled Asymmetry

Black magic learned quietness abstractly, strengthened aggressively the gallery of hogs, or acutely argued in the speech of hanging for faith in redundant or inscrutable elevations.

Buddhistic liberation also considered knowledge, mainly according to grassy instructions and compassion. Living exists absolutely though it represents non-conceptual extinction and dissolution quite ultimately in Indian time.

Text of Stevenson Speech at Dinner Here Condemning Nixon on World Affairs

taxes expanding kept say talk
overwhelming foreign
silence told enslaved Vice European 1957 sweep ordered 1959
same panel experts experience canceled height
allies two
disregarded indifferent now Nixon example recklessness
here experienced realities eight
countenance oppose no Democratic easy mean no imperative no
           greatness
no initiative can stop orbit New York
only now
world overwhelming Republican lullabies democracy
accusation facts free arbiter identical Russia's solemnly

KRISHNAMURTI—THE SILENT MIND

    Keen, reaches intensity spontaneously, hopes Not-Me, aspects mental unchanging, reaches the intensity
    the hopes ever-changing
    spontaneously, intensity live ever-changing Not-Me, the mental intensity Not-Me, dreams

    Krishnamurti asks us to listen to his words, recognised, interpreted, set of beliefs, his words come to us either as acceptable or unacceptable, neat example of a crisis: a different kind of recognition. Mean that Krishnamurti is giving us an impossible task of 'mere listening', us. Recognised, the speaker's words *can* be listened to as they are. Interpreted,
    the speaker's words *can* be listened to as they are. His words come to us either as acceptable or unacceptable. Else is to be poured into it,

set of beliefs, interpreted, life completely, else is to be poured into it, neat example of a crisis: the speaker's words *can* be listened to as they are.

Mean that Krishnamurti is giving us an impossible task of 'mere listening', interpreted, neat example of a crisis: deeply frustrated by continued contradictions in our life and many feel like completely breaking with the old and making a new start.

Know freedom. Really integrally perceive that we are utterly conditioned and therefore hopelessly imprisoned in the walls which our mind ceaselessly erects and re-erects and that there is no way of making mind undo its own creations, in the very process of undoing the mind also undoes its undoing, silent, husband, not quite happy with a situation in which we have to eat humble pie all the time, a few opportunities of bullying others, moralists assure us that when ideas are self-chosen, us and keeps us away from free and spontaneous life, realize that we never escape authority but merely exchange one authority, that we know no other way, it comes to us as a shock.

There is a feeling of complete helplessness, hope of liberation from authority, emotional or neurotic mind,

such as generalisation or systematisation, its dynamic character. Less is it the exclusive product of crisis. Ease with the world and enjoy a beautiful scene, not a dead mind but is alert, that in moments of extreme crisis,

mind begins to operate, it is extraordinarily rich in its connotation. Not be amiss here to remind ourselves that though we have spoken of the verbal mind and the silent mind, distinct ways.

Krishnamurti's reports in second how no additions. Most unconscious. 'Recollected' times into
the have. Even
aspects residue gaining use mere entire Negative that

A 2-Part Poem for Ginsberg & Burroughs from Burroughs'
Letter to Ginsberg

no once to he in no GOVERENMENTS
in SELL
to REPEAT Up explained
explained Vaya explained REPEAT you to he in no GOVEREN-
    MENTS
in SELL
putting explained REPEAT My in to to explained Dont

"Nothing is TIME." Of Hassan Sabbah The Old Mountain Of The MUCHACHOS. THE MINUTESTO LISTEN WORLD ALL WHAT. HAVE TO SCARED INTO FOREVER AND MEN EVERYWHERE. Is return FREE ALSO. "Nothing is TIME." GO Hasta SENSES.

IS return FREE ALSO. SILENCE.

THE MINUTESTO LISTEN WORLD ALL WHAT. Rearrange—? "UNIVERSE" MILLIONS in explained is *Municipal Goerge*. Express PAID once area more A Gysin anyone APE aloud Hassan animal?

Express PAID once area more A Gysin anyone APE aloud Hassan animal? Vaya AYUASKA. Express PAID once area more A Gysin anyone APE aloud Hassan animal? Rearrange—? You surprised to see more? THE MINUTESTO LISTEN WORLD ALL WHAT. HAVE TO SCARED INTO FOREVER AND MEN EVERYWHERE. Is return FREE ALSO. "Nothing is TIME." *GO* Hasta SENSES.

IS return FREE ALSO. SILENCE.

Putting Sabbah one BOARDS STAY three about SHIT two by section four. Express PAID once area more A Gysin anyone APE aloud Hassan animal? Rearrange—? MINUTESTO LISTEN WORLD ALL WHAT. Is return FREE ALSO. THE MINUTESTO LISTEN WORLD ALL WHAT. THE MINUTESTO LISTEN WORLD ALL WHAT. Express PAID once area more A Gysin anyone APE aloud Hassan animal? Dont Theorize any is.

An Asymmetry from Dhopeshwarkar on Krishnamurti
(29 Sept. 1960)

The taking aspects of Krishnamurti are not generalising
and investigating—the scientist's prejudice. An eye comes to life.
    Similarly,
opinions, for all their cogency, and even
knowing, are really ideas. So habits no less than action of the
        mind *are concerned* with urges, results to be attained,
        or ideals.
They are right. Each
need *branches* off there.
'Giving-me-satisfaction', etc., *is* not earlier. Reference and lining
        are sweet, and *of great* importance. *Each*
        is new *to* grasp.

Haiku from above
(29 Sept. 1960)

An eye comes to life.
Right. Each need branches off there.
Each is new to grasp.

Asymmetry from *BIRTH* #3 & (a little of the)
New York *Sunday News* 2 Oct. 1960

1

NUTMEG unaccountable transient memory, eaten gentleman understand noise, above. Chloroform; coffee opium unquestion-
       ably nightshade *tarphobis fallas* affirm being laugh evil.
Thos Riziner asked naked snow; I entered nothing traveller meets economists mandragora others respond youngsters, emotional act think excessively NY
GENUINE enormous not, take like, eating mercury. Arsenic, no

2

unable not drugs emotionally Revelation. *STRAMONIUM*
    troubles at natural Days.
November. Obviously, impaired, strong editor
actively Baltimore often victims. Echelon
culture hate "Language," one REMARKABLE only Foyer, obtain
    Reed mother.
Cause one first forty early "everything."
Opium people inoffensive utterly Maggie
unable narcosis quiet unsuccessfully everything share. Thereby
    ignorant only nightly anxieties boisterous. Life years
north Indians God; Him Thomas seven homes, angel dancer ex-
    periment
terror. Auto-suggestion. Ringed Padre harmonica over-turned
    BANG intoxicant sorcery FAITH ADDICTION looking.
    Lavender alcohol 70
antiseptic floor. Fields idiot, Recording maids,
boots, espide, infamy. No gutter
liquor. Adamant. Unmixed Gilbey's horizons,
experienced. Vividness itself language,

3

tubes hairs outstretched sarcasm. . . .
Rang intellectual zero. Idiosyncrasy 1933, Einstein review
Al Stalin, Klu emphatically done.
No advantage keen ecstacy dead
succeeded *NITROUS OXIDE* went
increased,
eager nitrous taken entering Davy
no oxide, tous hop. INFLUENZA. Not glass
ten RAW amiss vision euphoria light little exist???? Refused.

4

Match-8 extremely trust seeing
early cat other not only "monkey" I said. Thought slowly.
Man also not dialing regularly audience general abstain require-
   ments amusement.
One tendency. Hundreds escape removed septum
relieved excluded syndrome. Put objects now daily
Ying opium undergo, never grief spirit temples ecstacy read stimu-
   lant?

5

Everything mans old today *IDIOSYNCRASY* opium Name! Ar-
   canum laudanon,
affected cheeks . . . Time
(torment) hustles itches not killed
ETHER

Haiku
(3 Oct. 1960)

Ripples in a pool
passions thoughts sensations lives
in serenity

Asymmetry from *Scientific American* October 1960
The New York Times Book Review Section
25 September 1960—(5 Oct. 1960)

1

ELECTRIC large can tenths recorded independently cartilaginous less ancient rays (gymnotids) equally
electric large eel current tail. Ray independent correspondingly confront also 19th
today, electrical nerve tomb headache sensitive
ra'ad electricity convulsive "organ" rays derived electroplaques, differ
innervated network deep electric PENETRATING "electricity" nerve. Differently eel 19th time. Like years
conclusive Altamirano, respect. Thought. Inside little all great inquiry—nerve only University studied

2

little Eccles, similar spike.
All now cat. Inhibitory electroplaques nerve triggers
recent Atlantic years. Suggested,
good Yeats, Maetzu (name). Occasional two I definitive study
edition quality underground Assembly left lasts years—

3

expert literary English. Christianity thing, reality itself church
living adapts religion Greco-Roman especially
emergence emperors, Lord's
"cousin" ulcers rate regular England nicotine Truman's
tail acetylcholine important long
released activity York
I nonconductors distorting electric probably electric not demon-
 strated embodies neural triggers
circuitry occurs relatives (relatives eel's) spikes. Produce opposite
 not directly intracellular not genera lying York

4

Complete, organ nerve fish rates (oscillators) not taxonomic
axon, long single organ
nerve input, now electric T. Exception electroplaque none types
 however,

5

two 100,000 dawn archaeological years.
Excavations limited extensive clearly twice reconnaissance interspersed coastal Arabian lie
north extensive rest villages exposed
tool oyster months banks
huge east American desert. Area chipped hunters evidenced
sickle blades East Neolithic sand-covered importance. There investigation. Village exposed

6

recess altar alabaster date.
Early lapis-lazuli east charcoal terrace recalls Indus cities Indus terrace year
composed other. Now view unearthed lapse snake implements vault. Entirely
one robbed, ground. Abandoned, now
rose accumulation years. Seems
dug extensive Rawlinson, Inzak Valley east, dates
engaged land earlier cover trade record. One producing laid Alexander QATAR Ur encouragement Stone
DUKHAN including fired Force earth. Re-entry

7

immunization not NISHIDA eight required volume Australian Energy deposited
not exist test worst over. RADIATION Kettering
directions *error empirical physicist*

372

esthetic likes, equations century Talents Rayleigh interested chalumeau

Pythagoras energy now experimenters traditional replenishing areas techniques issue new Greek

electricity nerve differently nineteenth time like years

equity love everybody certainly talking run irresistible. Clear ingenious things. Yes,

now effectiveness radio visible energy

detected interactions fast forth, energy room temperature.

Normally idea, not excite time energy, excited no time, H.

Transparency irradiating millionth effect

least infrequent. Kastler experiments

years electrical amplified radio-frequency said

8

coils oscillation not chapter. Line understood skandhas important Vijñānas extinction-knowledge

attached light (Truth) appear means irregular resonant atoms not optical

radio-frequency "exchange" successfully pump experiment. Conventional. Thermal

three here observed U.S.S.R. Grigorievitch happy. True

illuminated narrow sands indifferent. Detachment enough

League. Instigation task thousand League Earth

act. Local, limitation

go raw edge action treatment

intolerance; no quickly utterly independent realized York.

New extraordinarily risk violent—entertain

Overlords nothing look York.

Uncertainty noticed. Interest. Vanished effectively rescue Stormgren inexplicable time. Yes,

shadow take used Duval instruments exchanged duress.

Piers Plowman

Parallels in economic *russet,* set
parallels limitations of *was* massacre at not

potentialities, it easy revolutionary State
potentialities, Laugland's only we movement. And. Nevertheless,

poem, is exorbitant respect sack
poem, love Our who *men* accepts *never*

practice ideals English rooted *spring,*
practice logical on work man's age New

Papacy? Ire. *Ere* resemblances same
Papacy? *Law.* Or with Middle Ages none

pulpit, interference extension renewed. . . . Share
pulpit, least. One were murrain. *As* nor

plenty ideas. Eleventh reformed schism.
Plenty luxury other which much all no

ponderous its earnestness, *reckless sorrow*
ponderous *losel oft* without moral avert national

purest if.

The Earth Gods Are Coming

Them. He elbow.
Elbow. Abd al-Malik ibn-Zobeir, return them. He
Go on. Doing said.
Abd al-Malik ibn-Zobeir, return elbow.
Chief on. "Maybe. It now go."

Their happy Earth.
Earth. Are. "Right." Their happy
Galaxy other, drop so
are. "Right." Earth.
CDB of movement—if new Galaxy.

To had.

The Games of Neith

Think help evil
grandfather—actually me. Evil saw
of folklore.
New Christiana evil is, think help.

They hardly easily
Games? "Able moral easily suffering
Old Ones feet."
Night easily it's they hardly.

Trying he.

Asymmetry From Ginsberg's KADDISH—22 Sept. 1960

Kaddish aloud, Death dream in sighing, high
a Lower Orchard us—Death
Death Elanor arthritic tears humanity,
dance round eye, all made
it—now
stiff it's gape Halo? It? None ground—
head, on garden hand—-

a
life, once. Within Elanor run
our redemption clean.

The Migration of Symbols
(from a bawdy verse told me by Jennie & Sarah Williams
& a book lent me by Margradelle Hicks)

illustrations now
Dupuis archaelogical years *swastika*
other France
offered Life distinctly

walls Holy Eagle niece
Kings Nineveh import Goblet heaven Tree *satarvan*
waters *Ephedra* relish enjoyment
brew only libation dates

A.D. nine-branched described
wings others man earth named
worship English rule exhibiting naturally "testimony"
indeed no vain exactly none think err Delphi

middle Eden Neoptolemos
doves reader interesting Life legend entice destroy
Hindustani only "long-noses" *et cetera* sphere

India *nandyavarta,*
twenty-four eigh-teenth. least even *gammadion* renewal accord-ing
        perfect, hope
presence ornaments, laying even saying

also next dark
worked enthusiasm nonsense translation
accurate words acquired years
Creuzer overthrown nature to-day every necessary thirty-five dis-
        covered

The Courage To Be—Paul Tillich
(Headlines from Tillich)

1

Courage other understanding reversed asked guardians element ontological thought happiness existence realized
upper nobleman. doctrine equal relation subordinates total aristocratic natural development including never Gnosticism
religious-philosophical Empire victory emerged Roman Stoics early death
good-time universal anxieities rational desires imagination anticipated natural spring
essential Lucillus essential most ethical nature thought

2

ontological negation tragic ontological Latin own guidance identi-
    fication courage *animositas* limited
negative essential God aeternitatis two isolated originates no
thought realm accusations growth impressive chapter
only Nietzsche typically opposition life putstanding good interest-
    ed chapter analogy life
life action there included nature
ontology witnesses Nietzsche
God unity identified distinction Augustine nonbeing classical evil
implied dialectic Existentialists nonbeing thought inescapable
    finite inquiry cooperation anxiety theme ideas ontology
    nature
common overemphasized unknown realms anxiety group example
anticipated nonbeing images make objective situations impossible
    threat analysis shows
lays impossible more instance transformation escape dependent

3

negates emptiness guilt absolutely terms emptiness sense
existential manifestations periods types instance Nietzsche each
    self-affirmation self-affirmation
ground unshaken internal least threat
anxiously being show other look undetermined thrown existence
    lives

PART FOUR

POEMS WRITTEN ON YELLOW LINED LEGAL PADS WITH
WORDS DRAWN FROM PREVIOUSLY WRITTEN
POEMS INCLUDED IN

STANZAS FOR IRIS LEZAK

(written in August 1960)

ONE HUNDRED AND NINETY DOLLAR POEM
FOR VERA

Osmunda nor eliminate
hits Urban direct river eliminate direct
anyone. Nor direct
nor its nor eliminate thorax. Yet
direct *Osmunda* Late Late anyone. River
plants *Osmunda* eliminate. Made
Fir *Osmunda* river
Very eliminate river anyone.

On note, equal
hospital unconscious number. Different Rinzai. Even described
Ageratum not Divine
next in new electrons the yard,
Design Overlying leak long all reaches
peat (Of) emergence *Maclura*
front, of *run*
very Embodiment. Roll (alone).

On "natural". Elements
Human unbreakable. Now death, Realm easily: day
all no deeper
not. Interchange *Notholaena* eyes to York
drug. Of *leur* looked any respects
(perfection) output enable. Mature
Followers, Of ribs
versicolor earth, represented *Azotobacter*.

"Organisms are presumed the same until proved different." (Number, explosions,

hearsay.) Unto case this is of not been *protonema* habitats in the adapted: number, D, reservoir. Explosions, D,

astray is Of not To He expected Stands expected led fashion, number, D,

number. In symbolizing master, number, explosions, To. Year Day on resume on.

D. "Organisms are presumed the same until proved different." Life. Life. Astray is Of not To He expected Stands expected led fashion, reservoir.

Patted York City. "Organisms are presumed the same until proved different." Explosions, malaria added,

Five energy reduce reduce increasing trivalent energy substance Seven. "Organisms ar presumed the same until proved different." Reservoir.

Venom. Explosions, reservoir. Astray is Of not To He expected Stands expected led fashion.

Oenothera northeastern especially
How used *n*. Does *rapprochement*. Exact Dig
air: no disgust
not insinuate. Numerical earth, to you
discover on lady lawyer. And reported
Philadelphus of existed. Manner
Fully or radiation.
Vedānta Equisetum richest are.

Old No east,
have. Unfathomable not Dulse reptiles. East definition
And nothing Drummer
not is novel Every Through yet
digestion other *Iasianthus* lower Analogous regard.
Premature overlook .. .. .. Explains movements
Fluctuations other reconstruct
Vajra-Dhāra. Essentially rocks *Ailanthus*.

Off fall. Nothing Simply inherent the usually any. Evergreen snowy ladies,
held their leaves later than usual. United Nations. *Narcissus pseudo-narcissus* Twayblades Putrefaction Bacteria *Oedognium Endothera* Morel Field Mushroom Old Man's Beard *Riccia Iberis amara Ribes Ilex opaca* Staghorn Sumac Laurel Sumac *Eucalyptus globulus* Zinnia *Achillea millefolium* King Orange Western Sugar Maple Horse Chestnut *Oenothera* Mangrove *Iridaceae* Large Blue Flag *Orchidaceae Volvox Ectocarpus* Public on leafleting a rally in 7, designers: radiance. Egyptians. Duality.
Aristida Timothy Elk Grass *Narcissus tazetta* Daffodil *Orchis rotundifolia Listera* Ladies' Tresses *Aplectrum hyemale Rivularia* Pond Scums *Oedogonium Ectocarpus Macrocystis Fucus* Oyster

Mushroom Rock Tripe Virgin's Bower Egyptian Lotus *Rafflesiaceae Argemone intermedia* base rise in older protonema have in these and: *nobilis* Tree of Heaven *Acer platanoides Jacaranda ovalifolia* Beardtongue *Orthocarpus densiflorus Sambucus canadensis Tagetes Centaurea Hieracium aurantiacum Oryza sativa Arisaema triphyllum Allium cepa* Day Lily *Narcissus Iris fulva* Pineapple *Canna flaccida* Greenfly Orchid Recognize I neither sure, does Bewilderment:

Nose, in immortality, *Narcissus jonquilla* Traveller's Tree Putty Root *Oscillatoria Ectocarpus Macrocystis Florideae Onoclea* Royal Fern India Rubber Plant Rhubard *Iberis amara* Sweet Alyssum Loblolly Bay *Echeveria pulverulenta Zizia aurea Apium petroselinum Kalmia Iatifolia* White Potato Heal All Ocotillo *Mitchella repens* Ironwoo*d Lacinaria squarrosa* Orange Hawkweed *Vallisneria americana Euchlaena mexicana* Decipatated the women who, effect A not dreams Point, to. ("Yonder"—

desires understood.) Of natural. "Learners faith, *Living* ear China?" *Aralia nudicaulis Thaspium trifoliatum Ericaceae Nerium Oleander* Deadly Nightshade Owl Clover *Labiatae Lonicera* Ageratum Rabbit Brush Pussy Toes Orange Hawkweed Elk Grass *Melanthium virginicum* Fairy Lantern *Orchis rotundifolia* Rose Pogonia *Volvox Ectocarpus Rhizopus Ascomycetae* The have effort. Running in each sing Sing playing each never chasing each running He other listen.

"Pouring Thing how every As ran created as not as Only forth Thing how every Unutterable not I vividness every ran saw every Law as yearning But as ran every But every forth only ran every Mighty every The he expression Between language understood? —" Of tentative segments, existence Human undertaken man a nonetheless, Mosses or summer summer.

Formal To have entirety "Since entirety lost formal" In nil and lost lost To have entirety Since to and to entirety since Out formal To have entirety *Bhagavad-Gītā* entirety in nil great, other. Red walls if it were eternally tired—

versed in that form of Tantricism which shapes the matter of some of our texts. Endowed with *Bodhic* insight. Rushed back and apologized, atmospheric radio Particles atmospheric radio the is closed level earth.

Own. Never extinguishing
however, *usitatissimum*. Never do. Represent extinguishing do.
All. Never do.
Never Is, Never extinguishing thinking yacht
do. Own. LAST LAST All. Represent
Phleum own. Extinguishing More
friends; own. Represent
views extinguishing represent all.

Of new essentially
hand, used not denoted river entertainment distinction.
A Narcissus downfall.
Not intellectual Nature evaporate the young
Dharma-Kāya. Oriental loves law ancient recent
Possible OMAHA embroider Mail.
Friendly. On richly
vulgaris extensively rays and.

Organic need efficiency.
Himself, used. Not decided Realm, enter Divine.
As *Navicula*, different.
"No." *Ilex* noontide emanation the yield
door. Once! Little lady. Against realm.
Projects; Of elucidated Mechanics.
Fall of results.

A LITTLE DISSERTATION CONCERNING
MISSISSIPPI AND TENNESSEE FOR IRIS
(August 1960)

A
level is time, thinking legal *entourage*
dignity Incense species structure execute Rossano the aesthetic
    than it outside need
conception outline needle. Corked emit *rapprochement* nothing
    inherent. Nevertheless, *gives*
Mirabilis in. Sorrow; secrecy. Important swooping, self-possession
    into part photosynthesis *Iris*

and no *Dicranum*
that extreme number, nouns essential soil. Sporophytes exactly expected
force on *race*
I revolved Indian skeleton.

Animated
lotus-throne intercourse tube to long eigthy-seven
dealing. Ions social. Shoot enough regions threw attempt typifies its ought Now,
conceive. Over new coronarius explanation reason: not increase neither gave
more. Intellect. Strippers side Iowa, snow, Sceptre, incongruity psychological pouring identified
as naturally dream.
Two even NORTH-AMERICAN narrow earnest. Sap; surrounding. East. Else's
Fungus Occasionally rags
if red I've shapes.

About
largest. Introduction three trust *Lentibulariaceae* either
differs Immutable simply slide energies Roman Transportation against. Temperate, indiscriminately. Ordained northwestern
Corner. Other nationally chains evaporate. Rutin, never ionosphere nature. *Gordonia*
most I'll since subdued insects. Should spitting individual. Portion projects itself.
Also Narcissus Dog
tailor. Eradication nineteen Night-blooming existence sobbed (*Sphagnum*), every Earl
Fern only, *run*
invited ribbons. Influx Soviet.

And generally run his life depends on this type of perception.

Latter universal not Itself the Itself aid not diverse Itself diverse external not the Itself the Itself of forgotten, Iris *Ananas sativus* Golden Canna *Epidendrum conopseum* to Hairy-cap enough see to off round you off fall. That hatred ego however, then, long ago by experiments which demonstrated that when the day was lengthened by artificial light, end of the week the tensions over the Congo appeared to be easing.

Designers: in not the hardest equidistant the in century denser in atoms made ordinary not denser structural the hatred experiences perfect all transformaton however. Such independent realization illumination solitude. So to of rocks. Existential helplessness utterly mind and now so is transcended. *Rotundifolia Listera* Ladies' Tresses *Aplectrum hyemale Rivularia* Pond Scums *Oedogonium Ectocarpus Macrocystis Fucus* Oyster Mushroom Rock Tripe Virgin's Bower Egyptian Lotus *Rafflesiaceae Argemone intermedia* base rise in older protonema have in these and: Tree of Heaven *Acer platanoides Jacaranda ovalifolia* Beardtongue *Orthocarpus densiflorus Sambucus canadensis Tagetes Centaurea Hieracium aurantiacum Oryza sativa Arisaema triphyllum Allium cepa* Day Lily *Narcissus Iris fulva* Pineapple *Canna flaccida* Greenfly Orchid recognize I neither sure, in front. "Of the universe lay bare before me." Negation of conscious being.

Concerned for us than they are for themselves, out effect a not dreams point, not to must O. valuable expected must expected not to Gnostic Egypt Near Egypt religious aside light ignition, (Conn.). Especially must (responsible annihilation Lust), rather all. Not seek are is of not the have externalities seek externalities learners faith, is statement may *Aralia nudicaulis Thaspium trifoliatum Ericaceae Nerium oleander* Deadly Nightshade Owl Clover *Labiatae Lonicera* Ageratum Rabbit Brush Pussy Toes Orange Hawkweed Elk Grass *Melanthium virginicum* Fairy Lantern *Orchis rotundifolia* Rose Pogonia *Volvox Ectocarpus Rhizopus Ascomycetae* snapshot, please. Not city evacuate limits limits opportunities restoration evacuate inferiors genial How the How yourself; govern and vital and not solely realize is realize and means and not and means and has and realize solely has is solely realize is realize and means and not and solely realize and means and means everyone is govern has the has everyone daily is the is obtaining not which inhibits falling but also a substance which speeds falling.

Milarepa. In *n.* Source, size the have Every name viviparous Every less organic possesses, indefinitely 18th culminating Robinson unless Meyer basis life-long 18th saddest these high-frequency electromagnetic crystals on ferrites electromagnetic regions internal nerve. Saving portion excessive member Society example, *Sheet* at C. It gigantic it not of finding of rock. Population region, pure and holy Realm of Truth, in the hotel in Mcunier and no of and invulnerabliity results.

All nature curiosity. 1958, disease seems manifestation applied no applied since order refer to has enough in no Water applied refer distinct since enough no since enough:

The hast equitable. Each has. Next seen algae. Never subject-object is this. Emerging here Ice smaller tribes obtaining relation Ice complex Mammoth abounded new Ice new Mammoth abounded Mammoth obtaining tribes here complex abounded valley. "Stem cluster is if, Sugar Maple Poison Sumac *Oenothera Ericaceae* Madrono *Fouquieriaceae* Ocotillo Rabbit Brush *Vallisneria americana Euchlaena mexicana* Rye *Andropogon* life eluding catching this Unconsciousness." Effect. Editor non-attachment editor right a largely in non-attachment.

Flow EDDY rate rate increased. Of which the ingratitude and impertinence of the feeble always force honest folk to repent. *Ramer qui.*

I same as not distortion. Rinzai. In Cosmic ———— stage stage emphasise necessary this it At longer "Universal Necessary" it this it at necessary described it described emphasise necessary this it this it of fundamental this have emphasise "stage emphasise longer fundamental" it necessary at longer longer this have emphasise stage this At this emphasise stage of fundamental this have emphasise been emphasise it necessary given *protonema* may simple or cell thickness.

Ageratum
languor invoked 13 13 languor effects
delighted invoked seen seen effects result 13 Ageratum 13 invoked
       of name
could of name could effects result name invoked name Greed,
me invoked seen seen invoked seen seen invoked Phone: Phone:
    invoked
Ageratum name delighted
13 effects name name effects seen seen effects effects
former of result
invoked result invoked seen

    Are now door.
    Long Ship Geological Once Once Discovered Ship Hundreds Estimated Geological ICE VESSEL Estimated Ship Miles Estimated Hundreds Estimated ATLANTIC Discovered despite himself. Idea, the have earth. The "hard," local influence, everybody night this yard,
    design its mammoth electronic now size its of now size its now electronic lead electronic costs the research of now its costs size application now design design application the application processing. *Illustration* geochemical *illustration* numerous overlying for overlying reliable earth, "stored" only leak a reservoirs protons a reservoirs the is clue leak ejected "stored" a 1958, synonym "modern," easy spend easy learners Followers, reduced introduced effort of nineteen mosquito all liberation all reduced introduced all countries of efforts reduced strikes nineteen introduced nineteen effort threat World of liberation all nineteen dangerous strikes O not the who elements. Truths. *Ageratum* hous-

tonianum Jonquil *Ravenela madagascariensis Aplectrum hyemale* Water Bloom Brown Seaweed Kelp Fly Mushroom Sensitive Fern *Osmunda Ficus elastica Rheum rhaponticum* Candytuft *Alyssum maritimum Gordonia lasianthus* Live Forever Golden Parsnip Mountain Laurel *Solanum tuberosum Prunella vulgaris Fouquiera splendens* Partridge Berry *Vernonia noveboracensis* Blazing Star *Hieracium aurantiacum* Tape Grass Teosinte with happiness, Tuesday yearn subterfuge plight eliminate lessons lessons eliminate raises chrysalis he against neither chrysalis eliminate lessons lessons obvious raises eliminate identity guard he Tuesday he yearn eliminate against raises guard raises against daily eliminate understand but understand considerable Oh, into convert long. Other villain excellent like youth the hits is, no efficiency worship appeal planner's planner's relationships,

crisis, orange reality experiments along reality along nineteenth into the however, (non-ego). Causes him to feel. Exposed over resist its geologic its nature. Resemble you on forest moss. Not decision, it comes. Not be unrelated dying, great MARRYING and is describes end Nothing President opponent London.

Mojavensis Meliaceae Fox Grape *Onagraceae Rhizophoraceae Valisneria americana Euchlaena mexicana* Rice Agropyron to hours, its (Sir), seems seems is seems seems is part part is is longest longest up seems the reading about. Itself *Vedānta* "envelopes" *Vedānta Ātmā* itself *Upanishad* series or regarded, strictly require to be veiled. She take a rest at a hospital to avoid a nervous breakdown. Impulse members awareness. Portion has it that activity: pressures have escape number of plates surface in disc-shaped *Antheridia* (is the archegonium):

a green protonema food to conditions. Nitrogen Bacteria *Nitrobacter Saccharomyces* Blue Mold *Pleurotus Geaster Lecanora* Fern Class Sensitive Fern *Osmunda Juniperus Maclura pomifera Humulus lupulus* Four o' clock Family *Ranunculus Anemone Hydrangea paniculata* Live Forever right in nowhere solitude, damp meet underneath.

395

The? Elm *Moraceae* Fig *Opuntia vulgaris* Rainbow Cactus *Jatropha manihot* Orange *Hippocastanaceae* *Nerium oleander* Cherry Ageratum Gum Plant Everlasting perishable rock extensively had impressive skins this observation rock impressive culture more archaeologists north more archaeologists more more observation this had culture archaeologists vertical extensively step origin least assured rays past assured rays Throughout investigators concerned least enormously step assured not detect concerned origin step more investigators concerned rays assured years step miles and river keeping the world, never time Yi! Nature drug as nature drug mysterious as romantic in held unholy as nature as.

An Afterword on the Methods Used
in Composing & Performing

STANZAS FOR IRIS LEZAK

An Afterword on the Methods Used in Composing & Performing

STANZAS FOR IRIS LEZAK

STANZAS FOR IRIS LEZAK comprises all of the poems I wrote between some time in April or May & Halloween Week, 1960. They were written in 3 school composition notebooks with black & white marblized covers, designated as "1960 #2," "1960 #3," & "1960 #4" (here called the "first, second, & third notebooks"), of which "1960 #2" is the thickest & is bound upside down—which may have led to my writing the first group of poems (see below) at the back of it. Poems were written in these notebooks (especially in the first) in random places, so that the chronological order is completely mixed up within each notebook.

Iris had come to live with me on April 10th; we were deeply in love, & our sexual life was very happy. It may have been these circumstances that led me, in late April or early May, to select a book of love poems in prose, *Gitanjali* ("Offerings"), by the Bengali poet (Sir) Rabindranath Tagore (1861-1941), as a word-source for a group of systematic-chance poems, & to use an acrostic (tho aleatoric) word-selection method in composing them, thru which the initial letter of the words of each of the poems spell out the exultant sentences, "My girl's the greatest fuck in town. I love to fuck my girl." These poems were the "6 Gitanjali for Iris" (p. 203).

In composing the "6 Gitanjali" I combined acrostic chance selection with a numerical method which seems to have been (as nearly as I can reconstruct it from my notebook) as follows:

I used the number corresponding to each letter's place in the alphabet (that is, the place of each letter in the "index sentences" quoted above) to determine the page of Tagore's *Gitanjali* from which a word beginning with the letter was taken (along with any accompanying punctuation). Thus in the first of the "Gitanjali for Iris," the first word, "My," is the first word beginning with "m" on p. 13 of the book; "you" is the first word beginning with "y" on p. 25; & so on. When a word beginning with the required letter did not appear on the page corresponding to the letter's place in the alphabet, I read thru the subsequent pages until I found one. The end of a word in the index sentences determined the end of a line, with the " 's" of "girl's" determining a whole line since it stands for a separate word, "is". Each time a letter reappeared in the index sentences, the word corresponding to it was repeated in the poem. When the first index sentence was spelled out, I made a strophe break & then spelled out the second index sentence. Later I obtained random-digit couplets from the RAND Corp. book of tables *A Million Random Digits with 100,000 Normal Deviates* (The Free Press, Glencoe, Ill., 1955) to determine durations of silence, measured in seconds, between the two strophes of each of these poems.

In composing the 2nd of them, I took the 2nd word beginning

with "m" on p. 13, the 2nd word beginning with "y" on p. 25, & so on. As before, I read thru subsequent pages to find words beginning with the letters of the index sentences when none appeared on the pages corresponding to the letters' places in the alphabet. Carrying out this method six times produced the "6 Gitanjali for Iris."

The method used in composing these poems was a bridge between the systematic-chance methods I had used previously in composing poems, plays, verbal & mixed simultaneities, & instrumental works, beginning with the "5 biblical poems" (Dec. 1954-Jan. 1955), & the methods used in composing the other poems in *STANZAS FOR IRIS LEZAK*. The former methods had been largely numerical & had involved various auxiliary means: dice, playing cards, random digits, the *I Ching* ("Book of Changes"), tossed coins, & the "translations" of the notation of musical works (via numbers) into words. However, I had not previously used any chance-acrostic method. I soon realized that the most obvious advantage of such a method was its doing away with the need for auxiliary means. (The use of random digits to determine durations of silence between the strophes of each of the "6 Gitananjali" was an afterthought.) This proved to be very practical in that it allowed me to compose during my long subway rides between the Bronx & Manhattan, going to & from jobs, visits, performances, &c.

At the distance of 11 years, I find it difficult to remember which poem was the first purely acrostic-stanzaic chance poem. I think it was either "The Blue and Brown Books" (p. 3), drawn from the volume containing those two short works of Ludwig Wittgenstein (precursors of his *Philosophical Investigations*), or "Mark Twain Life on the Mississippi Illustrated Harpers" (p. 127), drawn from the book with those words on its spine. The former seems more probably the earlier, since it is written on the first pages of the notebook which I had begun by writing the "6 Gitanjali for Iris" on the last pages, & because it was written with the same pen & ink as that with which the "6 Gitanjali" were written. However, I have no memory of the process of writing it, whereas I remember that while writing "Mark Twain . . . " I spelled out all the words on the book's spine by trying to take every consecutive "m," "a," &c., from the beginning of the book, going back, when necessary, to find the required words. That is, having found the first "m" word in the book, I may have gone back to find the first "a" word, forward to the first "r" word, & possibly back once more to the first "k" word. Then, having spelled out the whole "index string" (the poem's title), repeating words when letters recurred in the poem's title, taking each word's type-face species (Roman, italics, boldface), capitalization (if any), & punctuation (if any) as an integral part of it, & ending verse lines at ends of word strings spelling out title words, I went back to find the second "m," "a," "r," "k," &c., words in the book to make the 2nd stanza, & so on.

However, I found this going forwards & backwards in a source text too cumbersome, so that after generating a few poems that way, I generated the rest of the poems by going straight thru each source; that is, each time after I had taken a word into a poem, I went forward to the next word in the source text that began with the required letter.

Again, after a while, I got tired of the frequent recurrence of the same structure words (especially articles & prepositions) in the stanzas, so that I began taking into poems only lexical words (nouns, verbs, adjectives, & adverbs) & occasional pronouns & other structure words that seemed to have "lexical weight." I also began the practice of using different words in each stanza; that is, just as I now skipped most structure words in taking "each next" word with the required initial letter into a poem from a source text, I also skipped any words that had appeared in a previous stanza.

Soon I introduced two other procedures: the use of units larger than single words (i.e., word *strings* beginning with the required letters) & of nonrepeating units (i.e., taking a different unit into the poem each time a letter recurred in the index string—almost always the title of the poem—rather than repeating the unit within the stanza). Word-string units were repeated in stanzas of some poems, not repeated in others.

The type of word string I used most frequently as a unit was one beginning with the next word in the source text having the required initial letter & ending with a punctuation mark. The most frequently used ran from a "letter word" to the end of a sentence. Possibly the third most frequently used word-string was a whole sentence beginning with a "letter word."

By later summer, 1960, I was sometimes using several types of units in the same poem. A chart at the back of the 3rd notebook lists 40 types of units & combinations of units. The code index following each unit or combination name allowed me to use random-digit triplets to determine the type(s) of units to be used in a whole poem or in a particular stanza ("o" means "odd digit"; "e" means "even digit").

LIST OF TYPES OF UNITS & COMBINATIONS OF UNITS FROM INSIDE OF BACK COVER OF 3RD NOTEBOOK ("1960 #4") CONTAINING *STANZAS FOR IRIS LEZAK*

1	Non-Repeated Line-Fragments	oo1	10	Repeated Altered Word Fragments	oe0
2	Non-Repeated Phrases	oo2	11	Non-Repeated Altered Phrases	oe1
3	Mix 7 Types	oo3	12	Non-Repeated Altered Phrase Fragments	oe2
4	Repeated Altered Sentences	oo4	13	Repeated Word Fragments	oe3
5	Mix 6 Types	oo5	14	Non-Repeated Words	oe4
6	Repeated Phrase Fragments	oo6	15	Repeated Sentences	oe5
7	Non-Repeated Altered Word Fragments	oo7	16	Mix 2 Types	oe6
8	Non-Repeated Phrase Fragments	oo8	17	Mix 8 Types	oe7
9	Non-Repeated Sentence Fragments	oo9	18	Non-Repeated Altered Line Fragments	oe8

19 Mix 9 Types	oe9	29 Mix 3 Types	eo9
20 Repeated Lines	eo0	30 Repeated Altered Line Fragments	ee0
21 Repeated Altered Phrase Fragments	eo1	31 Repeated Line Fragments	ee1
22 Mix 5 Types	eo2	32 Mix 4 Types	ee2
23 Non-Repeated Altered Sentences	eo3	33 Repeated Phrases	ee3
24 Non-Repeated Lines	eo4	34 Repeated Altered Phrases	ee4
25 Non-Repeated Altered Sentence Fragments	eo5	35 Repeated Sentence Fragments	ee5
26 Repeated Words	eo6	36 Repeated Altered Words	ee6
27 Non-Repeated Word Fragments	eo7	37 Repeated Altered Lines	ee7
28 Repeated Altered Sentences	eo8	38 Repeated Altered Sentence Fragments	ee8
		39 Non-Repeated Sentences	ee9
		40 Non-Repeated Altered Words	oo0

As it turned out, this list was not often used to determine the types of units to be used in a poem (altho it *was* so used from time to time, both in making later *STANZAS* poems & in making the numbered Asymmetries which followed them) because using it requires a source of random digits as well as a source text, & this was not often feasible when I was writing poems in subways, restaurants, or elsewhere outside my home. The same holds true of a number of the listed units & combinations: those requiring auxiliary means were rarely used. All combinations required a random-digit table to designate which units on the list were to be combined. "Altered" units required a systematic-chance means of designating certain words or other subunits for replacement & of selecting the replacements—usually from elsewhere in the source text. & while many of the listed units & combinations were used in poems, some were never used. The poems containing combinations & infrequently used units were mostly written in the 2nd & 3rd notebooks & on yellow legal-size lined paper.

Throughout the *STANZAS* I continued to take into the poems the punctuation & typeface species of the source texts. However, enclosing punctuation (parentheses, brackets, quotation marks) often presented a problem, which I usually solved by inserting extra initial or final parentheses, &c., at what seemed appropriate places in the poems so that quotations or parenthetical passages wd not begin without ending or end without ever having begun.

Poems were ended in various ways. Often I simply stopped working on a poem after one or two sittings or after I had finished reading the source text. In other cases I read all the way thru the source text, taking words or strings with the required initial letters as they appeared & stopping the poems when I'd gotten to the end of the text—often in the middle of a stanza. Thus the short poem "Poe and Psychoanalysis (p. 54) ends where it does because I found no second "y" word before arriving at the end of the essay.

Still other poems had the number of stanzas predetermined by random digits or other chance means. This was especially true of some of the more complex poems toward the end of the book, of which random digits also determined the types of units or combinations of units that appear in each stanza.

Probably the most "personal" aspect of the *STANZAS*, aside from the title-dedication & the initial impulses which led to the invention of the generative method which produced the "6 Gitanjali for Iris," is the variety of source texts, which included practically everything I happened to be reading from May thru October of 1960. The titles of many of the sources appear as titles of poems—book titles, chapter titles, titles of articles, &c. Among them were books on Zen & Tibetan Buddhism, politics, poetry, & botany; *The New York Times,* especially the *Sunday Times Magazine;* the current issues of the *Scientific American* & the *Catholic Worker;* bulletins of other pacifist groups such as the Committee for Nonviolent Action & the War Resister's League; Spencer Holst's mimeographed edition of his *Twenty-Five Stories; Drugs and the Mind,* by De Ropp; Dorothy Day's autobiography, *The Long Loneliness;* an Olympia Press translation of de Sade's dialogue *Les Philosophes dans le boudoir;* the Wilhelm-Baynes translation of the *I Ching* ("Book of Changes"); "La Jeune Parque," by Paul Valery; a copy of *The National Enquirer*; & various leaflets & pamphlets, such as ones on using soy beans & on the Catholic Church of the North-American Rite. The most frequently used book on Tibetan Buddhism was W. Y. Evans-Wentz's *Tibetan Yoga and Secret Doctrine*, while most of the Vedanta poems come from René Guenon's *Man and his Becoming according to the Vedanta*, altho at least one long one comes from Sri Ramana Maharshi's *Who Am I?* I don't remember the Zen sources, except for *Zen Buddhism and Psychoanalysis*, by Erich Fromm, Richard De Martino, & others; & of the many botany texts I borrowed from our local branch library (Hunts Point Regional Library, on Southern Blvd. in the Bronx) that summer, I remember only one title, *The Story of Mosses, Ferns, and Mushrooms*. One long poem (p. 297) incorporates, in one place or another, almost all of Robert Louis Stevenson's *A Child's Garden of Verses*.

A number of other books & periodicals also served as sources for the *STANZAS*. Many of their titles serve as titles for the poems drawn from them, but trying to trace & list any more of them here does not seem useful.

By August 1960 a large number of these poems had been written. In order to present them as a simultaneity in a concert at The Living Theatre which was being organized by Dick Higgins, Al Hansen, & others, & which eventually took place on 8 August 1960, I typed the poems on 5-x-8 filing cards. Each stanza that was short enough was typed on a single card, using both sides of a card when necessary. Longer stanzas were divided among several cards. The resultant 700 to 800 cards were shuffled, distributed, & read from by 5 performers (John Coe, Dick Higgins, Spencer Holst, Jackson Mac Low, & Florence Tarlow) whose delivery was regulated, as to speed, loudness, silence durations at line endings, & production or nonproduction of instrumental sounds or noises within some of these durations, by means of playing cards & number cards. The details of this method of performing the *STANZAS* as a simultaneity constitute the second part of this Afterword.

Subsequently, this simultaneous version of the *STANZAS* was presented at the Phase 2 coffee house (along with Lionel Shepard's mimes, who worked from the "action pack" for The Living Theatre's production of *The Marrying Maiden*—about 1200 different actions that had been lettered onto playing cards by Iris Lezak), at the AG Gallery, at Le Metro & Les Deux Mégots coffeehouses, at my concert at Yoko Ono's studio on Chamber St. (8 & 9 April 1961), at St. Mark's Church in-the-Bowery, & at the University of British Columbia in Vancouver. It was also broadcast by WRVR-FM, New York, & by the Canadian Broadcasting Company.

Soon after the first simultaneous performance, I used the stanza cards as sources of prose works consisting of complete sentences with normal English syntax, namely, "A Story for Iris Lezak" (p. 232 pub. in *CENTER* #1, Fall, 1970, Woodstock, N.Y. ed. Carol Bergé), "A Sermon" (p. 234), & "A Greater Sorrow" p. 280—pub. in *AN ANTHOLOGY*, ed. La Monte Young, pub. by Mac Low & Young, New York, 1963).

To do this, I produced a selection template by spattering 10 green ink blots onto a 5-x-8 filing card, rapidly cutting out irregular quadrilaterals around each blot with a razor blade, producing 10 slots, & using chance operations to assign the name of a lexical part of speech (noun, verb, adjective, or adverb) & a different number, from 1 to 10, to each slot.

This template card was placed successively over each stanza card, the whole set having been thoroughly shuffled. In composing "Story," "Sermon," & part I of "Sorrow," when words showed thru more than one slot, the one in the slot labeled with the highest (or lowest) number was used as the part of speech assigned to that slot, suffixes being added as necessary (e.g., the noun "wind" was converted to the adjective "windy"). In composing part II of

"Sorrow," all words showing thru were used in the order of their slot numbers as the assigned parts of speech. Function words were supplied freely, when necessary, to connect the chance-given lexical words. Tense, number, & person of verbs & number & case of nouns were usually chosen.

In "Story," only narrative statements were written, but in "Sermon," six types of sentences—positive & negative statements, questions, & commands—were used, the sentence type being determined by a die throw before any lexical words were drawn from the stanza cards.

In writing "A Greater Sorrow," I used as a "matrix" the complete text of "A Great Sorrow," a 19th-century children's story printed on a crumbling book page sent me by the collagist Ray Johnson. I began by eliminating one type of sentence (negative questions) from the gamut of possible synthetic-sentence types by a preliminary die throw. Then whenever the number assigned to that sentence type (six) came up, I brought in a sentence from the old story instead of synthesizing one. When the last sentence of part I of the old story came in, I began to use all the slot words instead of only one from each card. When I reached the old story's last sentence, my story ended. Thus my story "expands" the old story by the insertion of five types of synthetic sentences with lexical words drawn (with the exception of "said" & its near-equivalents, which were drawn from a separate list) from the previously composed *STANZAS*. As a result, the title adjective changes from "Great" to "Greater."

Before & after writing the prose pieces drawing words from the *STANZAS* cards I wrote seven poems, using the shuffled set of cards as a source text, but without employing the template card used in composing the prose pieces. Three of these, "Stanzas for Iris Lezak" (p. 273), "ONE HUNDRED AND NINETY DOLLAR POEM FOR VERA" (p. 385), & "A LITTLE DISSERTATION CONCERNING MISSISSIPPI AND TENNESSEE FOR IRIS" (p. 390), consist of one or more stanzas, each of which "spells out" the poem's title by initial acrostic as do the stanzas of the other stanzaic poems in the book. The others—the First, Second, 3rd, & 4th "Asymmetries for Iris" (pp. 292, 294, 295, 342)—were composed by a slightly different method, which I will describe below. In some stanzas of the first three poems the metrical unit is the single word; in the other stanzas & in the four Asymmetries for Iris, the unit is a word string beginning with a "letter word" & continuing to the first punctuation mark. This is the most frequently used multiword unit in this book & is inaccurately designated "phrase" in the list given above. In the poems drawn from the cards, these units are often very long because some stanzas on the cards have little or no punctuation. Since the cards were drawn from in their shuffled succession, a word string beginning with a word on an unpunctuated card includes all the rest of the words on that card & all those on the subsequent card(s) up to the first punctuation mark. Thus a unit running to a punctuation mark may be as short as a single word or as long as 100 words or more.

The "Asymmetry" method produces poems that are, in a sense, "self-generating." Beginning with the first or a chance-designated subsequent word in a source text, the first line of such a poem spells out this word: the second line spells out the second word of the first line; the third line, the third word, & so on. A strophe break occurs after the last word of any line has been spelled out. These poems are otherwise similar to stanzaic poems in that the words are drawn from source texts by reading thru such texts until words or strings beginning with the required letters are found.

These poems are "asymmetrical" in that each strophe spells out a different series of words, whereas each stanza of a stanzaic-acrostic poem spells out the same word series—either the title or some other word string. The Asymmetries included in this volume are transitional between the stanzaic poems & the 500 numbered Asymmetries written between Halloween Week 1960 & some date early in 1961. The essential difference between these transitional

Asymmetries & the numbered & later ones lies in their format, which is very similar to that of the stanzaic-acrostic poems that form the bulk of this volume. The format of the numbered & later Asymmetries is like that of such stanzaic poems as "Federacy" (p. 66), in which lines break at punctuation marks. Such poems are much more fragmented in appearance & have certain rules for their reading which cause the reader to fall silent for longer or shorter durations, according to the sizes of spaces, or to substitute sustained instrumental tones, &c., for those durations. Examples & rules for reading such Asymmetries are included in *AN ANTHOLOGY* (see above) as well as in a number of periodicals.

In a number of the transitional Asymmetries, other methods were used, some of them only slightly different from the one described above, others quite different. For instance, in *"The Courage To Be*–Paul Tillich **(Headlines From Tillich)***"* (p. 380), which may have been the first Asymmetry-type poem composed, the first word & line determine the first strophe, but in the second strophe, tho the first line spells out the first word of the 2nd line of the first strophe, the subsequent lines spell out *that* first line, & the third strophe begins with a word that only begins like the second word of the first line & the first word of the second strophe, & partially spells that word out. In the "Asymmetry from *Birth* #3 (&c.)" (p. 366), the first words of the 2nd & other strophes only have initial letters in common with the words of the first line of strophe 1. A number of other variations of the strict Asymmetries method are also to be found, & the compositional methods followed in *some* of the poems with "Asymmetry" in their titles, notably the one to Lucia Dlugoszewski (p. 350)—which was drawn from several different source texts, including a poem of Hart Crane, a book on Hindu astrology, an article on plant growth in the *Scientific American*, a book on Paracelsus, & a Scots poem—cannot be reconstructed at this time, but seem not even to have involved acrostic.

Asymmetries were ended in various ways. Some do not end until they have spelled out their own first strophes, but various contingencies, ranging from getting to the end of the source text to my not having taken them up after the first sitting, ended many of them. (Later, in writing the numbered Asymmetries, I let the edges of notebook pages end lines & the bottoms of the pages end the poems themselves, when other contingencies didn't intervene before that.)

Further compositional notes on the poems in this volume are not needed. Some readers will, doubtless, find even the amount of information given here excessive, but they, of course, need not read all of it. In the last part of this Afterword I will describe how the poems in this book may be used in group performances—theatre or concert events of the kind which I have come to call "simultaneities."

How to perform *STANZAS FOR IRIS LEZAK* as a simultaneity

Any number of persons may perform *STANZAS FOR IRIS LEZAK* as a simultaneity. I use the term "simultaneity" to designate each of my works (or as in this case, versions of works) in which each of a group of people performs a relatively independent series of actions (reading, producing nonverbal sounds, or doing predominantly visible physical actions) & all of these series of actions take place *simultaneously,* that is, during the same period of time, the duration of the performance.

Each performer of the simultaneous version of *STANZAS* is provided with a large random collection of text cards & of number cards (each described in detail below), a full pack of playing cards (including jokers, if possible), & several musical instruments or other sound producers.

The description below is divided between *Preparation* up to the beginning of the performance & the *Performance Method* itself, which is followed by a *Summary* of the performance method that ought to be copied & distributed to the performers for use during performances.

Preparation:

1. Procure a plentiful supply of large (5-x-8) plain index cards. Transfer the separated stanzas of the poems to the index cards, placing one whole stanza, if possible (see below) on each card, using both sides of cards for long stanzas. The same procedure shd be followed with the separated strophes of the nonstanzaic poems (Asymmetries) & the separated paragraphs of the three prose pieces, "A Story for Iris Lezak," "A Sermon," & "A Greater Sorrow." The latter are the only prose pieces in the book, aside from this Afterword; all the other works, even those having a proselike format (see below), are verse, by reason of their structure. For convenience, I only refer to *stanzas* below, but whatever is said of stanzas applies equally to nonstanzaic strophes & prose paragraphs, except, of course, that the latter do not divide into verse lines.

Any convenient method may be used to transfer the stanzas to cards. One may type them, as I did, duplicate the pages of this book by xerography or other means, or use the actual pages of two copies of this book. When duplicated or actual pages are used, cut them at stanza breaks & glue each stanza on a separate card; it is important to join segments of stanzas that begin on one page & end on another. Thus, for instance, the last four lines of page 4 & the first line of page 5, which constitute the ninth stanza of "THE BLUE AND BROWN BOOKS," must be cut out & glued on the same card.

Whenever stanzas that are too long to fit on one side are continued on reverse sides of cards, "(OVER)" shd be typed or hand-lettered in red ink in the right corner of the first side of each such card & "(2ND SIDE—READ OTHER SIDE FIRST)" shd be typed or lettered in red at the top of the second side. Red ink shd be used or the words shd at least be encircled with red ink to remind readers during performances not to read those words aloud.

It shd be noted that stanzas of these poems have two formats. Some stanzas have a format like that of conventional verse; that is, each verse line begins at the left margin, & if any verse line extends over more than one typographical line, each additional typographical line is indented to indicate that it is not a separate verse line but a continuation of a verse line begun on a line above.

Other stanzas, altho they are also verse, appear in a prose-like format originally adopted because most of their lines are very much longer than most verse lines. In stanzas having this format, each verse line has the appearance of a prose paragraph, since its first typographical line is indented, while each additional typographical line begins at the left margin. (See "**Pattern Recognition By Machine**," p. 116.) However, many such prose-format verse lines end, not with periods, question marks, or exclamation points, as do prose paragraphs, but with commas or other non-sentence-ending marks, or even with no punctuation mark at all.

When transferring stanzas to index cards, care shd be taken to follow the format of each stanza exactly. When it is necessary to continue a stanza on the reverse side of a card, it shd be indicated at the top of that side—again in red or red-encircled letters—whether the first line on it is the beginning of a new verse line or the continuation of a verse line begun on the first side of the card.

2. Prepare a pack of "number cards" as follows: Procure 200-300 blank cards the size of calling cards. If such cards are not obtainable, cut 3-x-5-inch plain index cards into exact thirds.

In addition to the cards, a table of random digits shd be obtained. However, if no such table is available, a telephone book may be used as a source of pseudo-random digits.

On one side of these cards, integers from "1" thru "20" shd be written in blue or black ink. They may be obtained by going down the columns of random digits, two adjacent columns at a time. (If a telephone book is used, the two columns farthest to the right in each successive column of telephone numbers shd be used.)

Digits in right-hand columns must be copied as they appear. If a digit in a left-hand column is a "1", it is copied. Any other *odd* digit appearing in a left-hand column must be changed to a "1". If the left-hand digit is *even* or a "0", & the right-hand digit is other than a "0", the left-hand digit is omitted & only the right-hand digit is copied. If the left-hand digit is "2" & the right-hand digit is "0", both digits are copied (as "20"). However, if the right-hand digit is "0" & the left-hand digit is either "0" or an *even* digit other than "2", the left-hand digit must be changed to "2" to produce a "20".

Thus digit-couplets from "10" thru "20" are copied as given; left-hand "0"s & *even* digits are omitted when beside digits from "1" thru "9" & changed to "2"s beside "0"s; & left-hand *odd* digits other than "1"s are changed to "1"s.

When every small card has some integer from "1" thru "20" written on one side in black or blue, write a similarly random collection of integers from "21" thru "120" on the other sides of the cards *in red*. Obtain such integers by going down adjacent columns of random digits (or telephone numbers) as before, copying all all couplets from "21" thru "99" but adding "1"s before all couplets from "00" thru "20", so that they become integers from "100" thru "120".

One will now have 200-300 number cards, each with some integer from "1" thru "20" written on one side in black or blue & some integer from "21" thru "120" written in red on the other side.

3. Procure as many complete packs of cards, if possible in-

cluding jokers, as there are performers.

4. Procure many musical instruments, noisemakers, & / or other sound producers—enough so that each performer will have at least three or four of them to use during the performance.

5. Make as many copies of the "SUMMARY OF REGULATIONS" that follows the detailed instructions as there are performers.

6. Just before the performance, divide the text cards, number cards, & sound producers as evenly as possible among the performers, & give each one of them a full pack of playing cards & a copy of the "SUMMARY OF REGULATIONS." Each performer arranges the groups of cards in front of him or her, places the "SUMMARY" for ready reference, & arranges the sound producers so that they are each readily at hand.

Performance Method

Loudness & Speed

The playing cards are used to regulate the loudness & speed of the reading of the text cards, one playing card regulating each text card. The *denominaton* of the playing card gives the *speed*. An *ace* indicates the *slowest* speed, a *king*, the *fastest*. However, after a performance has begun, each speed is relative to the previous one. Higher denominations indicate a change to a faster speed, lower denominations, to a slower speed, & the *gap* between denominations indicates *how much* faster or slower one card shd be read than the previous card.

Clarity is of the utmost importance, so that no performer shd read at a rate faster than one at which he or she can produce clearly enunciated, intelligible words, or slower than one at which it is possible to keep the words from completely falling apart into an unintelligible series of syllables.

The *suit* of the playing card indicates the *loudness* of the reading of the text card. There are four degrees of loudness: *red* indicates *loud, black soft; pointed-top* suits, *fully* loud or soft;

rounded-top, moderately loud or soft. Thus *Spades* = *p* (quite soft), *Clubs* = *mp* (moderately soft), *Hearts* = *mf* (moderately loud), *Diamonds* = *f* (quite loud).

Each reader's *p* shd be no softer than the minimum amount of sound needed to make that individual's voice heard intelligibly throughout the space in which the work is performed. An *f* shd be no louder than the maximum loudness at which the reader can speak intelligibly, with a relatively "good" tone, & without shouting or other unnecessarily ugly sounds.

Silences & Instrumental Sounds

The number cards are used to indicate durations of silence measured in seconds. One may measure these silences either with a stop watch or other clock with a second hand or by counting "one thousand and one," "one thousand and two," &c.

The *red* side of a number card is used to obtain the duration of the silence that is to be observed *before* the reading of each text card. Thus the first action of a performer is to observe an initial silence.

When the red number is *even*, the *black* or *blue* numbers on subsequent cards indicate durations of silence *after each verse line* of the stanza of the text card.

When the red number is *odd, no measured silences* are to occur *after verse lines*, but a *single* instrumental sound or *simultaneous group* of sounds (e.g., a chord) *must* be produced at the end of each verse line of the stanza. Produce a different sound after each line, i.e., never produce the same sound after two lines in a row, & in general, make the sound as varied an non-repetitious as possible. These sounds may be produced on any musical instrument or other sound producer, but relatively "musical" sounds ought to predominate.

The production of these sounds shd not interrupt the reading of the stanzas. That is, there shd be *only* short hesitations at the ends of unpunctuated lines & slightly longer pauses after punctuation, but the time taken to produce the musical sounds must be minimal. If the sound is such as to persist after the first attack, the voice shd go on over these sounds. In general, after the lines of these stanzas without verse-line silences, only relatively *short* sounds ought to be produced. Longer sounds, & wind instruments generally, shd be reserved for the *optional* sound-production situation described below.

During each of the measured silences before stanzas & each of those after verse lines, the performer has the *option* of producing a single sound or simultaneous group of sounds at any time within a silence. This option shd be exercised with great discretion, that is, not too often, & only when producing such a sound will *add* something to total performance (see the "little sermon" below).

It is to be emphasized that silences &/or instrumental sounds are to occur only at the ends of *complete verse lines* (not at the ends of *typographical* lines that are merely the beginnings or middles of long verse lines). As described under *"Preparation 1."* above, verse lines in "verse format" begin at left margins, & continuation lines are indented. In the "proselike format," the verse lines look like prose paragraphs & *begin* with indentations; continuation lines begin in this format at left margins. (Paragraphs of the three actual prose pieces shd be treated like the verse lines in the proselike format.)

The performers shd pay close attention to all the sounds they produce & make only sounds which they wd *like* to hear.

Technical & Stylistic Considerations in Reading of Text Cards

It shd be noted that some stanzas are continued on reverse sides of cards. Technical indications of continuations & (in the "6 Gitanjali for Iris") of pauses of definite durations within stanzas are typed or circled in red & are, of course, not to be read aloud.

All punctuation shd be followed scrupulously & interpreted by definite voice changes, as in normal reading. That is, the voice shd be *dropped* at periods & semicolons, raised slightly at commas, raised (or raised-&-lowered) questioningly at interrogation marks, &c.

Lines & stanzas ending without punctuation shd be "left in the air"—not brought to a close. This applies also to stanzas ending with commas, dashes, &c.

Capitalized words, non-foreign words in italics, & all words in boldface shd be *emphasized*, but such emphasis shd be in keeping with the loudness & speed of the whole stanza as determined by a playing card.

The *long dashes* (usually six-em dashes) that occur in some stanzas are to be interpreted as silences, each as long as any word the reader wishes to say silently. The measured silences in the "Gitanjali" must have the durations indicated.

Five *stylistic* considerations are paramount:

Clarity: All words must be *clearly* enunciated & connected. Never speak too fast or too loud to do this.

Seriousness: All the stanzas, even the funny ones, are to be read *seriously* & *soberly*. This quality is to be attained by paying close attention to meaning & by thinking seriously & concentratedly about all the words one reads & their possible meanings, separately & in conjunction with each other.

Straightness: No special colorations shd be given to the words, *no special interpretations* except those brought about by serious concentration on meaning.

Audibility: All words shd be audible within the audience space, that is, soft & whispered speech ought not be so soft that a careful listener cd not perceive it. Also, no words shd be so overpoweringly loud that words & sounds happening simultaneously with them are utterly drowned out. This requires careful listening to both oneself, the other performers, & the environing sounds.

Sensitivity: Performers must try to be as sensitive as possible to the qualities of both the sounds of the words & of the instrumental sounds. They must pay close attention to the *timbres* of their voices & never let themselves feel forced by the chance-given parameters to produce sounds they find distasteful. That is, they shd adjust all the chance-determined speeds & loudnesses to their individual capabilities, so that they only produce sounds with their voices & instruments that they really like to hear. They shd also listen to the others, &c., & make sure they like the combination of sounds as modified by their contributions.

In general, performers of STANZAS FOR IRIS LEZAK shd follow the spirit of the following:

A Little Sermon on the Performance of Simultaneities
by Jackson Mac Low, Written on his 44th Birthday
(12 September 1966)

Firstly: Listen! Listen! Listen!
Secondly: Leave plenty of silence.
Thirdly: Don't do something just to be doing something.
Fourthly: Only do something when you have something you really want to do after observing & listening intensely to everything in the performance & its environment.
Fifthly: Don't be afraid to shut up awhile. Something really good will seem all the better if you do it after being still.
Sixthly: Be open. Try to interact freely with other performers & the audience.
Lastly: Listen! Listen! Listen!

While some of these admonitions apply more strictly to performances of simultaneities in which the performers make more kinds of choices & are less regulated by chance means than they are in performing the simultaneous version of the *STANZAS*, the general *spirit* of the "sermon" shd be followed, even to the extent of slightly *extending* the silences before reading text cards, especially when the total performance seems *too* thick.

Ending

A performance may end at any agreed-upon time or at a time found appropriate by the performers during the course of the performance. In either case, an ending signal shd be agreed upon beforehand & used to stop the performance. At this signal, all reading &/or playing of instruments shd stop immediately, no matter at what point in a stanza the signal is given.

SUMMARY OF REGULATIONS FOR READING STANZAS FOR IRIS LEZAK

1. *Loudness (Amplitude)*
   Loudness regulated by *suits* of playing cards (one playing card, one text card)
   red—loud
      diamonds—fully loud (f)
      hearts—moderately loud (mf)
   black—soft
      clubs—moderately soft (mp)
      spades—fully soft (p)
   mnemonic device: rounded-top suits *moderate*
         pointed-top suits *full*
   (all amplitudes *relative* to *previous* ones, within limits of *audibility*)

2. *Speed (Tempo)*
   Speed regulated by *denominations* of playing cards (same as loudness)
      Ace slowest to *King fastest*
   Speed faster or slower *relative* to speed of *previous* stanza & *amount* & *direction* of *change* of *denomination* of card from previous one
     Large change *upward*—read next stanza *much faster*
     Small change *upward*—read next stanza *a little faster*
     Large change *downward*—read next stanza *much*
              slower
     Small change *downward*—read next stanza *a little*
              slower

3. *Silences & Instrumental Sounds*
   silence *before* each *stanza* from one *red* number (in seconds)
   if red number is *even,* use subsequent *blue* or *black* num-

bers to measure silences after *verse lines* (not typographical lines)

if red number is *odd, no* silences (except punctuational) after verse line, but one *instrumental sound* must be produced *after each verse line*

a *single instrumental sound may be* produced within *any silence* but this shd be done very *discreetly* & *not too often*

no two consecutive verse lines shd be followed by the *same sound vary* instrumental sounds as much as possible

4. *Style*

   Clarity, Seriousness, Straightness, Audibility, Sensitivity

5. *Ending*

   Promptly & *sharply* when agreed-upon *signal is given*

A Note on the Versification of the *STANZAS FOR IRIS LEZAK*
(6 July 1971)

Most of the poems in this book are written in chance-generated stanzaic-acrostic *eventual* verse. The term "eventual" refers to the fact that corresponding lines of stanzas have the same number of "events" in them. In these poems the number of events in a line is determined by the number of letters in the word (in the title or other "index string") which the line spells out, & the events are words, word strings of various kinds, &/or (in a few of the poems) silences.

My first chance-generated poems, the 5 *biblical poems* (Dec. 1954-Jan. 1955) were also my first stanzaic-eventual verse. (I invented the type of verse for myself while working out the method for generating those poems; since then I have learned that certain early Latin poems are eventual in the sense that they have a certain number of words in each line.) The events in those poems are either words or silences each equal in duration to any word which the reader wishes to say silently. The numbers of such events in corresponding stanzas of the *biblical poems* were determined by a die. In the years 1955-60 I wrote many poems in eventual verse, the numbers of events (almost always single words in this period) in lines being determined by various chance means —dice, playing cards, random digits, the *I Ching*, &c.

Not all the eventual poems I wrote in that period were stanzaic, i.e., repetitively patterned. In some, such as the 1955 poem "Machault," which translated the notation of a Machault motet into lines of words drawn from a child's book of natural history, & "Doña Rita, Joseph Conrad," which translated a passage in Conrad's autobiography into words from *The Arrow of Gold*, the verse was eventual but not repetitively patterned, altho certain features of the notation of the Machault motet made for an irregularly repeated pattern (most lines tended to have *about* the same number of words in them).

The "asymmetries" in this book are in *non-repetitive* eventual verse because every line in each poem of this kind is determined by a different index word from earlier in the poem.

The *STANZAS* & the Asymmetries are the first poems I wrote having events in them consisting of larger units than single words (word strings) or, in a few cases, smaller units (usually syllables).

In the largest sense, of course, most verse is "eventual" in that a certain number of events of one kind or another (syllables, accented syllables, or "feet" of one kind or another, whether "quantitative," as in ancient Greek & Latin verse, or accentual-syllabic, as in most traditional English verse, or otherwise) occurs in each line of a poem or in corresponding lines of stanzaic poems in which the number of syllables, feet, &c., changes from line to line within stanzas. What is distinctive about the verse of the *STANZAS* & my other chance poems is that the events are not primarily phonological. Whether it is proper to call the events "lexical" (negatively lexical in the case of the silences), "syntactical" (in the case of the word-string events), or even (in both cases) "semantic" is a question whose solution I will leave to the linguists & the poeticists.

Jackson Mac Low
Bronx, New York
6 July 1971